The Complete Guide to

WALLS & CEILINGS

Framing • Drywall • Painting • Trimwork

COOL SPRINGS PRESS
Home and Garden Experts™

MINNEAPOLIS, MINNESOTA

COOL SPRINGS PRESS
Home and Garden Experts

First published in 2015 by Cool Springs Press, an imprint of Quarto Publishing Group USA Inc., 400 First Avenue North, Suite 400, Minneapolis, MN 55401 USA

Acquisitions Editor: Mark Johanson
Design Manager: Brad Springer
Layout: Danielle Smith-Boldt
Editor: Gary Legwold

Photography: Rau + Barber
Photo Assistance: Brad Holden

Cool Springs Press titles are also available at discounts in bulk quantity for industrial or sales-promotional use. For details write to Special Sales Manager at Quarto Publishing Group USA Inc., 400 First Avenue North, Suite 400, Minneapolis, MN 55401 USA. To find out more about our books, visit us online at www.coolspringspress.com.

ISBN: 978-1-59186-645-9

Printed in China

10 9 8 7 6 5 4 3 2 1

The Complete Guide to Walls & Ceilings
Created by: The Editors of Cool Springs Press, in cooperation with BLACK+DECKER.
BLACK+DECKER and the BLACK+DECKER logo are trademarks of The Black & Decker Corporation and are used under license. All rights reserved.

NOTICE TO READERS

For safety, use caution, care, and good judgment when following the procedures described in this book. The publisher and BLACK+DECKER cannot assume responsibility for any damage to property or injury to persons as a result of misuse of the information provided.

The techniques shown in this book are general techniques for various applications. In some instances, additional techniques not shown in this book may be required. Always follow manufacturers' instructions included with products, since deviating from the directions may void warranties. The projects in this book vary widely as to skill levels required: some may not be appropriate for all do-it-yourselfers, and some may require professional help.

Consult your local building department for information on building permits, codes, and other laws as they apply to your project.

Contents

The Complete Guide to **Walls & Ceilings**

Contents (Cont.)

Introduction

W hat did the fish say when he ran into the wall?
Dam!

OK, groan away, but when it comes to walls and ceilings, don't you feel for that fish? It can be daunting, the idea of building or tearing down walls. Same with creating, repairing, or improving a ceiling. You can run into an intimidating dam (maybe even a *damn!*) when you ponder taking on such projects in the very place where you live. Well, *The Complete Guide to Walls & Ceilings* will empower you and help you get over that dam.

Walls and ceilings are dramatic. Externally, they create and define a house where nothing existed previously, which alone is pretty cool. And then positioning and decorating the internal walls and ceilings are what makes that house a home, your special place.

The knowledge and can-do encouragement you'll gain from *The Complete Guide to Walls & Ceilings* will put you in the position of contributing to dramatic changes in your home. You'll have the power, tools, and ability to create a cozy, casual space for a home-theater room in the basement, to open up your dining-and-kitchen area by removing a wall, and to even put an addition onto your house—all while saving tons of money by doing it yourself.

The key word in the title is "complete." We cover it all in the most effective way, by going heavy on well-labeled how-to photos that fully inform someone who's excited to get into do-it-yourself projects as well as someone who has been there, done that— but still appreciates clear instructions as reference.

The Complete Guide to Walls & Ceilings opens with a chapter on framing. We cover the anatomy of a house and of a wall (king studs, jack studs, headers), framing windows, building loadbearing and non-loadbearing walls, building a kneewall, hanging a door, and framing a basement foundation.

The next key section makes you one with drywall. Included are drywall panel types; fasteners, adhesives, and caulks; tools, equipment, and finishing materials; planning layouts; how to make all sorts of drywall cuts; specialty tools; installing ceiling panels; hanging cementboard; building archways and domes; insulating interior basement walls; taping; and soundproofing.

Our painting section covers painting your walls and ceilings. You'll learn about paint sheens, painting tools, specialized roller techniques, and, of course, cleaning up.

The final section is on installing trim. Included are trim styles (Victorian, Arts & Crafts, etc.); tools and materials needed, especially power tools; fasteners; molding profiles; glues and adhesives; sanding; removing old trim and molding; mitering corners; crown molding; wainscoting; and making coped cuts.

The Complete Guide to Walls & Ceilings has what you need to get your project done—and we even throw in complete plans on practical-yet-decorative projects you may not have considered, such as installing a picture rail or chair rail.

As you take on your wall-and-ceiling projects, *The Complete Guide to Walls & Ceilings* has your back. If the book could talk, it would say exactly what a painter might say to a wall: *I got you covered.*

Framing Walls

Framing a wall is sometimes referred to as "rough carpentry" in the trades. It's a bit of a misnomer in that it suggests a kind of a freewheeling process where hammers are flying and accuracy is not particularly important. Compared to the precise angle-cutting, complicated joinery, and high-visibility of trim carpentry, rough carpentry does have somewhat more forgiving tolerances (and if you make an error you can fix it and cover it up with drywall). But taking the time to measure carefully and make strong, clean joints is definitely worth the effort. If your 16-on-center framing turns out to be 17-on-center, you'll regret it when installing the wallcoverings.

There are two basic approaches you can take to framing a wall. Many professional carpenters prefer to attach the studs to the sole plate and then raise the wall as a unit, attaching the tops of the studs to the cap plate on the ceiling once everything is lined up. This is probably faster, and nailing through the bottom of the sole plate and into the ends of the studs makes a very strong joint that is less likely to splinter the wood than toe-nailing. But since most of us homeowners are probably building only one or two walls, "stick-building" the framed wall by attaching each framing member one-at-a-time as you go is ultimately more controllable.

In this chapter:
- Anatomy of a House
- Building Walls
- Building a Kneewall
- Building a Wet Wall
- Installing Interior Doors
- Framing Basement Foundation Walls
- Removing a Non-loadbearing Wall

Anatomy of a House

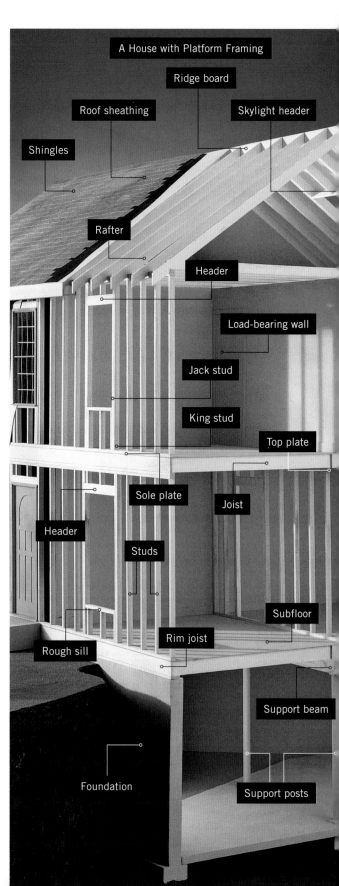

Before you start a do-it-yourself carpentry project, you should familiarize yourself with a few basic elements of home construction and remodeling. Take some time to get comfortable with the terminology of the models shown on the next few pages. The understanding you will gain in this section will make it easier to plan your project, buy the right materials, and clear up any confusion you might have about the internal design of your home.

If your project includes modifying exterior or load-bearing walls, you must determine if your house was

Anatomy of a House with Platform Framing

A House with Platform Framing

Ridge board

Roof sheathing

Skylight header

Shingles

Rafter

Header

Load-bearing wall

Jack stud

King stud

Top plate

Sole plate

Joist

Header

Studs

Subfloor

Rim joist

Rough sill

Support beam

Foundation

Support posts

Platform framing (photos, right and above) is identified by the floor-level sole plates and ceiling-level top plates to which the wall studs are attached. Most houses built after 1930 use platform framing. If you do not have access to unfinished areas, you can remove the wall surface at the bottom of a wall to determine what kind of framing was used in your home.

built using platform- or balloon-style framing. The framing style of your home determines what kind of temporary supports you will need to install while the work is in progress. If you have trouble determining what type of framing was used in your home, refer to the original blueprints, if you have them, or consult a building contractor or licensed home inspector.

Framing in a new door or window on an exterior wall normally requires installing a header. Make sure that the header you install meets the requirements of your local building code, and always install cripple studs where necessary.

Floors and ceilings consist of sheet materials, joists, and support beams. All floors used as living areas must have joists with at least 2 × 8 construction.

There are two types of walls: load-bearing and partition. Load-bearing walls require temporary supports during wall removal or framing of a door or window. Partition walls carry no structural load and do not require temporary supports.

Anatomy of a House with Balloon Framing

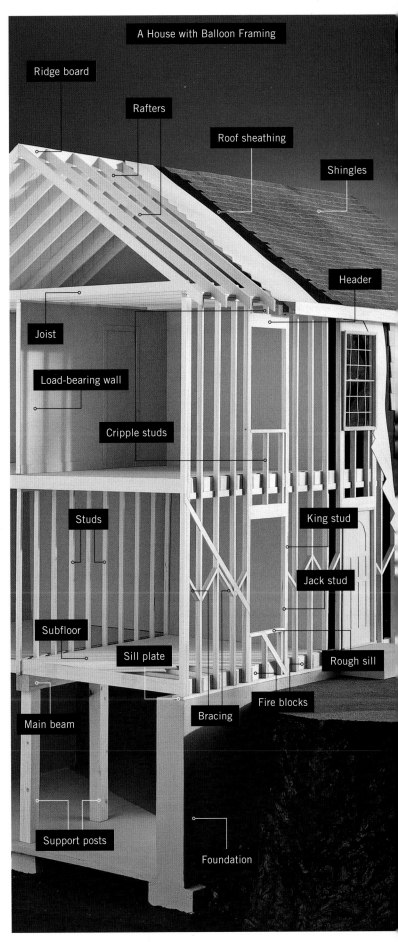

A House with Balloon Framing

Ridge board · Rafters · Roof sheathing · Shingles · Joist · Load-bearing wall · Cripple studs · Header · Studs · King stud · Jack stud · Subfloor · Sill plate · Rough sill · Main beam · Bracing · Fire blocks · Support posts · Foundation

Balloon framing (photos, right and above) is identified by wall studs that run uninterrupted from the roof to a sill plate on the foundation, without the sole plates and top plates found in platform-framed walls (page opposite). Balloon framing was used in houses built before 1930, and it is still used in some new home styles, especially those with high vaulted ceilings.

Anatomy Details

Many remodeling projects, like adding new doors or windows, require that you remove one or more studs in a load-bearing wall to create an opening. When planning your project, remember that new openings require a permanent support beam called a header, above the removed studs, to carry the structural load directly.

The required size for the header is set by local building codes and varies according to the width of the rough opening. For a window or door opening, a header can be built from two pieces of 2" dimensional lumber sandwiched around ⅜" plywood (chart, right). When a large portion of a load-bearing wall (or an entire wall) is removed, a laminated beam product can be used to make the new header.

If you will be removing more than one wall stud, make temporary supports to carry the structural load until the header is installed.

RECOMMENDED HEADER SIZES

ROUGH OPENING WIDTH	RECOMMENDED HEADER CONSTRUCTION
Up to 3'	⅜" plywood between two 2 × 4s
3 to 5'	⅜" plywood between two 2 × 6s
5 to 7'	⅜" plywood between two 2 × 8s
7 to 8'	⅜" plywood between two 2 × 10s

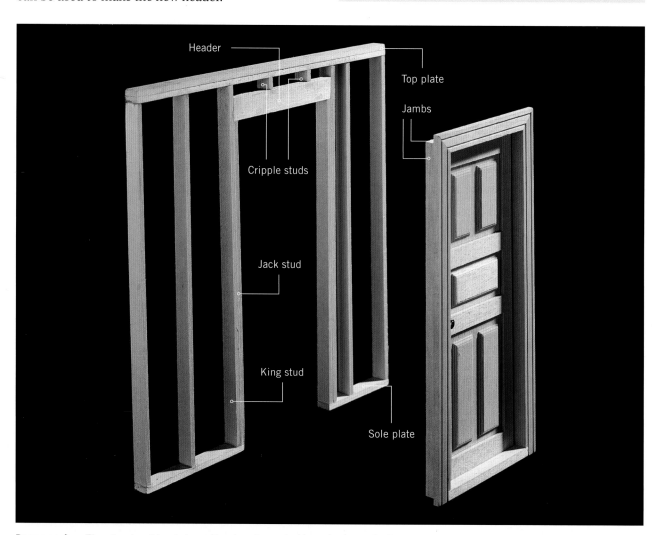

Door opening: The structural load above the door is carried by cripple studs that rest on a header. The ends of the header are supported by jack studs (also known as trimmer studs) and king studs that transfer the load to the sole plate and the foundation of the house. The rough opening for a door should be 1" wider and ½" taller than the dimensions of the door unit, including the jambs. This extra space lets you adjust the door unit during installation.

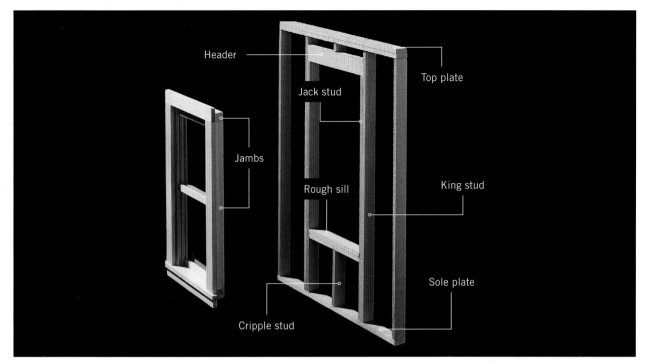

Window opening: The structural load above the window is carried by cripple studs resting on a header. The ends of the header are supported by jack studs and king studs, which transfer the load to the sole plate and the foundation of the house. The rough sill, which helps anchor the window unit but carries no structural weight, is supported by cripple studs. To provide room for adjustments during installation, the rough opening for a window should be 1" wider and ½" taller than the window unit, including the jambs.

Framing Options for Window & Door Openings (new lumber shown in yellow)

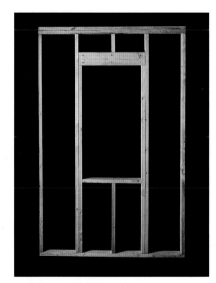

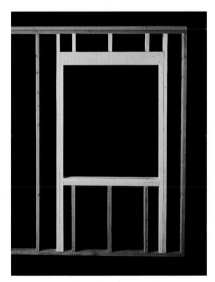

Using an existing opening avoids the need for new framing. This is a good option in homes with masonry exteriors, which are difficult to alter. Order a replacement unit that is 1" narrower and ½" shorter than the rough opening.

Framing a new opening is the only solution when you're installing a window or door where none existed or when you're replacing a unit with one that is much larger.

Enlarging an existing opening simplifies the framing. In many cases, you can use an existing king stud and jack stud to form one side of the new opening.

Building Walls

Partition walls are constructed between load-bearing walls to divide space. They should be strong and well made, but their main job is to house doors and to support wall coverings.

Anchoring New Partition Walls

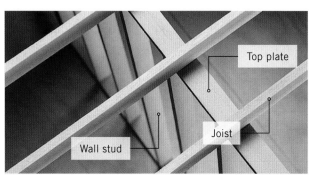

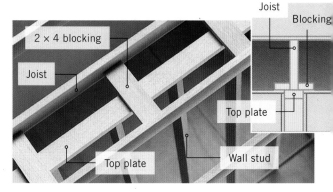

When a new wall is perpendicular to the ceiling or floor joists above, attach the top plate directly to the joists, using 16d nails.

When a new wall falls between parallel joists, install 2 × 4 blocking between the joists every 24". If the new wall is aligned with a parallel joist, install blocks on both sides of the wall, and attach the top plate to the joist (inset).

Wall Anatomy

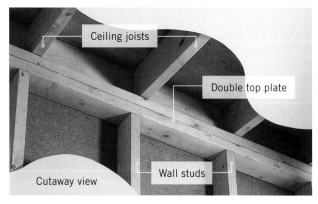

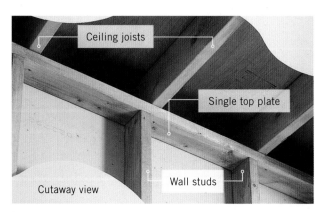

Load-bearing walls carry the structural weight of your home. In platform-framed houses, load-bearing walls can be identified by double top plates made from two layers of framing lumber. Load-bearing walls include all exterior walls and any interior walls that are aligned above support beams.

Partition walls are interior walls that do not carry the structural weight of the house. They have a single top plate and can be perpendicular to the floor and ceiling joists but are not aligned above support beams. Any interior wall that is parallel to floor and ceiling joists is a partition wall.

How to Build a Non-loadbearing Partition Wall

Mark the location of the new wall on the ceiling, then snap two chalk lines or use a scrap piece of 2× lumber as a template to mark layout lines for the top plate. Use a stud finder to locate floor joists or roof framing above the ceiling, and mark these locations with tick marks or tape outside the layout lines.

Cut the top and sole plates to length and lay them side by side. Use a speed square or framing square to draw pairs of lines across both plates to mark the stud locations. Space the studs at 16" intervals, on center.

Mark the location of any door framing on the top and sole plates. Refer to the door's rough opening specifications when marking the layout. Draw lines for both the king and jack studs.

Fasten the top plate to the ceiling using 3" deck screws or 10d nails. Be sure to orient the plate so the stud layout faces down.

OPTION: Rather than toe-nailing the studs to the sole plate, some builders prefer to attach them by face-nailing through the underside of the sole plate and into the bottom ends of the walls studs. Then, after the cap plate is installed on the ceiling, they tip the wall up, nail the sole plate in position, and then toe-nail or toe-screw the studs to the cap plate.

Hang a plumb bob from the edge of the top plate at several points along its length to find the sole plate location on the floor. The tip of the plumb bob should almost touch the floor. Wait until it stops moving before marking the sole plate reference point. Connect the points with a line to establish one edge of the sole plate. Use a piece of scrap 2× material as a template for marking the other edge.

(continued)

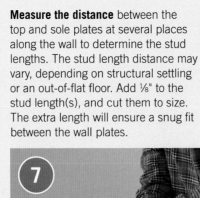

Measure the distance between the top and sole plates at several places along the wall to determine the stud lengths. The stud length distance may vary, depending on structural settling or an out-of-flat floor. Add ⅛" to the stud length(s), and cut them to size. The extra length will ensure a snug fit between the wall plates.

(7)

(8)

(6)

Drive the fasteners into the floor framing. For concrete floors, attach the sole plate with a powder-actuated nail gun or with hardened masonry screws. Cut out and remove a section of sole plate in the door opening or openings, if any (see page 30).

Fasten the end wall studs to adjoining walls. If the new studs do not fall at stud locations, you'll need to install blocking in the old walls (see page 19).

(9)

(10)

(11)

Nail the king studs, jack studs, a header, and a cripple stud in place to complete the rough door framing. See page 29 for more information on framing a door opening. (Inset) An option for attaching wall studs to plates is to use metal connectors and 4d nails.

If building codes in your area require fire blocking, install 2× cutoff scraps between the studs, 4 ft. from the floor, to serve this purpose. Stagger the blocks so you can endnail each piece.

Drill holes through the studs to create guide holes for wiring and plumbing. When this work is completed, fasten metal protector plates over these areas to prevent drilling or nailing through wiring and pipes later. Have your work inspected before proceeding with drywall.

JOINING SECTIONS USING STEEL STUDS

Steel studs and tracks have the same basic structure—a web that spans two flanged sides—but, studs also contain a ¼" lip to improve their rigidity.

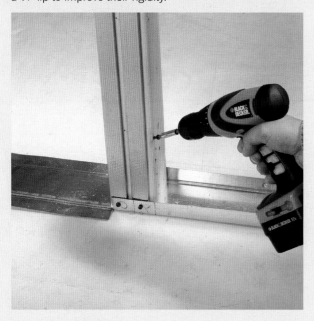

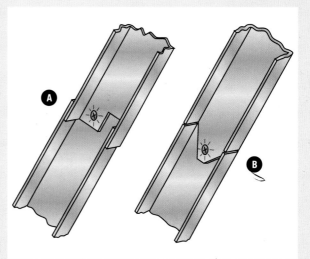

Join sections with a spliced joint (A) or notched joint (B). Make a spliced joint by cutting a 2" slit in the web of one track. Slip the other track into the slit and secure with a screw. For a notched joint, cut back the flanges of one track and taper the web so it fits into the other track; secure with a screw.

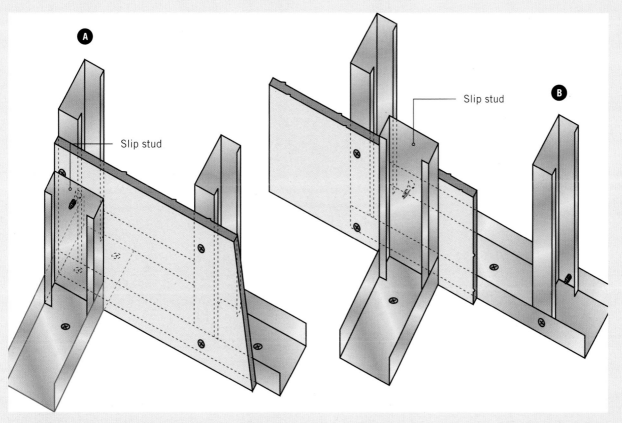

Slip stud

Slip stud

Slip stud

Build corners using a slip stud: A slip stud is not fastened until the adjacent drywall is in place. Form L-shaped corners (A) by overlapping the tracks. Cut off the flange on one side of one track, removing enough to allow room for the overlapping track and drywall. Form a T-shaped corner (B) by leaving a gap between the tracks for the drywall. Secure each slip stud by screwing through the stud into the tracks of the adjacent wall. Also screw through the back side of the drywall into the slip stud, if possible. Where there's no backing behind the slip stud, drive screws at a 45° angle through the back corners of the slip stud and into the drywall.

Building a Kneewall

Kneewalls are shortened versions of conventional walls that usually stand three to four feet tall. They typically fasten to an adjoining wall and tie into it with matching base moldings. The top surface may be trimmed with a wood cap and moldings or simply wrapped with wallboard. Kneewalls can also be constructed from glass block for a more contemporary look or modified into a deeper built-in display case or bookshelf.

From a design standpoint, a kneewall helps to divide a large room into smaller spaces without losing the openness of a large space. A pair of kneewalls can even provide an attractive entryway into a living or dining room if the ends terminate in matching posts. Depending on the house design, these posts could serve a load-bearing purpose as well. Large bathrooms can benefit from a kneewall that creates a modesty divider next to a toilet or bath changing area.

TOOLS & MATERIALS

Utility knife	10d nails or pneumatic framing nails
Tape measure	Drywall
Framing and combination squares	Wood casing material
Hammer or nail gun	6d finish nails or 16-gauge pneumatic brad nails
Nailset	Deck screws
Drill/driver	Construction adhesive
Level	Wallboard finishing supplies
Drywall finishing tools	
Framing lumber	

Kneewalls are straightforward projects that require only basic wall-building skills. You can even build the kneewall in the workshop and carry it to the job site for installation. Unless you are building a kneewall with a load-bearing post or installing wiring in it, there's no need to get a permit or have the project inspected.

How to Build a Kneewall

Mark the kneewall location on an adjacent wall. It helps to position the kneewall in front of a wall stud for convenient attachment.

Option: If you cannot hit a wall stud, you'll need to remove the wallboard between two wall studs and install blocking between them to bridge the cavity and create an attachment point. See "Removing a Non-loadbearing Wall," page 38.

(continued)

Mark the kneewall layout area on the floor with masking tape, dark marker, or pencil lines. If the kneewall will be installed on a carpeted floor, cut out the carpet and pad within the layout lines. Use a sharp chisel to remove the carpet tack strip against the wall. Carefully pry off the wall base molding; you can reuse it if it doesn't break.

Construct the kneewall frame from framing lumber. Build it with a top plate, sole plate, and studs, just as you would a conventional wall. Space the studs 16" on center. Keep in mind that top and sole plates will add height to the kneewall. Be sure to account for this when measuring the length of the kneewall studs.

Set the kneewall frame in position and check it for level. Shim beneath the sole plate, if necessary. Fasten the kneewall to the adjacent wall stud with 3" deck screws. Use shorter deck screws and a bead of construction adhesive to fasten the sole plate to the subflooring. Arrange the sole plate screws in a zigzag pattern for added strength.

NOTE: If you're installing a kneewall over ceramic tile, drill pilot holes for attachment screws with a masonry bit to prevent cracking the tile.

Fasten drywall to the sides and end of the kneewall (and over the top if the project does not include a wooden top cap). Nail strips of metal corner bead to the outside corners, then tape and mud the corners and seams (see pages 59 to 83). Prime and paint the wall coverings.

Nail a wooden top cap to the kneewall top plate with 6d casing nails or brads. Size the cap so it overhangs the drywall and any moldings you plan to apply beneath it. Miter-cut these molding strips and install them beneath the top cap to hide the drywall joint.

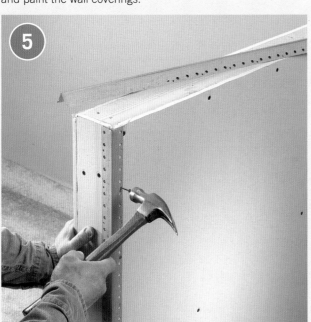

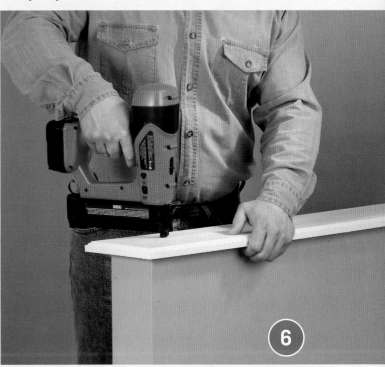

7

Cut and reinstall the moldings you removed earlier on the existing wall. Then wrap the base of the kneewall with mitered base moldings that match the room moldings.

Building a Wet Wall

A wet wall is simply a wall that contains plumbing for water supply and drainage. To accommodate the drain and vent pipes, which range from 1½ to 3 inches in diameter for branch lines, the wall framing needs to be built with 2 × 6 or larger dimensional lumber. You can also attach furring strips (usually 2 × 2) to existing 2 × 4 framing members to increase wall thickness. The chart on the next page describes how deeply you are allowed to notch wall framing members under various load conditions, as well as the maximum-diameter holes you may drill for running plumbing and wiring.

Building a new wet wall or converting an existing wall to house new plumbing requires a building permit and an on-site inspection once all of the hook-ups are made. Do not install any wallcoverings until after your plumbing and wiring have been inspected and approved.

TOOLS & MATERIALS

Circular saw	Basic plumbing tools
Wrecking bar or pry bar	Reciprocating saw
Drill/driver	Protective plates
Caulk gun and adhesive	Plumbing pipes and hangers
Hammer	Dust mask
8d common nails	Goggles
Masking tape	Gloves
Hole saw	
Jigsaw	

MAXIMUM HOLE & NOTCH CHART

FRAMING MEMBER	MAXIMUM HOLE SIZE	MAXIMUM NOTCH SIZE
2 × 4 loadbearing stud	1 7/16" diameter	7/8" deep
2 × 4 non-loadbearing stud	2 1/2" diameter	1 7/16" deep
2 × 6 loadbearing stud	2 1/4" diameter	1 3/8" deep
2 × 6 non-loadbearing stud	3 5/16" diameter	2 3/16" deep
2 × 6 joists	1 1/2" diameter	7/8" deep
2 × 8 joists	2 3/8" diameter	1 1/4" deep
2 × 10 joists	3 1/16" diameter	1 1/2" deep
2 × 12 joists	3 3/4" diameter	1 7/8" deep

The framing member chart shows the maximum sizes for holes and notches that can be cut into studs and joists when running pipes. Where possible, use notches rather than bored holes, because pipe installation is usually easier. When boring holes, there must be at least 5/8" of wood between the edge of a stud and the hole, and at least 2" between the edge of a joist and the hole. Joists can be notched only in the end 1/3 of the overall span; never in the middle 1/3 of the joist. When two pipes are run through a stud, the pipes should be stacked one over the other, never side by side.

SIZING FOR WATER DISTRIBUTION PIPES

FIXTURE	UNIT RATING
Toilet	3
Vanity sink	1
Shower	2
Bathtub	2
Dishwasher	2
Kitchen sink	2
Clothes washer	2
Utility sink	2
Sillcock	3

SIZE OF SERVICE PIPE FROM STREET	SIZE OF DISTRIBUTION PIPE FROM WATER METER	MAXIMUM LENGTH (FT.)— TOTAL FIXTURE UNITS					
		40	60	80	100	150	200
3/4"	1/2"	9	8	7	6	5	4
3/4"	3/4"	27	23	19	17	14	11
3/4"	1"	44	40	36	33	28	23
1"	1"	60	47	41	36	30	25
1"	1 1/4"	102	87	76	67	52	44

Water distribution pipes are the main pipes extending from the water meter throughout the house, supplying water to the branch pipes leading to individual fixtures. To determine the size of the distribution pipes, you must first calculate the total demand in "fixture units" (above, left) and the overall length of the water supply lines, from the street hookup through the water meter and to the most distant fixture in the house. Then, use the second table (above, right) to calculate the minimum size for the water distribution pipes.

SIZES FOR BRANCH PIPES & SUPPLY TUBES

FIXTURE	MIN. BRANCH PIPE SIZE	MIN. SUPPLY TUBE SIZE
Toilet	1/2"	3/8"
Vanity sink	1/2"	3/8"
Shower	1/2"	1/2"
Bathtub	1/2"	1/2"
Dishwasher	1/2"	1/2"
Kitchen sink	1/2"	1/2"
Clothes washer	1/2"	1/2"
Utility sink	1/2"	1/2"
Sillcock	3/4"	N.A.
Water heater	3/4"	N.A.

TYPE OF PIPE	PIPE SUPPORT INTERVALS	
	VERTICAL-RUN SUPPORT INTERVAL	HORIZONTAL-RUN SUPPORT INTERVAL
Copper	10 ft.	6 ft.
PEX	5 ft.	3 ft.
CPVC	10 ft.	3 ft.
PVC	10 ft.	4 ft.
Steel	12 ft.	10 ft.
Iron	15 ft.	5 ft.

Branch pipes are the water supply lines that run from the distribution pipes toward the individual fixtures. Supply tubes are the vinyl, chromed copper, or braided tubes that carry water from the branch pipes to the fixtures.

Minimum intervals for supporting pipes are determined by the type of pipe and its orientation in the system. Remember that the measurements shown above are minimum requirements.

How to Build & Plumb a Wet Wall

Clear the work area. If you are remodeling an existing wall to contain plumbing for a new kitchen or bathroom, you'll need to completely remove the wall coverings so you can fur out the wall studs. This project requires a building permit and at least one on-site inspection. Shut off power at the main service panel before cutting into walls.

Begin removing wallcoverings on the entire wall. There are many ways to go about this. One is to set your circular saw to a cutting depth equal to the wallcovering thickness and make a few starter cuts. Remove any cover plates on the wall before you start.

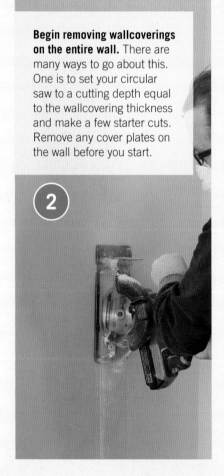

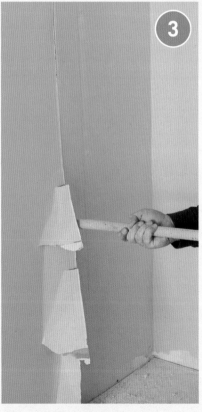

Next, use a wrecking bar to pry the wallcovering loose. Work in sections that are large, but manageable. Discard the material you remove immediately.

Remove old drywall screws or nails that remain in the wall-framing members.

Cut 2 × 2 furring strips to length. Start with the sole plate of the wall. Apply a bead of construction adhesive to the 2 × 2.

Attach the furring strips to the wall framing members with 8d finish or casing nails. Drive a nail every 12 to 16 inches.

Install the vertical furring strips next, using nails and construction adhesive. Finally, attach furring strips to the wall cap plate. Re-route wiring in the wall according to your plan. If you are keeping receptacles or switches in the same place, you'll still need to move the boxes forward in the wall cavity so the edges will be flush with the new wall surface.

If you are installing a drain for a tub or shower, mark out the location of the drain onto the subfloor. Remove floorcoverings first. Mark a center point for the drainage pipe onto the sole plate. The pipe should align with the location for the drain trap. If your plan calls for it, drill additional holes for fixture drains, such as the wall sink stub-out being installed in this wall.

Drill holes for the drain pipes using a hole saw that's slightly larger than the outside diameter of the new pipe. In most cases, a 2"-diameter pipe is adequate for this type of branch drain (see table, page 23), so a 2½" hole saw is a good choice.

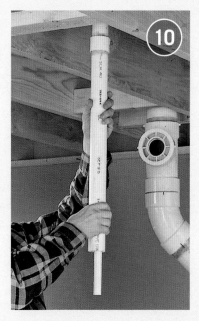

Feed sections of drain pipe up through the holes in the sole plate and floor (if you are tying in to the plumbing on the floor below—the easiest way to tap into the existing plumbing system). Connect the drain line to a drainage stack, maintaining a slope of at least ¼" per ft. It is always a good idea to include a cleanout on the new branch line.

(continued)

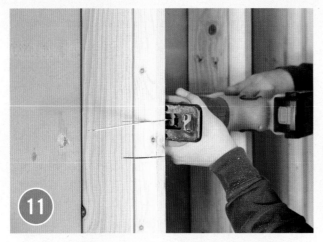

Cut notches in the wall-framing members to hold the horizontal plumbing in the drain lines. See chart on page 23. Cut no deeper than needed to hold the pipes.

Cut the horizontal lines to length and set them into the notches. You can hold them in place with tape if they don't stay put.

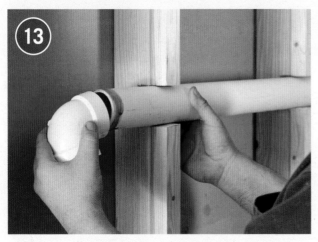

Attach a 90° elbow to the end of the new horizontal line so it aligns with the drain pipe coming up through the floor. The other end of horizontal pipe is fitted with a tee fitting so the vent line can be extended up through the cap plate and ceiling.

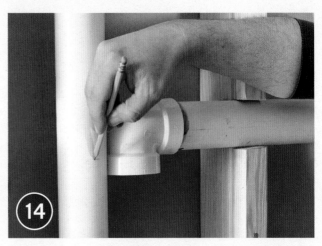

With the drain pipes seated in the fitting below the floor (but not cemented), mark the free ends of the vertical pipes for cutting at the points where they will join the fittings on the horizontal line. Dry-fit this union. Do not cement yet.

Remove the subfloor in the section you've laid out for the drain. Cut with a jigsaw, using a starter hole if you need to. If you've planned the drain location wisely it will not fall over a floor joist.

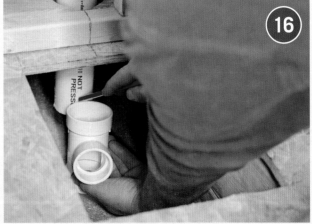

Reach into the hole in the subfloor and mark the vertical pipe for cutting to accept a tee fitting. The tee should have a slight sweep downward. Normally, the open end of the tee is sized for a 1½"-diameter drain tube to run from the vertical drain line to the drain trap.

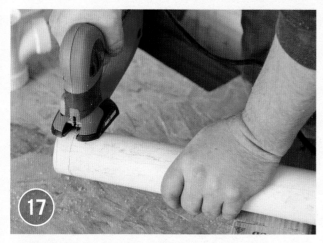

Remove the drain pipes and cut them to the lengths you've marked.

Cement the reducing tee into the drain line for the tub, making sure to orient the sweep correctly and to align the opening with the drain trap location.

Cement a reducing tee into the drain line for the sink stub-out.

Cement the drain lines into the drain fittings from below. Solvent-cement the brand drain line components on the floor below, tying the line into the main drain stack or another large branch drain.

Install cold and hot water supply lines, connecting from the floor below.

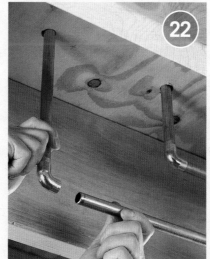

Connect the vent pipe from the wet wall with another vent line in the attic or, if you prefer, run it out through the roof and flash and cover it according to your local plumbing codes.

Solder supply stub-outs onto the new water lines. Install protective metal plates on the wall studs to cover pipe (and electrical cable) penetrations. Have your work inspected and, when approved, you may go ahead and install wallcoverings.

Installing Interior Doors

Creating an opening for a door in a wall involves building a framework about 1 inch wider and ½ inch taller than the door's jamb frame. This oversized opening, called a rough opening, will enable you to position the door easily and shim it plumb and level. Before framing a door, it's always a good idea to buy the door and refer to the manufacturer's recommendations for rough opening size.

Door frames consist of a pair of full-length king studs and two shorter jack studs that support the header above the door. A header provides an attachment point for wallboard and door casings. On load-bearing walls, it also helps to transfer the building's structural loads from above down into the wall framework and eventually the foundation.

Door framing requires flat, straight, and dry framing lumber, so choose your king, jack, and header pieces carefully. Sight down the edges and ends to look for warpage, and cut off the ends of pieces with splits.

TOOLS & MATERIALS

Tape measure

Framing square

Hammer or nail gun

Handsaw or reciprocating saw

Framing lumber

10d or pneumatic framing nails

½" plywood
   (for structural headers)

Construction adhesive

Creating a square, properly sized opening for a door is the most important element of a successful door installation project.

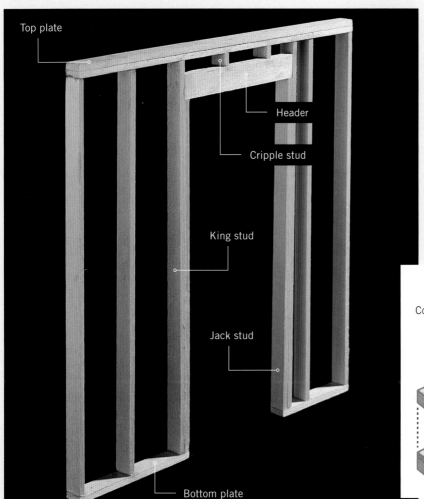

Top plate

Header

Cripple stud

King stud

Jack stud

Bottom plate

Door frames for prehung doors (left) start with king studs that attach to the top and bottom plates. Inside the king studs, jack studs support the header at the top of the opening. Cripple studs continue the wall-stud layout above the opening. In non-loadbearing walls, the header may be a 2 × 4 laid flat or a built-up header (below). The dimensions of the framed opening are referred to as the rough opening.

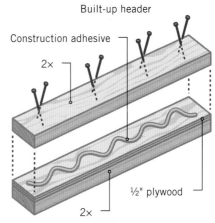

Built-up header

Construction adhesive

2×

½" plywood

2×

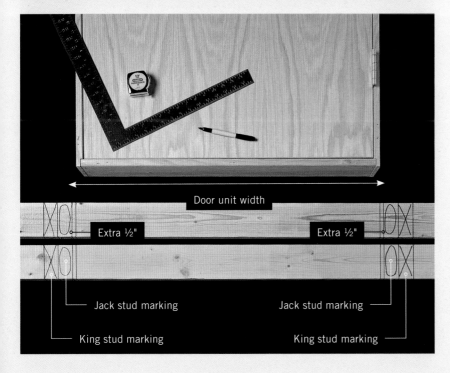

Door unit width

Extra ½"   Extra ½"

Jack stud marking   Jack stud marking

King stud marking   King stud marking

To mark the layout for the door frame, measure the width of the door unit along the bottom. Add 1" to this dimension to determine the width of the rough opening (the distance between the jack studs). This gives you a ½" gap on each side for adjusting the door frame during installation. Mark the top and bottom plates for the jack and king studs.

Door framing on load-bearing walls will require a structural header that transfers loads above the wall into the jack studs, sole plate, and down into the house foundation. Build it by sandwiching a piece of ⅜" plywood between two 2 × 4s. Use construction adhesive and nails to fasten the header together.

Mark layout lines for the king and jack studs on the wall's top and sole plates (see page 29). Cut the king studs slightly longer than the distance between the wall plates, and toenail them in place with 10d nails or 3" pneumatic nails.

Cut the jack studs to length (they should rest on the sole plate). The height of a jack stud for a standard interior door is 83½", or ½" taller than the door. Nail the jack studs to the king studs.

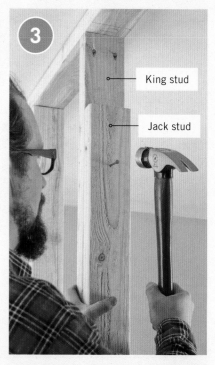

King stud

Jack stud

Install the built-up header by resting it on the jack studs and endnailing through the king studs. Use 10d nails or 3" pneumatic nails.

Fasten a cripple stud above the header halfway between the king studs for use as a nailing surface.

Cut a sole plate opening for the door with a reciprocating saw or handsaw. Trim the sole plate flush with the jack studs. Install the saw blade teeth-up for better access.

How to Frame an Opening for a Non-loadbearing Wall

VARIATION: In a non-loadbearing wall, the header can be a piece of 2× framing lumber that lays flat on top of the jack studs. Cut it to length, and install by endnailing through the king studs or down into the jack studs. Toenail a cripple stud between the top plate and header, halfway between the king studs. It transfers structural loads into the header.

 ## OPTION: FRAMING OPENINGS FOR SLIDING & FOLDING DOORS

The same basic framing techniques are used, whether you're planning to install a sliding, bifold, pocket, or prehung interior door. The different door styles require different frame openings. You may need to frame an opening two to three times wider than the opening for a standard prehung door. Purchase the doors and hardware in advance, and consult the hardware manufacturer's instructions for the exact dimensions of the rough opening and header size for the type of door you select.

Most bifold doors are designed to fit in an 80"-high finished opening. Wood bifold doors have the advantage of allowing you to trim the doors, if necessary, to fit openings that are slightly shorter.

Installing a Prehung Interior Door

Install prehung interior doors after the framing work is complete and the drywall has been installed. If the rough opening for the door has been framed accurately, installing the door takes about an hour.

Standard prehung doors have 4½-inch-wide jambs and are sized to fit walls with 2 × 4 construction and ½-inch wallboard. If you have 2 × 6 construction or thicker wall surface material, you can special order a door to match, or you can add jamb extensions to a standard-sized door (photo, below).

TOOLS & MATERIALS

Level	Prehung interior door
Hammer	Wood shims
Handsaw	8d casing nails

TIP: JAMB EXTENSIONS

Jamb extension

If your walls are built with 2 × 6 studs, you'll need to extend the jambs by attaching wood strips to the edges of the jamb after the door is installed. Use glue and 4d casing nails when attaching jamb extensions.

How to Install a Prehung Interior Door

Insert pairs of wood shims driven from opposite directions into the gap between the framing members and the hinge-side jamb, spaced every 12". Check the hinge-side jamb to make sure it is still plumb and does not bow.

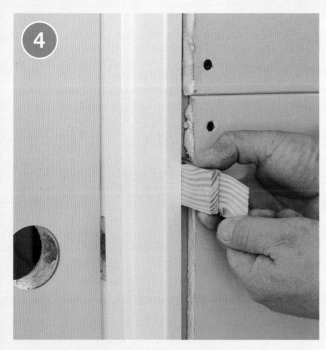

Slide the door unit into the framed opening so the edges of the jambs are flush with the wall surface and the hinge-side jamb is plumb.

Anchor the hinge-side jamb with 8d casing nails driven through the jamb and shims and into the jack stud.

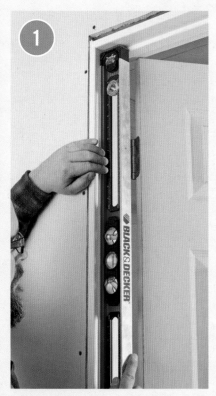

Insert pairs of shims in the gap between the framing members and the latch-side jamb and top jamb, spaced every 12". With the door closed, adjust the shims so the gap between door edge and jamb is ⅛" wide. Drive 8d casing nails through the jambs and shims, into the framing members.

Cut the shims flush with the wall surface, using a handsaw. Hold the saw vertically to prevent damage to the door jamb or wall. Finish the door and install the lockset as directed by the manufacturer. See pages 244 to 255 to install trim around the door.

Framing Basement Foundation Walls

You can use conventional wall-framing techniques to turn an unused basement into a warm, inviting living space. Stud walls provide deep bays for insulation and allow you to use ordinary receptacle boxes for wall outlets. Fully framed walls will be stronger than the furring strip method discussed on pages 102 to 103, and they may be your only option if your basement walls aren't flat and plumb. The downside to framing your basement walls is that the material costs will be greater than using furring strips and foam insulation. Stud walls will also reduce the size of the room, which may be an issue if you have a small basement.

Assembling a stud wall next to a foundation wall is essentially the same process as building a wall elsewhere. However, since there's always the potential for water infiltration through cinder block or poured basement walls, it's a good idea to build your walls about ½" away from the foundation to create an airspace. This gap will also be useful for avoiding any unevenness in your foundation walls.

How to Frame a Basement Foundation Wall

Mark the location of the new wall on the floor joists above, then use a scrap piece of 2 × 4 as a template to draw layout lines for the new top plate. Position the top plate about ½" away from the foundation wall to create an airspace. If the joists run parallel to the foundation wall, nail blocking between them to create attachment points for the new wall.

Hang a plumb bob from the top plate layout lines to mark the sole plate position on the floor. Move the bob along the top plate and mark the sole plate at several points on the floor. Set a piece of scrap 2 × 4 in place on the floor to make sure the sole plate will still allow for an air gap. Draw pairs of lines across both plates with a combination square to mark stud locations.

Fasten the top plate to the floor joists using 3" deck screws or 10d nails (top). Be sure to orient the plate so the stud layout faces down. Attach the sole plate to the concrete floor with a powder-actuated nailer (lower) or with hardened masonry screws. Drill pilot holes for the screws with a hammer drill.

4

Measure the distance between the top and sole plates at several places along the wall to determine the stud lengths. The stud length distance may vary, depending on structural settling or an out-of-flat floor. Add ⅛" to the stud length(s), and cut them to size.

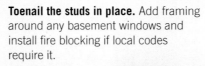

Toenail the studs in place. Add framing around any basement windows and install fire blocking if local codes require it.

5

Drill holes through the studs to create raceways for wiring and plumbing. Install these systems and fasten metal protector plates over these areas to prevent drilling or nailing through wiring and pipes later. Have your work inspected before proceeding with insulation and wallboard.

6

7

Install rolled insulation in the stud bays. Using plastic encapsulated insulation is a good preventive measure against mold growth. Otherwise, use kraft-faced insulation.

Staple 6-mil plastic sheeting to the wall studs to form a vapor barrier behind the finished wall. Cut holes in the plastic for receptacle openings.

NOTE: There is considerable debate over whether or not you should employ a vapor barrier on a basement wall, mostly because the barrier can trap water that enters from the exterior. Check with your local building inspector.

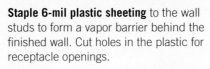

8

Install your wallcovering of choice. If you choose drywall, finish the seams with drywall compound and tape as usual. Be sure to use moisture-resistant drywall for basement walls (some new drywall products are also mold- and mildew-resistant—ask at your building center).

9

1

Install 2 × 4 blocking between floor joists to form a square framework around the obstruction. Use 3" deck screws to fasten the framework in place.

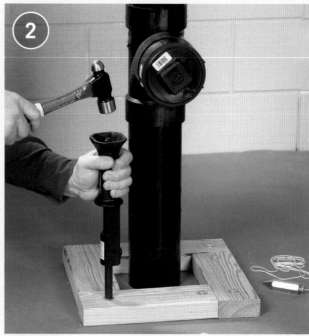

2

Build another square framework on the floor that matches the size of the top frame. Make this frame from treated lumber, and fasten it to the concrete with a powder-actuated nailer or a hammer drill and masonry screws. Hang a plumb bob down from the top frame to find the exact location of this bottom frame before attaching it.

3

Toenail four 2 × 4 studs between the two frames to complete the chase framework. Finish the chase with drywall, metal corner bead, and drywall compound.

4

If the chase encloses a DWV stack or other plumbing with valves or cleanouts, be sure to build an access panel in the chase to keep these areas accessible. Use furring strips or plywood behind two sides of the access opening to form tabs that hold the access panel in place. Attach the panel with screws, and glue on decorative trim to hide the drywall edges.

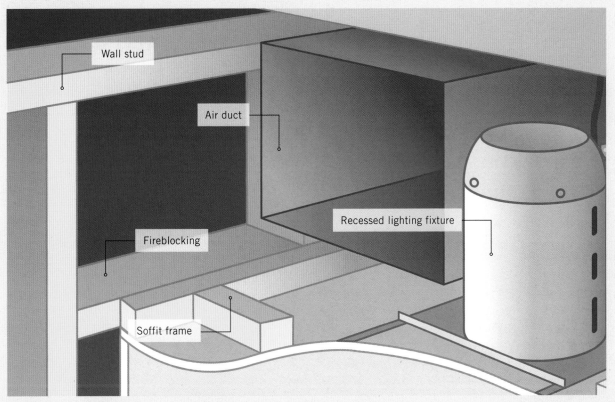

Wall stud

Air duct

Recessed lighting fixture

Fireblocking

Soffit frame

Hide immovable obstructions in a soffit built from dimension lumber or steel and covered with drywall or other finish material. An extra-wide soffit is also a great place to install recessed lighting fixtures.

How to Frame a Furnace Duct

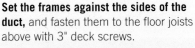

Set the frames against the sides of the duct, and fasten them to the floor joists above with 3" deck screws.

Build a pair of ladder-like frames that match the side dimensions of the furnace duct from standard 2 × 2s. Fasten the parts together with 3" deck screws.

Install 2 × 2 crosspieces between the frames to provide attachment points below the duct for drywall. Then finish the soffit with drywall, metal corner bead, and drywall compound.

Removing a Non-loadbearing Wall

Removing an existing interior wall is an easy way to create more usable space without the expense of building an addition. Removing a wall turns two small rooms into a large space perfect for family living. Adding new walls in a larger area creates a private space to use as a quiet study or as a new bedroom.

Be sure the wall you plan to remove is not load-bearing before you begin (see page 14). If you need to remove a load-bearing wall, check with a contractor or building inspector first. Load-bearing walls carry the weight of the structure above them. You'll need to install a temporary support wall to take the place of the structural wall you're removing.

Remember that walls also hold the essential mechanical systems that run through your home. You need to consider how your project affects these mechanicals. Turn off electrical power at the service panel before you begin demolition.

TOOLS & MATERIALS

Stud finder	Pry bars
Tape measure	Reciprocating
Utility knife	or circular saw
Hammer	Drill

How to Remove a Non-loadbearing Wall

Use a utility knife to score the intersections where the wall you're removing meets the ceiling to keep from damaging it during wall removal. Pry away baseboard trim and remove receptacle plates and switch covers to prepare for demolition.

Use the side of a hammer to punch a starter hole in the drywall, then carefully remove the drywall with a pry bar. Try to pull off large sections at a time to minimize dust. Remove any remaining drywall nails or screws from the wall studs.

Reroute outlets, switches, plumbing, or ductwork. Have professionals do this for you if you are not experienced with these systems or confident in your skills. This work should be inspected after it is completed.

Locate the closest permanent studs on the adjacent wall or walls with a stud finder, and carefully remove the drywall up to these studs. Score the drywall first with a utility knife, then cut through it with a circular saw.

Remove the wall studs by cutting through them in the middle with a reciprocating saw and prying out the upper and lower sections. Remove the endmost studs where the wall meets an adjacent wall or walls.

Cut through the wall's top plate with a circular saw or reciprocating saw. Pry out the top plate sections carefully to avoid damaging the ceiling.

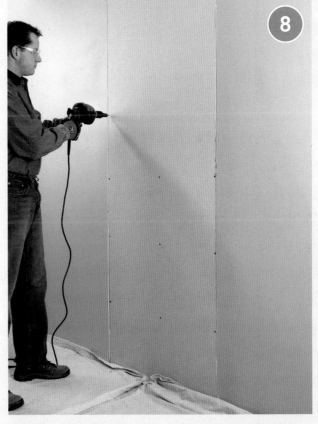

Remove the sole plate just as you did the top plate by cutting through it and prying up the long pieces.

Patch the walls and ceiling with strips of drywall, and repair the floor as needed with new floor coverings.

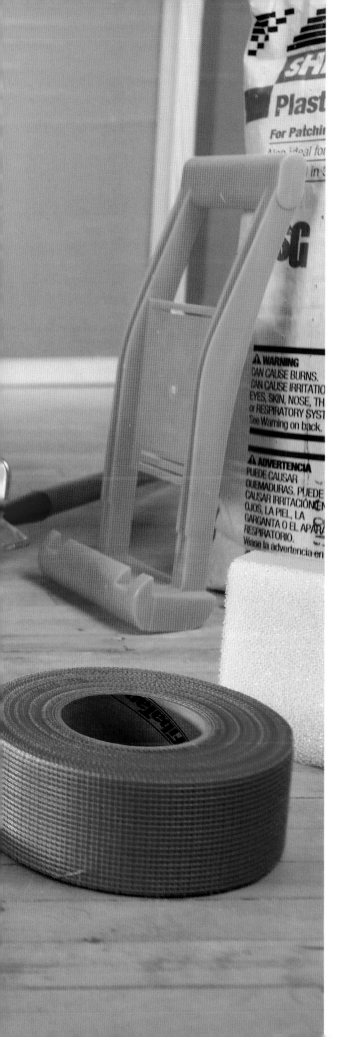

Drywall Materials & Equipment

A successful drywalling job depends heavily on selecting the best materials and equipment for the task. The process starts with the drywall panels themselves. Not only is choosing the right panel type for your application important to get good results, it can mean the difference between passing a building inspection and having to tear out your work and start over. Contact your local building department early on in the planning stage to get information relevant to your job. Of most concern to building departments are ceilings and firewalls that separate distinct parts of the house—the wall between a house and an attached garage is a typical example—because these areas must meet strict fire code standards.

Another factor to consider when choosing materials is moisture. If the room you're working on is in a high-moisture environment, use panels that resist moisture damage and mold. You may also need special seaming, taping, and mudding products. The information that follows provides a comprehensive guide to help you make these decisions.

Although you can hang drywall using only a hammer and a utility knife, good tools make the job go faster and yield better results. From professional drywall guns with self-feed screws to laser levels, joint compound paddles, and hoppers for applying textured finishes, this chapter provides a comprehensive guide to tools that can be used in any phase of the process.

In this chapter:
- Drywall Panel Types
- Fasteners, Adhesives & Caulks
- Finishing Materials
- Drywall Tools & Equipment

Drywall Panel Types

Up until the 1930s, interior walls were created by troweling wet plaster onto wood or metal lath that had been nailed to the wall framing members. The finished wall required three coats of plaster, each of which had to be permitted to dry or set. The first generation of drywall panels replaced the lath and the heavy "scratch" coat of plaster. Today, even when a traditional plaster wall finish is desired, special blue-papered drywall panels are anchored to the framing to form the base of the wall instead of a hand-troweled scratch coat. This reduces labor and drying time greatly. Since the end of World War II, the typical drywall panel wall requires no finish layer of plaster. Only minor surface corrections are required, including the filling of seams and covering of fastener dimples with joint compound. Eliminating hand-troweled finishes saves time, labor, and money.

Drywall usually consists of a strong paper skin adhered to a gypsum core. The finish-ready face paper wraps around to the back of the panel at the sides, where it overlaps the coarser, more rigid paper used on the back. For handling purposes, sheets of drywall are joined at the ends by removable strips of tape. To facilitate finishing, panels are typically tapered at the long edges. The shallow depression formed where panels meet is easily covered with tape and filled with joint compound for a flat surface that appears continuous. The short, butt-end joints are not recessed and are more challenging to finish.

Drywall is a broad category of building materials that covers many types of panels with various purposes, including common gypsum-based wallcovering panels as well as specialty wallcoverings and tile backers.

 GYPSUM

Gypsum is a naturally occurring crystal mined from the earth. It is formed when calcium sulfate chemically combines with water. The scrubbers that neutralize sulfuric acid emitted from power plants also create gypsum synthetically. Today much of our gypsum drywall is a byproduct of this effort to protect the environment from acid rain. When buildings burn, the water is driven out of gypsum crystals in drywall, producing steam. This characteristic makes gypsum a fire suppressant, though eventually the dehydrated gypsum will collapse.

Piles of mined gypsum await processing into the basic constituent material used to make drywall.

Types of Panels

Standard drywall is used for most walls and ceilings in dry, interior areas. It comes in 4-ft.-wide panels in lengths ranging from 8 to 16 ft. and in thicknesses of ¼", ⅜", ½", and ⅝". There are also 54"-wide panels for horizontal installations on walls with 9-ft. ceilings.

Flexible drywall, specially made for curved walls, is a bendable version of standard ¼"-thick drywall. It can be installed dry or dampened with water to increase its flexibility.

Fire-resistant drywall has a dense, fiber-reinforced core that helps contain fire. Thicknesses are ½", ⅝", and ¾". Most fire-resistant drywall is called "Type X." Fire-resistant panels are generally required in attached garages, on walls adjacent to garages, and in furnace and utility rooms.

Moisture-resistant drywall, commonly called "greenboard" for the color of its face paper, is designed for areas of high-humidity. It is no longer allowed as a backer for tub and shower surrounds.

Abuse-resistant drywall withstands surface impacts and resists penetrations better than standard drywall. It's available in ½" regular and ⅝" fire-resistant types.

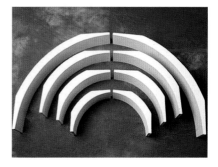

Decorative drywall products include prefinished vinyl-coated panel systems, decorative corner treatments, prefabricated arches, and drywall panels that look like traditional raised-panel paneling.

Sound-resistant drywall products have up to eight times as much sound-deadening capability as standard drywall. These products are good for home theaters.

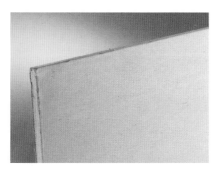

Plaster-base drywall, sometimes called "blueboard," is used with veneer plaster systems instead of a traditional hand-troweled scratch coat. Panels have two layers of paper—a blue-colored face paper that's highly absorptive over a moisture-resistant paper to protect the gypsum core.

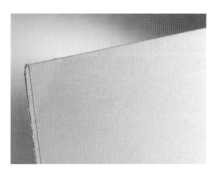

Mold-resistant drywall is a specialty board designed for areas that are regularly damp, have high humidity, or that are otherwise susceptible to mold and mildew growth.

If you're planning to tile new walls in wet areas, such as tub and shower enclosures, use tile backer board as a substrate rather than drywall. Unlike drywall, tile backer won't break down—and ruin the tile job—if water gets behind the tile. There are three basic types of tile backer (see page 267 for supplier information).

Cementboard is made from Portland cement and sand reinforced by a continuous outer layer of fiberglass mesh. It's available in $\frac{5}{16}$", $\frac{1}{2}$", and $\frac{5}{8}$" thicknesses. See page 84 to 85 for installation instructions.

Fiber-cement board is similar to cementboard but is somewhat lighter, with fiber reinforcement integrated throughout the panel material. It comes in $\frac{1}{4}$" and $\frac{1}{2}$" thicknesses. Cementboard and fiber-cement board cannot be damaged by water, but water can pass through them. To prevent damage to the framing, install a water barrier of 4-mil plastic or 15# building paper behind the backer.

Dens-Shield®, commonly called glass mat, is a water-resistant gypsum board with a waterproof fiberglass facing. Dens-Shield cuts and installs much like standard drywall but requires galvanized screws to prevent corrosion. Because the front surface provides the water barrier, all untaped joints and penetrations must be sealed with caulk before the tile is installed. Do not use a water barrier behind Dens-Shield.

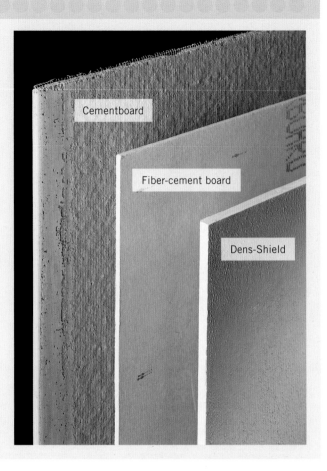

Cementboard

Fiber-cement board

Dens-Shield

TIP

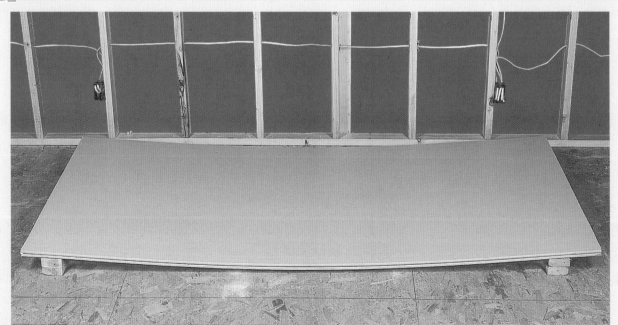

Pre-bowing panels helps ensure a tight seal with the framing when using adhesives. The day before installation, stack panels face up, supporting each end with a pair of 2 × 4s. This helps create pressure between the panel and the studs as the memory of the panel tries to revert to the bowed shape.

Using Specialized Drywall Panels

Upgrade to thicker ⅝" panels to achieve greater sag resistance on ceilings with 24" joist spacing or when a finish coat of water-based texture will be applied. The greater thickness also improves fire- and sound-transmission ratings. Look for Type X drywall.

Flexible ¼" panels can be bent in a tight radius and applied two-layers thick on curved walls. Regular ¼" and ⅜" panels can be attached directly over damaged wall surfaces in remodel and repair work. They also bend well when dampened. The ⅜" panels may also be used in double-layer applications or in a single layer under paneling.

Greenboard panels hold up well under damp conditions in bathrooms, kitchens, and laundry rooms, although they do require closer joist spacing on ceilings. The composition of the panel is the same as standard drywall, but the paper is replaced with vinyl facing to repel moisture. For wet areas behind tile or shower and tub surround, use a tile backerboard like Dens-Shield or cementboard.

Scratch pass

Plaster-base panels are used when a tough plaster surface is needed to match traditional lath and plaster walls. Plaster-base panels can be attached to the wall or ceiling framing. The special blue paper face allows a strong adhesion with the gypsum plaster while protecting the gypsum core from moisture damage as the plaster dries.

Fasteners, Adhesives & Caulks

Drywall is best fastened with drywall screws—typically black phosphate-coated, coarse-threaded screws that are 1¼ inches long. Until the rise of the countersinking screwgun, drywall was installed with hammers and ring-shank drywall nails. Nails still have some uses: for example, the initial securing of hard-to-reach portions of wall and ceiling panels. Nails are also often used for securing metal corner bead because they create less distortion of the bead than an over-driven screw. Ring-shank drywall nails should penetrate framing by at least ¾ inch. Nails cannot be used with metal wall studs and framing. Because screws hold drywall more securely than nails, you may employ greater fastener spacing with them (see table on page 73).

Drywall screws are categorized by letters, indicating the type of framing they are best suited to be used with. For wood framing, select Type W screws that penetrate the framing by at least ⅝ inch. For steel framing or to secure gypsum panels to resilient channels, use fine-threaded Type S screws that penetrate the metal by at least ⅜ inch. Use drill-point Type S screws for heavy-gauge steel. To screw gypsum to gypsum in double layers until an adhesive sets, use course threaded Type G screws. Alternatively, use longer Type S or W screws to attach panels to the framing.

Special screws are made for other non-drywall panels. Cementboard is best fastened with cementboard screws that self-tap into the hard cementboard surface and then resist corrosion in the damp, alkaline environment. Use fine threads for steel framing and coarse threads for wood framing. Hot-dipped galvanized roofing nails may also be used to secure cementboard and other tile backers to wood framing.

Some drywall installations also call for the use of adhesives. Ordinary joint compound can function as an adhesive when applied between drywall layers in a two-layer wall. Panel adhesive may be used to laminate drywall panels also. Panel adhesive applied to studs or joists can reduce fastener needs by 75 percent and eliminate the possibility of panels rattling. A spray-on adhesive is used to attach vinyl corner bead to drywall.

Acoustical sealant (caulk) fills openings and cracks that let sound through walls and ceilings and helps isolate drywall panels from the vibration of adjacent surfaces. Used around electric boxes and floor-to-wall seams, it's the least expensive way to improve sound-transmission class ratings. It can also reduce heating and cooling needs by blocking air gaps.

Drywall screws are the fastener of choice for hanging drywall on walls and ceilings, largely because they grip better, are more controllable, and don't pop out like nails can. Many pros still use nails, however, to tack panels into place prior to screwing.

Fastening Drywall Panels

Drywall fasteners include: Type W for screwing panels to wood framing (A); Type G for drawing panels together in multilayer installations (B); Trimhead drywall screws for fastening wood trim to metal studs (C); Type S standard (D) and Self-tapping (E) for attaching panels to steel framing; Cementboard screws (F); Ring-shank drywall nails (G); and Smooth drywall nails (H).

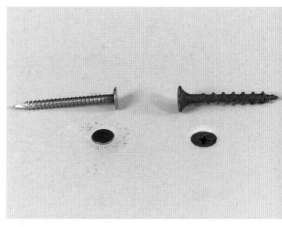

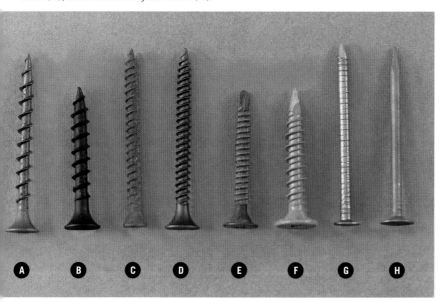

A   B   C   D   E   F   G   H

Drywall screwheads and nail heads are shaped to provide maximum holding power for the panel without tearing the facing paper. Screws have a bugle head that preserves the paper integrity as long as the screw is not overdriven. The undersides of the nail heads have slight, smooth tapers so the heads may be countersunk without tearing through the paper.

DRYWALL ADHESIVES

Adhesives can be used in drywall installation and offer a number of benefits: They create a much stronger bond between framing and panels, reduce the number of fasteners needed by up to 75 percent, and can bridge minor irregularities in framing members. There are several types of adhesives and caulks used for installing drywall:

Construction adhesive is used with screws for gluing panels directly to framing or a solid base, such as concrete basement walls.

Panel or laminating adhesive is used for gluing drywall panels to other panels in multi-layer installations, or to bond panels with concrete walls or rigid foam insulation. A few Type G drywall screws may be needed to support panels while the adhesive sets up.

Contact cement is used for attaching other coverings to drywall panels, such as mass-loaded vinyl sheeting for soundproofing.

Acoustical sealant, while not an adhesive, is used during multiple layer installations to seal all gaps around the perimeter of installed panels and along corners, ceilings, and floors. Acoustical sealant comes in a tube and is applied with a caulk gun.

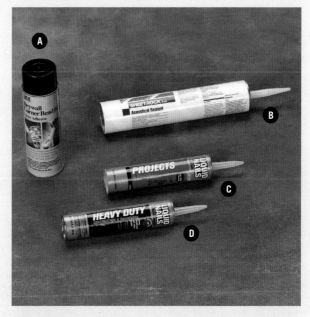

Adhesives useful for installing and finishing drywall include: spray-on adhesive (A) for attaching corner bead; acoustical sealant (B) for filling gaps around panel perimeters in multi-layer installations; and panel adhesive (C) and construction adhesive (D) for bonding panels to framing members or other panels.

Finishing Materials

Finishing drywall is the more difficult part of surfacing walls and ceilings, but it's a project well within the ability of a DIY homeowner. Armed with a basic understanding of the variety of finish materials available, you'll be able to walk out of your local home center or drywall supplier with the exact supplies you need to cover all joints, corners, and fasteners for a successful drywall project.

The primary materials used in finishing are corner bead, tape, and joint compound. Corner bead is the angle strip—usually made of metal or vinyl—that covers a drywall corner, creating a straight, durable edge where walls intersect. Joint tape is combined with joint compound to create a permanent layer that covers the drywall seams as well as small holes and gaps. Without tape, thick applications of compound are highly prone to cracking. There are two types of joint tape: paper and self-adhesive fiberglass mesh. Joint compound, commonly called "mud," seals and levels all seams, corners, and depressions in a drywall installation. It's also used for skim coating and some texturing treatments. There are several types of compounds, with important differences among them, but the two main forms are used for setting and drying (setting-type and drying-type).

ESTIMATING MATERIALS

The following tips will help you determine how much of each material you will need for your project. Add 10 to 15 percent to your estimate to cover waste and mistakes.

Corner Bead: Count the number of corners and the lengths of each, and purchase enough bead to cover each in one piece. Beads are available in standard lengths of 8 to 10 feet.

Joint Tape: Approximately 375 feet of tape will finish 1000 square feet of drywall.

Compound: The following are estimates. Check with the manufacturer for actual coverage information. For every 100 square feet of drywall, you'll need approximately:

- 1 gallon of pre-mixed, drying-type compound (taping, topping, and all purpose)

- 8 lbs. of powder drying-type compound

- 7½ lbs. of standard powder setting-type compound

- 5½ lbs. of lightweight powder setting-type compound

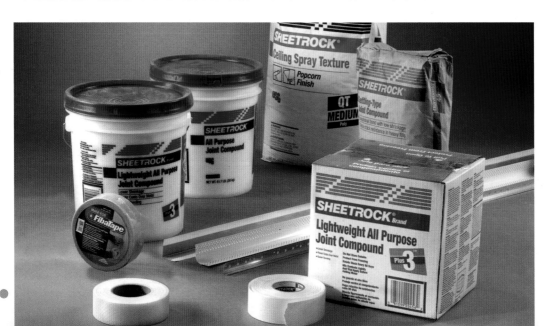

Materials for finishing your drywall-coated wall include: bead and tape (for covering corners and seams), joint compound (for covering dimples, dents, bead, and tape) and texturing materials (for creating a spray-texture surface).

Corner Bead

Corners, seams, and edges of drywall should not be left unprotected. Instead, apply preformed corner strips (called *bead*) or pre-seamed tape to make a crisp edge and protect the drywall from damage. A 90° inside corner is usually finished with drywall joint tape, but outside and off-angle inside corners are best finished with corner beads.

Metal corner bead is a rigid, tough corner bead that's installed with drywall nails or screws driven through the drywall and into the framing. It also may be installed with a crimping tool.

Vinyl outside corner bead is applied with staples or a spray-on adhesive.

Paper-faced metal or plastic corner bead is embedded in joint compound on outside corners. No fasteners are needed but a special roller tool is recommended to bed the legs properly.

Off-angle corner bead makes inside and outside corners greater than 90° much easier to finish.

Off-angle corner bead comes in rolls or straight lengths and features a flexible center. Some have a raised ridge that, when facing out, may be used for outside corners. Others have a rubberized center to allow for movement as the house settles.

Bullnose outside-corner bead and inner-cove bead leave a curved corner. Outside bullnose corners require that the drywall not overlap at the corner to leave room for the radius corner.

Corner bead for arches has one edge cut into segments for bending along an arch.

J-bead and L-bead are attached to the edges of drywall that are left open or that meet a non-drywall surface, such as wood or brick. J-bead must be installed before the drywall panel is fastened at the finished edge. L-bead may come with a tear-away masking strip to protect adjacent surfaces while finishing.

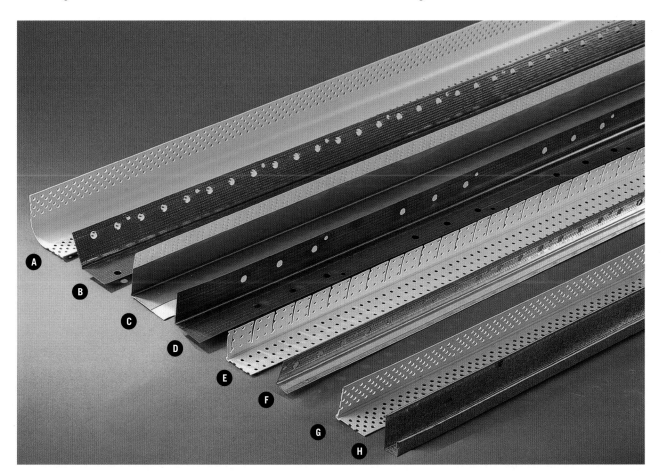

Corner bead options include: bullnose and inner-cove corner beads (A); off-angle corner beads for inside or outside corners (B); paper-faced metal or plastic outside corner bead (C); metal outside corner bead (D); corner bead for arches (E); L-bead (F); vinyl outside corner bead (G); and J-bead (H).

Joint Tape & Compound

Made of paper or fiberglass mesh, joint tape is sold in rolls usually 75 or 150 feet long. Paper tape makes crisper inside corners because it is pre-creased lengthwise. It is also resistant to accidental cutting with a taping knife. The self-adhesive, fiberglass-mesh tape applies easily to flat joints and does not need to be set into a joint compound bed (whereas paper tape must be). Fiberglass mesh tape works better for making quick repairs.

Joint compound is used as both a bonding agent and filler. It goes on smoothly, dries hard, and sands easily (albeit with much dust). It is sold in two forms: as a dry powder in a bag and as a premixed compound in a tub. Setting-type (powder) joint compounds are mixed with water on site. It sets stronger, harder, and faster than pre-mixed compounds and it doesn't shrink as much. Setting-type compounds are best mixed with a mixing paddle used with a power drill. It is important that the blend be well-mixed, as any lumps will affect the finished surface and make it very difficult to smooth out the mud. Unlike premixed compound, setting-type compound hardens in the bucket if it sits longer than the set time, and even "easy sand" varieties resist sanding more than drying-type compounds. Set times of compounds vary from forty-five minutes to as much as six hours. They harden by chemical reaction.

Drying-type joint compounds come premixed in one- and five-gallon tubs. They set by drying and are not as strong or fast-setting as setting-type compounds. Drying-type joint compounds come in taping, topping, and all-purpose formulas. Advantages to drying-type compounds include convenience, ability to save leftover compound for months, and ease of sanding. Use topping compound for second and third coats only. Lightweight, all-purpose joint compound may be used for both taping and topping when convenience dictates.

Fire-rated tape is another convenient self-adhesive tape, used for surfaces that are finished just enough to meet fire codes. It doesn't need a coat of compound to achieve its fire rating. It is a popular choice in attached garages where common walls between the garage and house must meet fire-rating standards.

Joint tape comes in two primary types: pre-creased paper tape that can be used on inside corners, outside corners, or flat seams, and self-adhesive fiberglass mesh, which is best suited for flat seams and repairs.

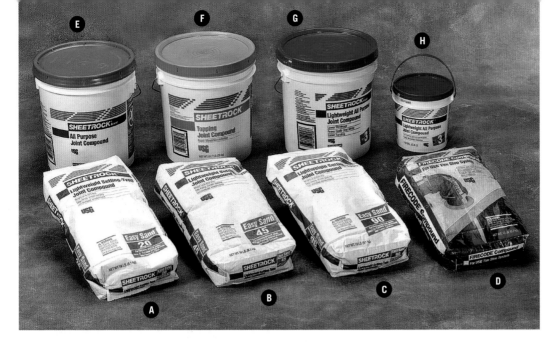

Drywall joint compounds include: setting-type joint compounds in 20-minute, 45-minute, and 90-minute grades (A, B, C); fireproof taping compound (D); premixed all-purpose joint compound (E); premixed topping compound (F); premixed lightweight all-purpose compound (G, H).

TEXTURING MATERIALS

Texturing mud can be ready-mix topping compound or specially designed for the look you are trying to achieve. Texturing compounds often come in dry powder form and are blended with water using a hand mixer or a drill and paddle.

Aggregated ceiling textures have coarse to fine aggregates like polystyrene or perlite particles already mixed in to achieve popcorn or cottage cheese texture and other rough surfaces.

Orange peel and knock down textures are for walls and ceilings. The effects are produced with smooth (unaggregated) compound, such as lightweight, all-purpose joint compound.

Acoustical textures, used for ceilings and other non-contact surfaces, are made from a compound designed to absorb sound.

Texturing mud is applied to walls and ceilings with pneumatic spray equipment, such as a hopper gun, which can be rented along with an air compressor to drive the sprayer. Texture may also be applied with a long-handled paint roller. When mixed to a thicker consistency, texturing mud may be applied like joint compound using finishing trowels or knives.

Adjacent finished surfaces need to be protected diligently when texturing. A paper roller that lays 12" masking paper with masking tape along one edge comes in very handy, as does a spray shield. Use a knock-down knife to flatten the peaks when creating a knock-down texture. A 12" knife can also be used, though it may leave edge tracks. Any number of brushes can be used to stipple or swirl compound into interesting textures.

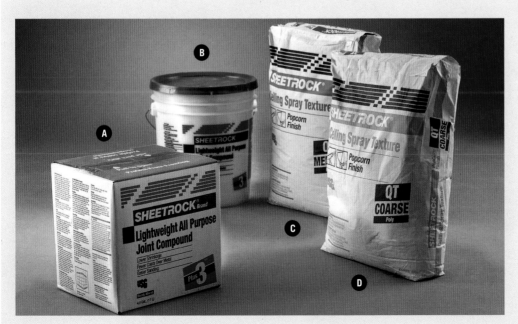

Products for applying textured finishes include: lightweight pre-mixed joint-compound (A, B); medium aggregate ceiling texture (C); coarse aggregate ceiling texture (D).

Drywall Tools & Equipment

To hang drywall, you'll need a variety of tools to measure, mark, and cut panels to size, as well as fasten them to the framing. A tape measure is a necessity for measuring and marking drywall—a 25-footer is a versatile choice. A T-square saves time by helping you make straight, square cuts across the entire width of a panel; a chalk line creates layout and cutting lines across greater spans. To check the framing for plumb and square, a framing square and four-foot level are handy.

The principal tool for cutting drywall is a utility knife. Make sure you have plenty of fresh blades on hand, swapping out the dull ones often. Use a drywall rasp to smooth cut panel edges. A standard compass is necessary for scribing adjacent surfaces onto a panel and creating small circles for cutouts. For larger circles, use a drywall compass to score the panel. A drill can also be outfitted with a hole saw for pipes and other small round cutouts. A keyhole saw makes quick work of small holes, such as those for electrical boxes. A drywall saw quickly cuts notches for doors,

windows, and other openings. For faster speed in making cutouts, use a spiral saw to cut through panels after they have been installed.

The best tool for hanging drywall is a screw gun. Similar to a drill, a screw gun has an adjustable clutch that stops driving the screw at a preset depth. For large jobs, it's practical to rent a screw gun; otherwise, use a variable speed ⅜-inch drill with a dimpling tool and carefully drive the screws. A drywall lifter helps you prop up panels while fastening them, but a flat bar can perform the same function. Apply adhesives and caulking using a caulk gun.

Drywall hand tools can be purchased at home centers at reasonable prices. If you don't wish to buy power tools, most of them can be found at rental centers, along with a variety of specialty tools. During every phase of a drywall project, make sure to protect yourself from the dust and debris generated; always wear protective eyewear and a dust mask or respirator, especially when sanding.

Tools for installing drywall include: flat pry bar (A), speed square (B), 4" taping knife (C), cordless drill/driver (D), 12" taping knife (E), chalkline (F), dust mask (G), drywall hammer (H), 6" taping knife (I), carpenter's square (J), drywall lifter (K), drywall tape (L), joint compound tray (mud tray) (M), drywall rasp (N), utility knife (O), drywall keyhole saw (P), 3-ft. level (Q), caulk gun (R), drywall T-square (S).

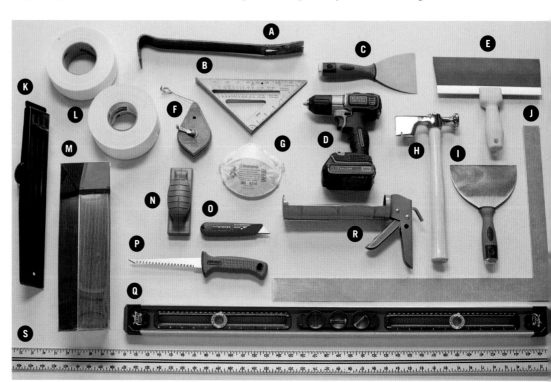

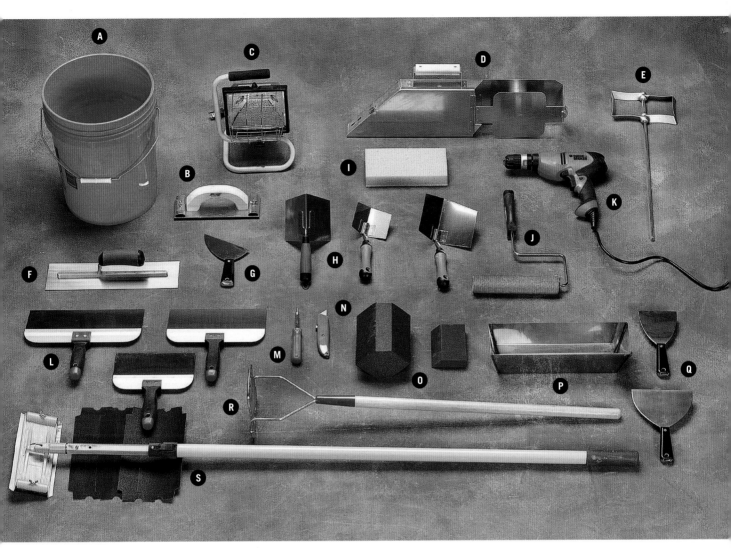

Drywall finishing tools include: 5-gallon bucket (A); hand/block sander (B); work light (C); drywall banjo (D); mixing paddle (E); 12" finishing trowel (F); 6" angled taping knife (G); corner taping knives (H); wet sanding sponge (I); paint roller with tight-nap roller cover (J); ½" drill (K); taping knives (8, 10, 12") (L); screwdriver (M); utility knife (N); dry sanding sponges (O); mud pan (P); taping knives (4, 6") (Q); hand masher (R); 120-, 150-, 220-grit sanding screens, sandpaper, and pole sander (S).

A successful drywall finish job is one that isn't seen once the paint or wallcovering is applied. A flawless finish is a lot easier to obtain when you use the proper tools for the job. Mixing joint compound with a ½-inch heavy-duty drill and a mixing paddle, for example, yields superior product and takes far less time than mixing by hand (although using a hand masher will improve your results). Another useful tool is a mud pan that holds the compound while you work. It fits nicely into your hand and has sharp edges for scraping excess mud from taping knives.

As for knives, the minimum you'll need are a 6-inch knife for taping and a 12-inch knife for the filler and final coats—though a 4-inch taping knife is handy for tight spots, and some prefer a 10-inch knife for the filler coat. There are a number of specialty knives available that can help make taping easier, such as a double-bladed knife for inside corners and angled knives for

tight spots. Many drywall installers also find a 12-inch finishing trowel handy for feathering the final coat. Don't buy bottom-line or plastic knives, even for a small job—the money saved won't justify the frustration.

Sanding completes the job. Professionals use a pole sander with replaceable fiberglass sanding screens—a versatile and effective tool, and quite handy for ceilings. For hand sanding, sanding blocks and dry sanding sponges will take care of the finish work, and a bright work light can help draw attention to overlooked areas.

If you will be skim-coating surfaces, you'll also need a 5-gallon bucket for thinning down compound and a paint roller with a tight-nap roller cover for application. Finally, keep a few general tools on hand for making adjustments as you work, such as a utility knife for trimming tape or panels at butt joints, and a screwdriver to drive protruding heads.

Specialty Tools

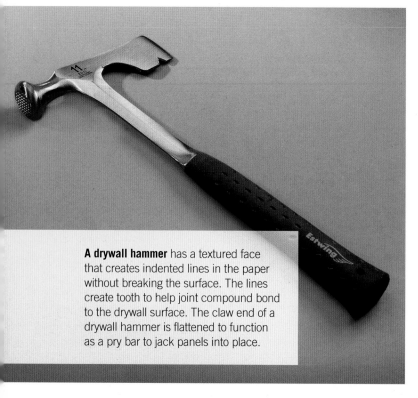

A drywall hammer has a textured face that creates indented lines in the paper without breaking the surface. The lines create tooth to help joint compound bond to the drywall surface. The claw end of a drywall hammer is flattened to function as a pry bar to jack panels into place.

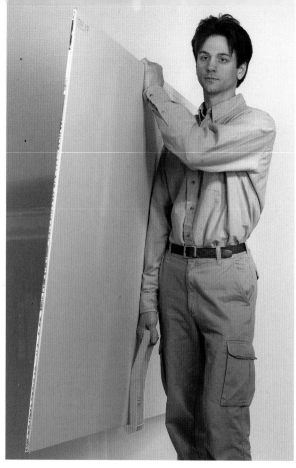

A panel carrier supports drywall panels from below and includes a carrying handle so panels can be easily carried by one person.

Drywall clips are used to isolate corner joints from the movement of adjacent framing members. They also facilitate optimal thermal insulation of walls by reducing the number of studs and backers needed.

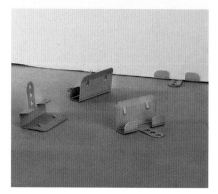

Drywall stilts are a useful way to reach the ceiling and retain mobility. Use them only for finishing drywall and only after the room has been cleared of debris and drop cloths. Do not use them when installing drywall panels—it is a very dangerous practice.

A drywall lifter is basically a one piece metal lever that slips underneath the panel at floor level. Stepping on the lift pedal causes the panel to rise about ½", which is the recommended minimum gap between the floor and the bottom of the panel.

Drywall benches have broad bench tops so they can be used as step stools as well as sawhorses for holding panels to be cut. Most are adjustable for ideal access to upper walls and ceilings.

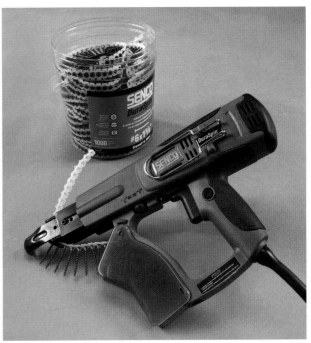

Drywall guns feature a special chuck for automatic depth control of the screw head. Self-feeding models automatically load drywall screws collated on plastic strips, saving time. If you do not use self-feeding guns regularly, calibrating them can be tricky. Also, the cost-per-screw is much higher. They can be rented at most building or rental centers.

A panel lift is a rented tool that allows you to lift drywall to a ceiling or high wall. It is stable and will hold the panel as long as necessary, making it an indispensable tool if you will be working alone.

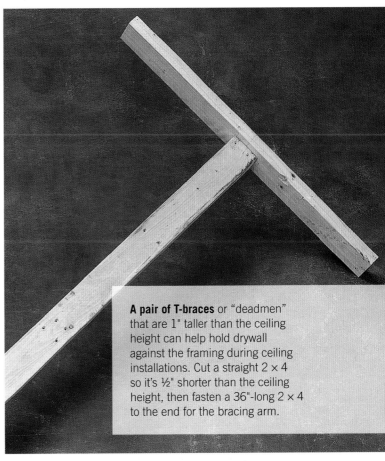

A pair of T-braces or "deadmen" that are 1" taller than the ceiling height can help hold drywall against the framing during ceiling installations. Cut a straight 2 × 4 so it's ½" shorter than the ceiling height, then fasten a 36"-long 2 × 4 to the end for the bracing arm.

(continued)

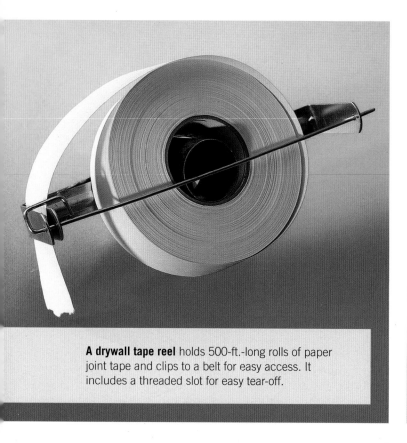

A drywall tape reel holds 500-ft.-long rolls of paper joint tape and clips to a belt for easy access. It includes a threaded slot for easy tear-off.

A mortar hawk can be loaded with joint compound and toted around so you can take just as much as you need for each dimple or seam.

A drywall banjo is a relatively inexpensive taping machine that passes paper tape through a box filled with thinned joint compound for simultaneous tape and mud application. These also can be rented at larger rental centers.

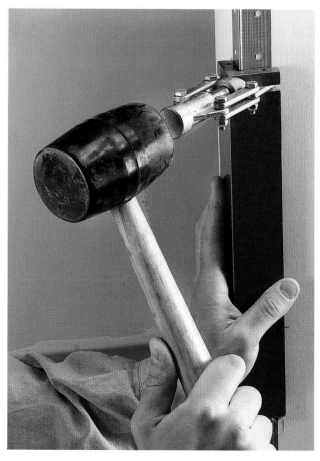

A corner crimper attaches metal corner bead to outside corners without the use of fasteners. It's especially useful for metal-framed walls where nails don't grip.

Sanding systems can reduce airborne dust by up to 95%. Most systems are available with both pole and hand sanding attachments that connect to a wet/dry vacuum. Water filters are also available for catching dust before it reaches the vacuum.

Air compressors and sprayguns with handheld hoppers are used to apply texture to walls and ceilings, and are available for rent. While they are relatively easy to use, get an operator's manual or lesson at the rental center, then practice on a scrap of cardboard before attempting your project.

 ## CLEANING DRYWALL FINISHING TOOLS

Taping tools can be cleaned easily with water. Rinse and wipe off taping knives, mud pans, and mixing paddles immediately after use. Do not clean tools in a sink—compound can settle in pipes where it will harden and clog drains. Wipe down and dry tools thoroughly to prevent rust.

Hang taping knives to store them so the blades will not be bent or damaged by other tools. A pegboard hanger system is perfect for this task, and the knives will be easy to locate when you need them.

Drywall Installation

Hanging drywall panels can be an awkward task marked by heavy lifting and strenuous physical feats. Or it can be an efficient process that exploits the mechanical advantages of specialized drywall tools and accessories. Unless you are counting on home improvement work for exercise and conditioning, the recommendations in this chapter will help take the pain and frustration out of the drywalling process.

As a general rule, use the smallest number of drywall panels possible to minimize seams and potential cracks. Unfortunately, bigger panels are heavier, which is a particular issue when you're drywalling a ceiling. If you have ever tried to hold a full sheet of ⅝-inch drywall overhead for several minutes while someone else fumbles to get a screw in place, you can probably still feel the strain in your arms and shoulders. Instead, use a panel lift (page 55)—a miraculous rental tool that does the heavy lifting for you.

In this chapter:
- Making a Layout Plan
- Preparing for Drywall Installation
- Measuring & Cutting Drywall
- Fastening Drywall
- Hanging Drywall
- Hanging Cementboard
- Curved Walls
- Architectural Details
- Archways
- Preformed Domes
- Garage Drywall
- Basement Prep: Solution 1
- Basement Prep: Solution 2
- Soundproofing
- Multiple Drywall Layers
- Soundproof Room

Making a Layout Plan

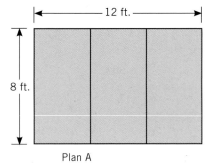

12 ft.
Acceptable
8 ft.

Plan A

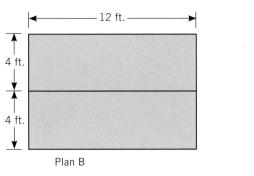

12 ft.
Better
4 ft.
4 ft.

Plan B

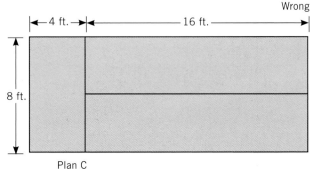

4 ft. — 16 ft.
Wrong
8 ft.

Plan C

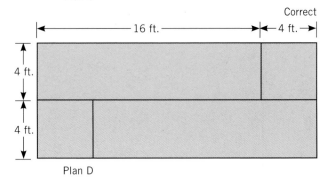

16 ft. — 4 ft.
Correct
4 ft.
4 ft.

Plan D

Planning the layout of drywall panels prior to installation makes it a lot easier to create a materials list, minimize seams, and solve potential problems before they crop up. Take careful measurements and sketch each wall and ceiling to be covered. Note the center-to-center (O.C.) spacing of the framing members, which can determine the thickness of drywall you install as well as how you install it (either parallel or perpendicular to the framing). See the chart on the opposite page for maximum framing spacing allowances.

Standard drywall is commonly available in widths of 4 feet and 54 inches and lengths of 8, 10, 12, 14, and 16 feet. It's in your best interest to use the longest drywall panels you can: It'll save you a lot of work during the finishing phase. Home centers and lumberyards always have 4 × 8 foot panels in stock and usually carry smaller quantities of the other sizes, or you can special order them.

The goal of planning the optimal drywall layout is to minimize seams. Seams require joint tape, compound, and sanding, which means the less of them there are, the less work you have ahead of you. For wall or ceiling surfaces 48 inches wide or less, cover the entire area using a single drywall panel. With no seams to tape, you'll only have to cover the screw heads with a few thin coats of compound.

Walls that are wider than 48 inches will require at least two panels. While there are a number of ways you can hang them, some possibilities yield better results than others. For example, for a wall that is 8 feet high and 12 feet long (as shown in first two plans at the top right), three panels could be installed vertically (Plan A), resulting in only tapered seams and no butt joints. However, this plan requires 16 linear feet of vertical taping, working from floor to ceiling, which is more difficult than taping a horizontal seam. Using two 4 × 12 foot panels (Plan B) reduces the amount of taping by 25 percent and places the seam about waist high, easing the finishing process. While a reduction of 25 percent of the finish work may not mean much on a small project, on a large remodel or new construction it can save you a lot of time and money.

Avoid butt joints where possible, but if they are necessary, locate them as far from the center of the wall as possible to help mask the seam. While it is best to use full panels, do not butt a tapered edge to panel ends (Plan C). This configuration produces an 8-foot long butt seam that will be difficult to finish. The best solution is to stagger the long panels and fill in with pieces cut from another (Plan D). For all butt joints, panel ends must break on a framing member unless you plan to use back blocking to recess the seam (see page 83).

In rooms with ceilings over 8 feet in height, use 54-inch-wide panels. If ceilings are taller than 9 feet, consider using longer panels installed vertically.

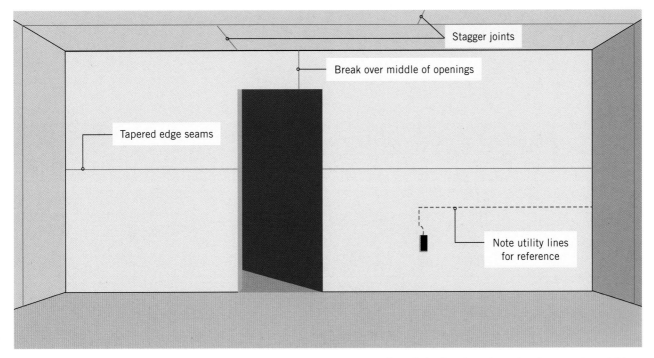

Drywall seams must fall on the centers of framing members, so measure and mark the framing when planning your layout. Use long sheets horizontally to span an entire wall. Avoid butted end joints whenever possible; where they do occur, stagger them between rows so they don't fall on the same framing member. Don't place seams over the corners of doors, windows, or other openings; joints there often crack or cause bulges that interfere with trim. Where framing contains utility lines, draw a map for future reference, noting locations of wiring, pipes, and shutoff valves.

MAXIMUM FRAMING SPACING

PANEL THICKNESS	INSTALLATION	MAXIMUM FRAMING SPACING
⅜"	Ceilings, perpendicular to framing	16" O.C.
	walls	16" O.C.
½"	Ceilings, parallel to framing	16" O.C.
	Ceilings, perpendicular to framing	24" O.C.
	walls	24" O.C.
⅝"	Ceilings, parallel to framing	16" O.C.
	Ceilings, perpendicular to framing	24" O.C.
	walls	24" O.C.

Estimating Materials

To estimate the number of drywall panels you'll need, simply count the number used in your layout sketch. For larger projects, you can do a quick estimation for 4 × 8 foot panels by measuring the length of the walls and dividing the total by 4. For each window, subtract a quarter panel; for doors, half a panel. Keep in mind that panels are sold in pairs, so round odd numbered totals up to an even number.

The number of screws you'll need depends on the spacing of your framing and the fastener spacing schedule required (see page 73). For a rough estimate, calculate the square footage of the wall and ceiling surfaces, and multiply by one fastener per square foot. Drywall screws are sold in pounds; one pound of screws equals roughly 320 screws. Construction adhesive is available in tubes. Check the manufacturer's specifications on the tube for coverage.

Preparing for Drywall Installation

TOOLS & MATERIALS

Work gloves
Eye protection
Hammer
Tape measure
Framing square
Handsaw
Plane
Screwgun or drill
2× framing lumber
10d framing nails
Wood shims
Drywall screws
Metal protector plates
Foam insulation
Furring strips
Cardboard strips
Stapler

Begin your installation project by checking the framing—and adding blocking, if necessary—and planning the layout of the panels. Minor flaws in the framing can be hidden by the drywall and joint compound, but a severely bowed or twisted stud or crowned or sagging joists will result in an uneven finished surface.

Check the framing using your eye, a straight board, or a string. Bad studs or joists can be planed down, furred out, or replaced. But for serious ceiling problems, it's sometimes easiest to add a grid of furring strips or install a steel channel ceiling system (see page 65).

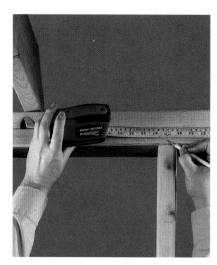

Following your layout plan, measure and mark the location of seams to ensure there is adequate backing for panels. Install 2× blocking where needed to provide additional fastening support.

Drywall Preparation

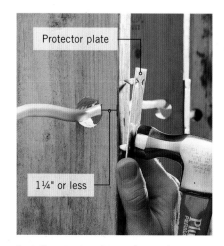

Install protector plates where wires or pipes pass through framing members and are less than 1¼" from the front edge. The plates keep drywall screws from puncturing wires or pipes.

Protector plate

1¼" or less

Wrap water pipes along the ceiling with foam insulation before covering them with drywall. This prevents condensation on the pipes that can drip onto the drywall and cause staining.

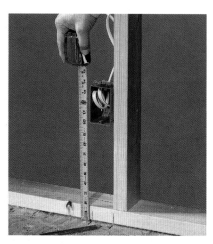

Mark the location and dimensions of electrical boxes on the floor. This makes it easier to locate them during drywall installation.

Installing Blocking

Add backing to support panel edges that don't fall over framing. When installing new panels next to an existing wall surface, or where the framing layout doesn't coincide with the drywall edges, it's often easiest to add an extra stud for backing.

Add crossblocking with 24" O.C. spacing between framing members where needed to help support edges of drywall panels at joints.

Fasten 2 × 4 nailers to the top plate of walls that run parallel to joists. This provides a fastening surface for ceiling panels. The nailer should overhang the plate by half its width.

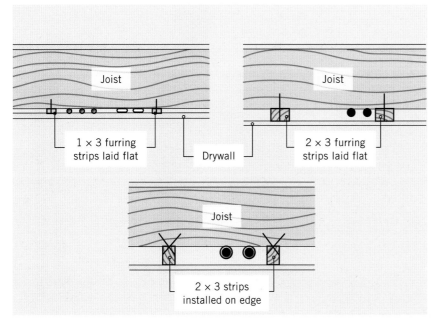

Joist — 1 × 3 furring strips laid flat — Drywall

Joist — 2 × 3 furring strips laid flat

Joist — 2 × 3 strips installed on edge

Attach furring strips where service lines and other obstacles project beyond the framing. The strips create a flat surface for attaching drywall and can also be used to compensate for uneven joists. Use 1 × 3 or 2 × 3 furring strips, and attach them perpendicularly to the framing with drywall screws. Space the strips 16" O.C., and use wood shims secured behind the strips to adjust for unevenness.

Use wood strips to join panel edges in problem areas between framing, creating a floating seam. This method does not provide a substitute for structural backing; the panels still must be supported by framing or blocking.

Straightening Bowed Studs

Use a long, straight 2 × 4 as a guide to check the alignment of studs. Hold the 2 × 4 against the studs both horizontally and diagonally, looking for gaps. To check a corner for square, use a 24" framing square.

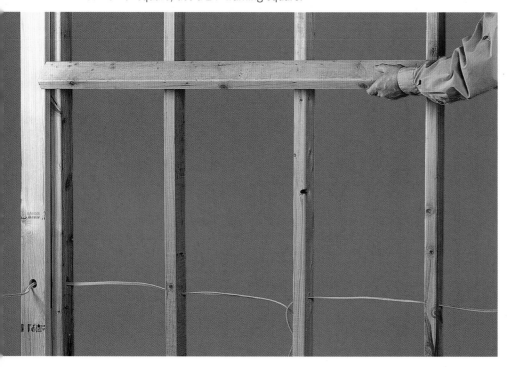

For studs that bow outward slightly, use a plane or chisel to trim the facing edge just enough so it is flush with the surrounding framing.

Studs in non-loadbearing walls bowed inward more than ¼" can be straightened. Using a handsaw, make a 2" cut into the stud at the midpoint of the bow. Pull the stud outward, and glue a tapered wood shim into the saw cut to hold the stud straight. Attach a 2-ft.-long 2 × 4 brace to one side of the stud to strengthen it, then trim off the shim. Replace any studs that are severely twisted.

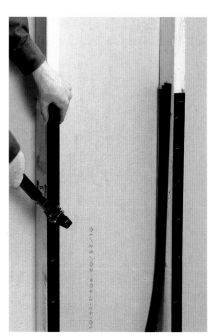

Staple cardboard strips to stud faces. Use solid strips (not corrugated), which are available from drywall suppliers, or mat board from an art supply store. For extreme bows, start with a 12 to 24" strip and add layers of successively longer strips.

Installing a Suspended Ceiling System for Drywall

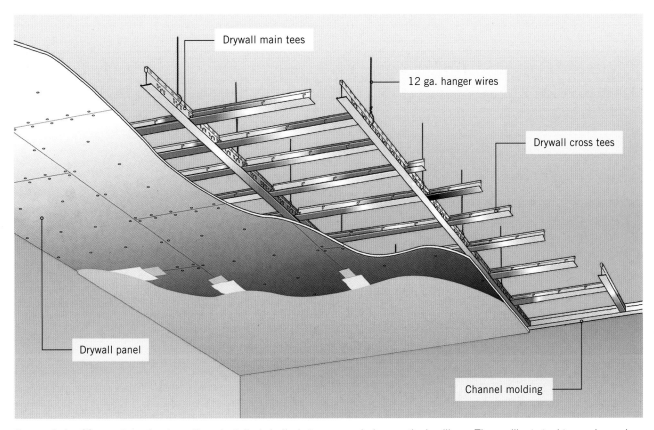

Drywall main tees

12 ga. hanger wires

Drywall cross tees

Drywall panel

Channel molding

Suspended ceiling systems for drywall are installed similarly to suspended acoustical ceilings. The resilient steel tees, channels, and heavy-gauge wire work together to create a base grid strong enough to support up to two layers of ⅝" fire-rated drywall. Like steel framing, steel channels and tees can be cut to length using aviation snips or a saw outfitted with a metal cutting blade. Once the ceiling system is in place, drywall panels are installed as in a conventional installation. For ½" and ⅝" panels, use 1" Type S (fine thread) drywall screws.

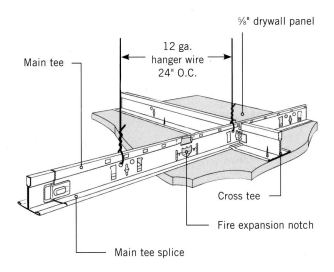

Main tee

12 ga. hanger wire 24" O.C.

⅝" drywall panel

Cross tee

Fire expansion notch

Main tee splice

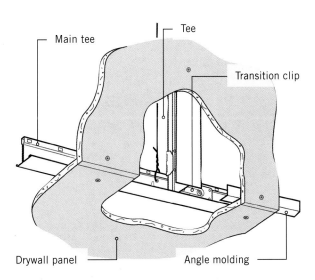

Main tee

Tee

Transition clip

Drywall panel

Angle molding

Main tees should be supported every 24" O.C. for ½" and ⅝" ceiling panels, and a maximum of 16" O.C. for thicker panels. Use 12-gauge hanger wires fastened to the ceiling joists. Fasten the channel molding to framing members with 1¼" drywall screws.

Form vertical surfaces for ceiling soffits or ductwork raceways by screwing drywall panels to tees that are attached to the main tees with transition clips.

Measuring & Cutting Drywall

Drywall is one of the easiest building materials to install, partly because it allows for minor errors. Most professionals measure and cut to the nearest ⅛ inch, and it's perfectly acceptable to trim off a little extra from a panel to make it easier to get into a tight space. The exceptions to this are cutouts for electrical boxes and recessed light fixtures, which must be accurate because the coverplates usually hide less than you think they will.

Make sure your utility knife is sharp. A sharp blade ensures clean, accurate cuts that slice through the face paper and score the gypsum core in one pass. A dull blade can slip from the cutting line to snag and rip the face paper and is more likely to cause injury.

With a sharp utility knife, you can make cuts from either side of panels. But when using drywall and keyhole saws, make all cuts from the front side to prevent tearing the face paper. For projects that require a number of cutouts, use a spiral saw. This tool makes short work of large openings and electrical boxes, though it generates a lot of dust; make sure to wear a dust mask. Inexpensive spiral saws are available at home centers, or you can use a standard router outfitted with a piloted drywall bit.

How to Make Straight Cuts

Mark the length on the face of the panel, then set a T-square at the mark. Hold the square in place with your hand and foot, and cut through the face paper using a utility knife with sharp blade.

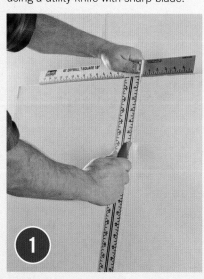

1

2

Bend the scored section backward with both hands to snap the gypsum core.

3

Fold back the waste piece and cut through the back paper with the utility knife.

How to Make Angled Cuts

1

Measure both the vertical "rise" and horizontal "run" of the area, and mark the dimensions along the corresponding edges of the panel.

2

Connect the marks with a T-square, hold down firmly, and score the drywall from point to point. Finish the cut using the "snap cut" method on page 66. Be careful not to damage the pointed ends.

 ## TIP: MAKING ROUGH CUTS

Make horizontal cuts using a tape measure and utility knife. With one hand, hold the knife blade at the end of the tape. With the other hand, grip the tape at the desired measurement; slide this hand along the panel edge as you make the cut.

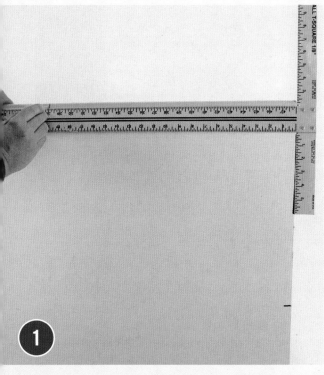

3

Smooth rough edges with a drywall rasp. One or two passes with the rasp should be sufficient. To help fit a piece into a tight space, bevel the edge slightly toward the back of the panel.

How to Cut Notches

Using a full-size drywall saw, cut the vertical sides of the notch. (These saws are also handy for cutting out door and window openings after the drywall is installed.)

Cut the face paper along the bottom of the notch using a utility knife. Snap the waste piece backward to break the core, then cut through the back paper.

How to Cut Large Openings

Measure the location of the cutout and transfer the dimensions to the backside of the panel. Score along the line that represents the header of the opening using a straightedge and utility knife.

Install the panel over the opening. The scored line should fall at the header. Cut the drywall along the jambs and up to the header using a drywall saw. Snap forward the waste piece to break the core, then cut through the face paper and remove.

How to Cut an Electrical Box Opening: Coordinate Method

Transfer the coordinates to the panel and connect the points, using a T-square. Measure from the panel edge that will abut the fixed edge you measured from. If the panel has been cut short for a better fit, make sure to account for this in your measurements.

Locate the four corners of the box by measuring from the nearest fixed edge—a corner, the ceiling, or the edge of an installed panel—to the outside edges of the box.

Drill a pilot hole in one corner of the outline, then make the cutout with a keyhole or drywall saw.

 # How to Cut an Electrical Box Opening: Chalk Method

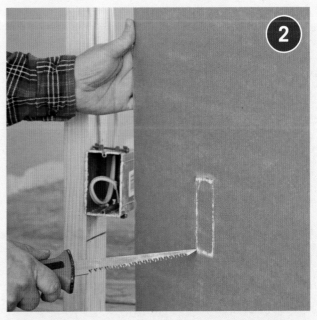

Rub the face of the electrical box with chalk or lipstick, position the panel where it will be installed, and press it against the box.

Pull the panel back from the wall; a chalk outline of the box is on the back of the panel. Drill a pilot hole in one corner of the outline, then make the cut with a keyhole or drywall saw.

How to Cut Round Holes in Drywall

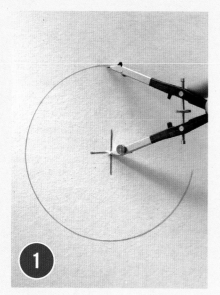

1

To make round cutouts, measure to the center of the object, then transfer the centerpoint to the drywall panel. Use a compass set to half the diameter of the cutout to mark the circle on the panel face.

Force the pointed end of a drywall saw through the panel from the face side, then saw along the marked line. (These saws work well for all internal cuts.)

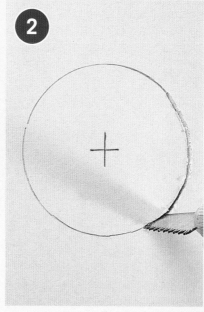

2

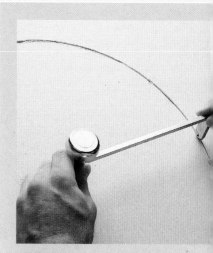

VARIATION: Drive the point of a drywall compass into the center marking, then rotate the compass wheel to cut the face paper. Tap a nail through the centerpoint, score the back paper, then knock out the hole through the face.

 # How to Make a Cutout for a Round Fixture Box

1

Locate the four outermost edges of the round box by measuring from the nearest fixed edge—a corner, the ceiling, or the edge of an installed panel—to the outermost edges of the box.

Transfer the coordinates to the panel, measuring from the panel edge that will abut the fixed edge you measured from, then connect the points using a T-square. The point where the lines intersect is the centerpoint of the circle.

NOTE: If the panel has been cut short for a better fit, make sure to account for this in your measurements.

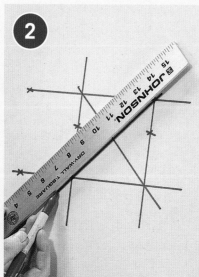

2

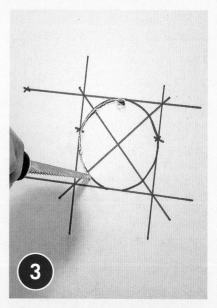

3

Use a compass to draw the outline of the round box on the panel (see above). Drill a pilot hole at one point of the outline, then make the cutout with a keyhole saw.

NOTE: To avoid the need for stainblocking primer, substitute a pencil for a permanent marker.

Making Cuts with a Compass

For out-of-square corners, cut the panel 1" longer than necessary, then hold it in position so it is plumb. Set a compass at 1¼", then run it along the wall to scribe the corner onto the face of the panel. Snap cut along the line using a utility knife (see page 66).

Irregular surfaces can be scribed onto panels using the same method. Cut along the scribe line with a keyhole saw, then test fit the piece and make adjustments as necessary.

Cutting Drywall with a Spiral Saw

Spiral saws (or drywall routers) are handy for cutting holes for electrical boxes and openings. You can use a spiral saw made for the purpose or outfit a standard router by removing the router base and installing a piloted drywall bit.

For electrical boxes, mark the floor at the locations of the box centers. Hang the drywall, fastening only at the top edge. Plunge the bit into the box center, move the bit sideways to the edge, then carefully work the bit to the outside. Follow the outside of the box, cutting counterclockwise.

For doorways and other openings, install the drywall over the opening. Moving clockwise, let the bit follow the inside of the frame to make the cutout. Always work clockwise when cutting along the inside of a frame; counterclockwise when following the outside of an object, like an electrical box.

Fastening Drywall

The key to fastening drywall is to countersink screwheads to create a slight recess, or "dimple," without breaking the face paper. The best tool for the job is a screwgun, which has an adjustable clutch that can be set to stop screws at a preset depth. A variable speed drill/driver and a light touch will also get the job done.

When driving screws, hold the screwgun or drill at a right angle to the framing, placing the fastener ⅜ inch from the panel edge. Space screws evenly along the perimeter and across the field of the panel, following the chart on the opposite page. Do not fasten the entire perimeter and then fasten the field; work along the length or width of the panel, moving across to the sides as you push the drywall tight against the framing. Construction adhesive can be used in addition to screws to create a stronger bond between panel and framing.

Pre-drive fasteners near the edges of panels at the location of each framing member to help facilitate installation. Drive fasteners deep enough to hold their place but not enough to penetrate the backside of the panel. This lets you hold the panel in place as you finish driving the screws one-handed.

TOOLS & MATERIALS

Work gloves	Screwgun or ⅜" drill	Drywall	Drywall screws
Eye protection	Caulk gun	Drywall nails	Construction adhesive

FASTENING DRYWALL

Adhesives create stronger bonds than fasteners and reduce the number of screws needed for panel installation. Apply a ⅜" bead along framing members, stopping 6" from panel edges (left). At butt joints, apply beads to both sides of the joint (right). Panels are then fastened along the perimeter.

At panel edges, drive fasteners ⅜" from the edges, making sure to hit the framing squarely. If the fastener tears the paper or crumbles the edge, drive another about 2" away from the first.

Recess all screws to provide a space, called a "dimple," for the joint compound. However, driving a screw too far and breaking the paper renders it useless.

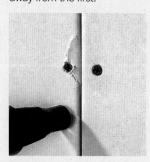 

SIZE OF FASTENERS

FASTENER TYPE	DRYWALL THICKNESS	MINIMUM FASTENER LENGTH	FASTENER TYPE	DRYWALL THICKNESS	MINIMUM FASTENER LENGTH
Wood screws	⅜"	1"	Steel screws	⅜"	¾"
(Type W;	½"	1⅛"	(Type S;	½"	⅞"
coarse thread)	⅝"	1¼"	fine thread, self-tapping)	⅝"	1"

*For multiple layers of drywall, fasteners must penetrate the framing by ⅞". Add the thickness of the two layers plus ⅞" to determine the minimum fastener length.

MAXIMUM FASTENER SPACING

FRAMING	O. C. SPACING	INSTALLATION STYLE	MAXIMUM SCREW SPACING
Wood joists	16" O.C.	Single panel w/screws	12" O.C.
		Single panel w/adhesive & screws	16" O.C.
		Multiple layers w/screws	
		Base layer:	24" O.C.
		Face layer:	12" O.C.
		Multiple layers w/adhesive & screws:	
		Base layer:	12" O.C.
		Face layer:	12" O.C. (perimeter) 16" O.C. (field)
	24" O.C.	Single panel w/screws	12" O.C.
		Single panel w/adhesive & screws	16" O.C.
		Multiple layers w/screws	12" O.C.
		Multiple layers w/adhesive & screws:	
		Base layer:	12" O.C.
		Face layer:	12" O.C. (perimeter) 16" O.C. (field)
Wood studs	16" O.C.	Single panel w/screws	16" O.C.
		Single panel w/adhesive & screws:	
		Load-bearing partitions	24" O.C.
		Nonload-bearing partitions	24" O.C.
		Multiple layers w/screws	
		Base layer:	24" O.C.
		Face layer:	16" O.C.
		Multiple layers w/adhesive & screws:	
		Base layer:	16" O.C.
		Face layer:	16" O.C. (at top & bottom only)
	24" O.C.	Single panel w/screws	12" O.C.
		Single panel w/adhesive & screws:	
		Load-bearing partitions	16" O.C.
		Nonload-bearing partitions	24" O.C.
		Multiple layers w/screws	
		Base layer:	24" O.C.
		Face layer:	12" O.C.

FRAMING	O. C. SPACING	INSTALLATION STYLE	MAXIMUM SCREW SPACING
Wood studs (cont.)	24" O.C.	Multiple layers w/adhesive & screws:	
		Base layer:	12" O.C.
		Face layer:	16" O.C. (at top & bottom only)
Steel studs	16" O.C.	Single panel w/screws	16" O.C.
		Multiple layers w/screws:	
		Base layer:	
		Parallel panels	24" O.C.
		Perpendicular	*(see below)
		Face layer:	16" O.C.
		Multiple layers w/adhesive & screws:	
		Base layer:	24" O.C.
		Face layer:	12" O.C. (perimeter) 16" O.C. (field)
Steel studs & resilient channel walls	24" O.C.	Single panel w/screws	12" O.C.
		Multiple layers w/screws:	
		Base layer:	
		Parallel panels	24" O.C.
		Perpendicular	*(see below)
		Face layer:	12" O.C.
		Multiple layers w/adhesive & screws:	
		Base layer:	24" O.C.
		Face layer:	12" O.C. (perimeter) 16" O.C. (field)
Resilient channel ceilings	24" O.C.	Single panel w/screws	12" O.C.
		Multiple layers w/screws:	
		Base layer:	
		Parallel panels	24" O.C.
		Perpendicular	*(see below)
		Face layer:	12" O.C.
		Multiple layers w/adhesive & screws:	
		Base layer:	24" O.C.
		Face layer:	12" O.C. (perimeter) 16" O.C. (field)

*1 screw at each end and 1 screw centered in the field, at each fastener location.
NOTE: The above information is subject to manufacturer installation specifications.

Hanging Drywall

Hanging drywall is a project that can be completed quickly and easily with a little preplanning and a helping hand.

If you're installing drywall on both the ceilings and the walls, do the ceilings first so the wall panels add extra support for the ceiling panels. When it comes time to install the walls, hang all full panels first, then measure and cut the remaining pieces about ⅛ inch too small to allow for easy fit.

In nearly every installation, you'll deal with corners. For standard 90° corners, panels most often can butt against one another. But other corners, such as those lacking adequate nailing surfaces or ones that are prone to cracking, may require the use of drywall clips or specialty beads.

Drywall is heavy. While it's possible to hang drywall by yourself, work with a helper whenever possible. A panel lift is also a time and back saver, simplifying installation to ceilings and the upper portion of walls. If you don't want to rent a panel lift, you can make a pair of T-braces, called "deadmen" (see page 55) to hold ceiling panels tight against framing for fastening.

Use a panel lifter to position drywall for fastening. Slide the front end of the lifter beneath the panel edge, then rock backward with your foot to raise the panel into place.

TIP

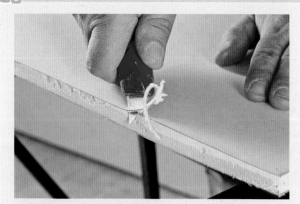

Where untapered panel ends will be butted together, bevel-cut the outside edges of each panel at 45°, removing about ⅛" of material. This helps prevent the paper from creating a ridge along the seam. Peel off any loose paper from the edge.

TOOLS & MATERIALS

Work gloves	Drywall panels
Eye protection	Drywall screws
T-square	Deadmen
Utility knife	Ladders
Screwgun or drill	Metal flashing
Panel lift	Self-tapping steel screws
Chalk line	Drywall clips

How to Install Drywall on Flat Ceilings

Snap a chalk line perpendicular to the joists, 48⅛" from the starting wall.

1

2

Measure to make sure the first panel will break on the center of a joist. If necessary, cut the panel on the end that abuts the side wall so the panel breaks on the next farthest joist. Load the panel onto a rented panel lift, or use a helper, and lift the panel flat against the joists.

3

Position the panel with the leading edge on the chalk line and the end centered on a joist. Fasten the panel with appropriately sized screws following the fastener spacing chart on page 73.

4

After the first row of panels is installed, begin the next row with a half-panel. This ensures that the butted end joints will be staggered between rows.

How to Install Ceiling Panels Using Deadmen

Construct two 2 × 4 deadmen (see page 55). Lean one against the wall where the panel will be installed, with the top arm a couple inches below the joists. Have a helper assist in lifting the panel and placing the lead edge on the arm. Angle the deadman to pin the panel flush against the joists, but don't use so much pressure you risk damage to the panel.

Use the other deadman to hoist the panel against the joists 24" from the back end. Place ladders at each deadman location and adjust the panel's position by loosening the braces with one hand and moving the panel with the other. Replace the braces and fasten the panel to the framing, following the fastener spacing chart on page 73.

 ## SETTING YOUR CLUTCH

Professional drywallers drive hundreds, even thousands, of screws per day. Consequently, they invest in pro-quality screwdriving equipment, often with self-feeding coils of screws for rapid-fire work. For DIYers, this equipment can be rented—and may be worth the investment for a very large project. But in most cases, a decent quality cordless drill/driver will do nicely. If the drill/driver has a clutch (and most do these days), so much the better. Essentially, a clutch stops the drill's chuck from spinning when the screw encounters a specific amount of resistance. This prevents overdriving of the screw, which is especially important when drywalling (you want to avoid driving the screw far enough into the drywall to break the surface paper). But for the clutch to work properly you need to make sure it is set to the appropriate level of sensitivity. A drill/driver normally has several settings indicated on a shroud or ring near the drill chuck. The highest setting is used for drilling. Basically, the clutch won't disengage the chuck unless it encounters so much resistance that the drill could be damaged. On the lowest setting, the drill will disengage when it encounters only very slight resistance,

as when completing driving a screw into drywall. Before you start driving any drywall screws, test your clutch setting by driving a screw into a piece of scrap drywall and a 2 × 4. Re-set the clutch as needed until it stops driving the moment the screwhead becomes countersunk, creating a very slight dimple. Having the clutch set correctly ensures that your fasteners will have maximum holding power with just enough of a surrounding dimple to give the joint compound a place to go.

Installing Floating Ceiling Joints

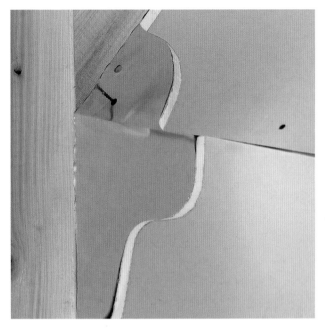

Use metal flashing to prevent cracks along the peak of pitched and cathedral ceilings (left) and the angle between pitched ceilings and sidewalls (right). For both applications, cut metal flashing 16" wide and to the length of the joint, then bend it lengthwise to match the angle of the peak or corner. Fasten flashing to the framing on one side only, then fasten the panels on that side to the framing. However, fasten the panels at the unfastened side to the flashing only, using self-tapping steel screws. Drive the first row of screws into the framing not less than 12" from the "floating" edge of the panels.

NOTE: Flexible vinyl bead can also be used for corners prone to cracking.

BENDING FLASHING ● ● ● ● ● ● ● ● ● ●

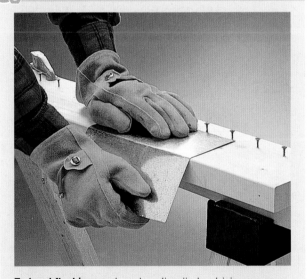

To bend flashing, make a bending jig by driving screws into a piece of wood, creating a space one-half the width of the flashing when measured from the edge of the board. Clamp the bending jig to a work surface. Lay a piece of flashing flat on the board, and bend it over the edge.

For a ceiling with trusses, use drywall clips to eliminate cracks caused by "truss uplift," the seasonal shifting caused by weather changes. Slip clips on the edge of the panel prior to installation, then fasten the clips to the top plate. Fasten the panel to the trusses not less than 18" from the edge of the panel.

How to Install Drywall on Wood-framed Walls

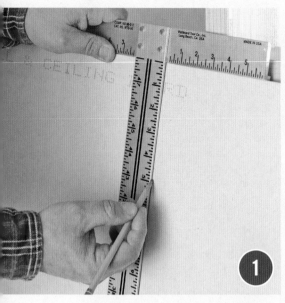

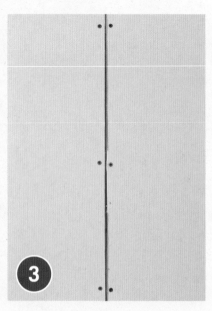

Measure from the wall end or corner to make sure the first panel will break on the center of the stud. If necessary, trim the sheet on the side or end that will be placed in the corner. Mark the stud centers on the panel face, and pre-drive screws at each location along the top edge to facilitate fastening. Apply adhesive to the studs, if necessary (see page 72).

With a helper or a drywall lifter, hoist the first panel tight against the ceiling, making sure the side edge is centered on a stud. Push the panel flat against the framing, and drive the starter screws to secure the panel. Make any cutouts, then fasten the field of the panel, following the screw spacing on page 73.

Measure, cut, and install the remaining panels along the upper wall. Bevel panel ends slightly, leaving a ⅛" gap between them at the joint. Butt joints can also be installed using back blocking to create a recess (see page 83).

VARIATION: When installing drywall vertically, cut each panel so it's ½" shorter than the ceiling height to allow for expansion. (The gap will be covered by base molding.)

Measure, cut, and install the bottom row, butting the panels tight to the upper row and leaving a ½" gap at the floor. Secure to the framing along the top edge using the starter screws, then make all cutouts before fastening the rest of the panel.

Installing Drywall at Inside Corners

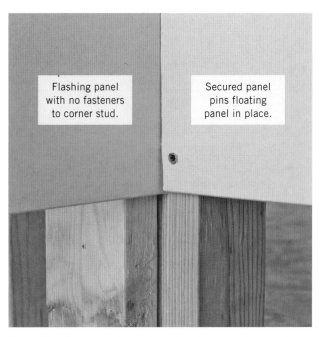

Flashing panel with no fasteners to corner stud.

Secured panel pins floating panel in place.

Standard 90° inside corners are installed with the first panel butted against the framing and the adjacent panel butted against the first. The screw spacing remains the same as on a flat wall (see page 73). If the corner is out of plumb or the adjacent wall has an irregular surface, see page 71 for cutting instructions.

Use a "floating corner" to reduce the chances of popped fasteners and cracks. Install the first panel, fastening only to within one stud bay of the corner. Push the leading edge of the adjacent panel against the first to support the unfastened edge. Fasten the second panel normally, including the corner.

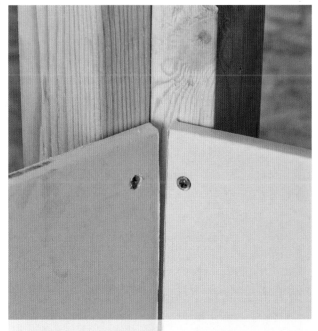

Drywall clips can be used at corners that lack an adequate nailing surface, allowing two panels to be secured to the same stud. Slide clips onto the leading edge of the first panel, with the metal nailing flange outward. Install the panel, fastening the flange to the stud on the adjacent wall with drywall screws. Install the adjacent panel normally.

For off-angle corners, do not overlap panel ends. Install so the panel ends meet at the corner with a ⅛" gap between them.

Installing Drywall at Outside Corners

At outside corners, run panels long so they extend past the corner framing. Fasten the panel in place, score the backside, and snap cut to remove the waste piece.

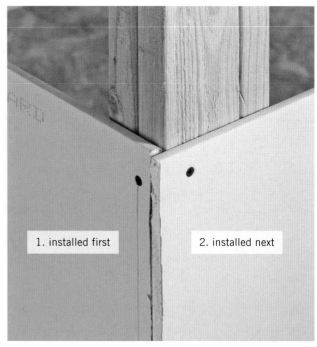

1. installed first   2. installed next

For standard 90° outside corners, install the first panel so the outside edge is flush with the framing, then install the adjacent panel so it overlaps the end of the first panel.

For off-angle corners or corners where bullnose bead will be installed, do not overlap panel ends. Install each panel so it's leading edge breaks ⅛" from the outside edge of the framing.

NOTE: Bullnose beads with a slight radius may require a larger reveal.

For drywall that abuts a finished edge, such as paneling or wood trim, install panels ⅛" from the finished surface, then install an L-bead to cover the exposed edge (see page 119).

How to Install Drywall Abutting a Finished Surface

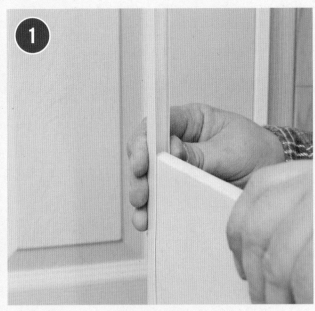

Cut the J-bead (see page 49) to size, then position it flush against the finished surface. Fasten it to the adjacent framing with drywall screws.

NOTE: Make sure to install J-bead that matches the thickness of your drywall.

Cut a piece of drywall to size, but let the end run long for final trimming. Slide the end of the drywall into the J-bead until it fits snugly, then fasten the panel to the framing. Score the backside flush with the face of the wall, then snap cut to remove the waste.

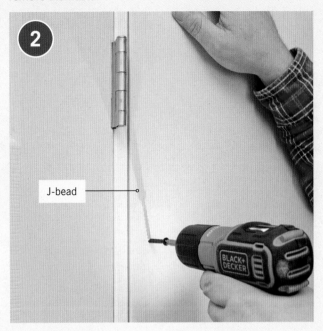

J-bead

Installing Drywall On Gable Walls

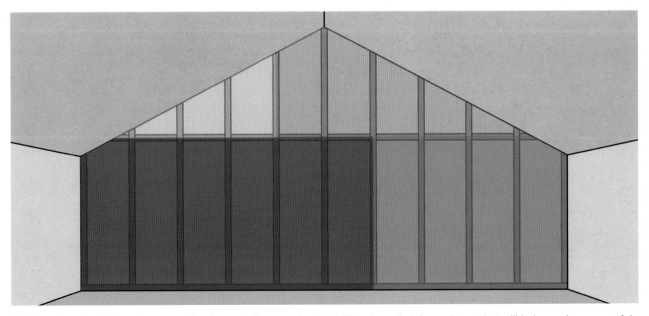

Gables and cathedral ceilings present unique challenges when installing drywall. A few pointers that will help you be successful include: Use as many of the panel's factory edges as possible; test-fit each piece directly on the wall; do not force pieces into place, but trim edges as needed instead; install pieces horizontally, with 2 × 4 blocking between the framing member; align horizontal seams, but not vertical seams—stagger these to minimize any twisting in the framing members.

Metal stud walls in residential construction are generally created with C-shaped 20- to 25-gauge steel studs that are secured at the top and bottom with flanged tracks. If the wall is built correctly, all of the open sides of the C-shaped studs will face in the same direction. Before you begin installing drywall, note which direction the open sides are on.

Begin installing drywall panels in the corner of the room that's closer to the open sides of the metal studs. The first panel should fall midway across a stud, coming from the direction of the open side. Attaching the panel this way will stabilize it; if you install the panel so the free end of the stud flange is loose, it may flex when you attach the drywall screws.

Screw the first panel at each corner using Type S drywall screws (1" is recommended for ½" drywall). These screws have a fairly sharp point that can penetrate the light-gauge metal flanges of the steel studs. As when attaching drywall to wood framing, take care not to overdrive the screws; they tend to take off rather aggressively once they engage in the metal.

Install the second drywall panel, leaving a slight gap at the joint. The new panel should be crossing the closed side of the C-shaped stud. Continue working in this direction until the wall is covered. Taping and seaming are done the same way as for wood framing.

Installing Back Blockers

No matter how good a job you do installing and finishing a butt joint, there's always a chance it'll be visible, even after a coat of paint or layer of wallcovering. Drywall panels can expand and contract as the temperature and humidity in your home changes, causing butted panel ends to push outward and create ridges. While ridging eventually stops (up to a year after installation), you can install back blocking to help prevent the problem before it even starts.

Back blocking creates a recessed butt joint by slightly bending panel ends into the bay between framing members, where they are secured to a floating blocking device with drywall screws. The result is a recessed joint that approximates a tapered joint and can be finished just as easily using standard techniques. And because the joint floats between framing members, it's unlikely to crack or ridge. Back blocking can be used for both walls and ceilings.

Although commercial back blockers are available, you can easily make your own back blocker by attaching narrow strips of ¼-inch hardboard to the edges of a 6 to 10-inch-wide strip of ¾-inch plywood. When placed behind a drywall butt joint, the hardboard strips will create a thin space, into which the edges of the drywall will be deflected when it's screwed to the back blocker. The instructions below show a homemade back blocker in use.

How to Install a Back Blocker

Hang the first drywall panel so the end breaks midway between the framing members. Position the back blocker behind the panel so the end covers half of the wood center strip, then fasten every 6" along the end.

Install the second panel so it butts against the first panel. Fasten the end of the second panel to the back blocker with drywall screws every 6". The screws will pull the end of the panel into the blocker, creating the recessed joint.

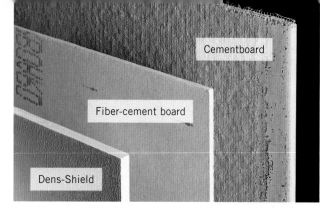

Cementboard

Fiber-cement board

Dens-Shield

Hanging Cementboard

Use tile backer board as the substrate for tile walls in wet areas. Unlike drywall, tile backer won't break down and cause damage if water gets behind the tile. The three basic types of tile backer are cementboard, fiber-cement board, and Dens-Shield.

Though water cannot damage either cementboard or fiber-cement board, it can pass through them. To protect the framing members, install a water barrier of 4-mil plastic or 15# building paper behind the backer.

Common tile backers are cementboard, fiber-cement board, and Dens-Shield. Cementboard is made from Portland cement and sand reinforced by an outer layer of fiberglass mesh. Fiber-cement board is made similarly, but with a fiber reinforcement integrated throughout the panel. Dens-Shield is a water-resistant gypsum board with a waterproof acrylic facing.

Dens-Shield has a waterproof acrylic facing that provides the water barrier. It cuts and installs much like drywall, but requires galvanized screws to prevent corrosion and must be sealed with caulk at all untaped joints and penetrations.

TOOLS & MATERIALS

Work gloves	T-square	Taping knives	1¼" cementboard screws	Latex-Portland cement mortar
Eye protection	Small masonry bits	Stapler	Cementboard joint tape	15# building paper
Utility knife or carbide-tipped cutter	Hammer	4-mil plastic sheeting	Spacers	Screwgun
	Jigsaw with a carbide grit blade	Cementboard		

 How to Hang Cementboard

1

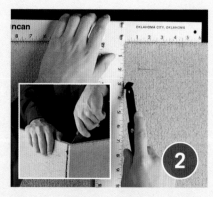

2

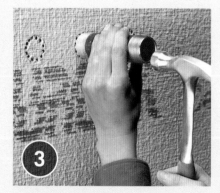

3

Staple a water barrier of 4-mil plastic sheeting or 15# building paper over the framing. Overlap seams by several inches, and leave the sheets long at the perimeter.

NOTE: Framing for cementboard must be 16" on-center; steel studs must be 20-gauge.

Cut cementboard by scoring through the mesh just below the surface with a utility knife or carbide-tipped cutter. Snap the panel back, then cut through the back-side mesh (inset).

NOTE: For tile applications, the rough face of the board is the front.

Make cutouts for pipes and other penetrations by drilling a series of holes through the board, using a small masonry bit. Tap the hole out with a hammer or a scrap of pipe. Cut holes along edges with a jigsaw and carbide grit blade.

Install the sheets horizontally. Where possible, use full pieces to avoid butted seams, which are difficult to fasten. If there are vertical seams, stagger them between rows. Leave a ⅛" gap between sheets at vertical seams and corners. Use spacers to set the bottom row of panels ¼" above the tub or shower base. Fasten the sheets with 1¼" cementboard screws, driven every 8" for walls and every 6" for ceilings. Drive the screws at least ½" from the edges to prevent crumbling. If the studs are steel, don't fasten within 1" of the top track.

Cover the joints and corners with cementboard joint tape (alkali-resistant fiberglass mesh) and latex-Portland cement mortar (thin-set). Apply a layer of mortar with a taping knife, embed the tape into the mortar, then smooth and level the mortar.

Finishing Cementboard

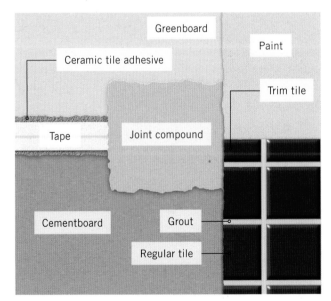

Greenboard
Paint
Ceramic tile adhesive
Trim tile
Tape
Joint compound
Cementboard
Grout
Regular tile

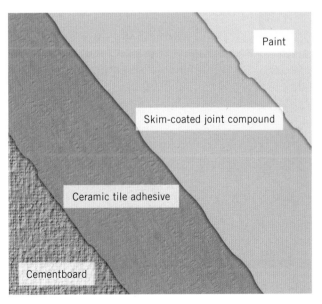

Paint
Skim-coated joint compound
Ceramic tile adhesive
Cementboard

To finish a joint between cementboard and greenboard, seal the joint and exposed cementboard with ceramic tile adhesive, a mixture of four parts adhesive to one part water. Embed paper joint tape into the adhesive, smoothing the tape with a taping knife. Allow the adhesive to dry, then finish the joint with at least two coats of all-purpose drywall joint compound.

To finish small areas of cementboard that will not be tiled, seal the cementboard with ceramic tile adhesive, a mixture of four parts adhesive to one part water, then apply a skim-coat of all-purpose drywall joint compound using a 12" drywall knife. Then prime and paint the wall.

Curved Walls

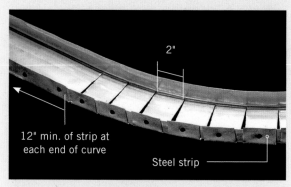

2"

12" min. of strip at each end of curve

Steel strip

As a substitute for flexible track, use standard 20- or 25-gauge steel track. Along the curved portion of the wall, cut the web and flange along the outside of the curve at 2" intervals. From the web of a scrap piece, cut a 1"-wide strip that runs the length of the curve, plus 8". Bend the track to follow the curve, then screw the strip to the inside of the outer flange, using 7/16" Type S screws. This construction requires 12" of straight (uncut) track at both ends of the curve.

Curved walls have obvious appeal and are surprisingly easy to build. Structurally, a curved wall is very similar to a standard non-loadbearing partition wall, with two key differences: the stud spacing and the materials used for the top and bottom wall plates.

Traditionally, plates for curved walls were cut from ¾-inch plywood—a somewhat time-consuming and wasteful process—but now a flexible track product made of light-gauge steel has made the construction much easier (see Resources, page 267). Using the steel track, frame the wall based on a layout drawn onto the floor. Shape the track to follow the layout, screw together the track pieces to lock-in the shape, then add the studs.

The ideal stud spacing for your project depends upon the type of finish material you plan to use. If it's drywall, ¼-inch flexible panels (usually installed in double layers) require studs spaced a maximum of 9 inches O.C. for curves with a minimum radius of 32 inches. For radii less than 32 inches, you may have to wet the panels.

By virtue of their shape, curved walls provide some of their own stability. Half-walls with pronounced curves may not need additional support if they're secured at one end. If your wall needs additional support, look for ways to tie it into the existing

framing, or install cabinets or other permanent fixtures for stability.

If you are planning a curved wall of full height, use a plumb bob to transfer the layout of the bottom track up to the ceiling for the layout of the top track. Check the alignment by placing a few studs at the ends and middle, and then fasten the top track to the ceiling joists with drywall screws.

When hanging drywall on curved walls, it's best to install the panels perpendicular to the framing. Try to avoid joints, but if they are unavoidable, note that vertical seams are much easier to hide in the curve than horizontal seams. If panels have been wetted for the installation, allow them to dry thoroughly before taping seams.

A curved wall can be created in several ways using traditional framing and drywall methods or modern products that eliminate much of the work.

How to Frame a Curved Wall

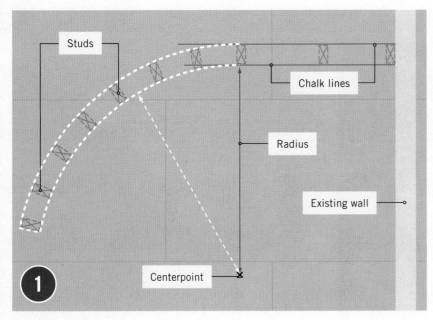

Studs

Chalk lines

Radius

Existing wall

Centerpoint

1

Draw the wall layout. Mark straight portions with parallel chalk lines representing the outside edges of the wall track. Use a framing square to make sure the lines are perpendicular to the adjoining wall. At the start of the curve, square off from the chalk line and measure out the distance of the radius to mark the curve's centerpoint. For small curves (4 ft., or so), drive a nail at the centerpoint, hook the end of a tape measure on the nail, and draw the curve using the tape and a pencil as a compass; for larger curves, use a straight board nailed at the centerpoint.

2

Position the track along the layout lines, following the curve exactly. Mark the end of the wall onto the track using a marker, then cut the track to length with aviation snips. Cut the top track to the same length.

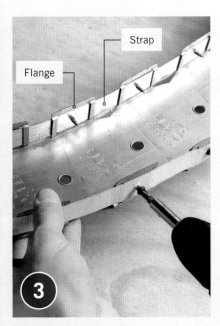

Strap

Flange

3

4

5

Reposition the bottom track on the layout, then apply masking tape along the outside flanges. Secure the track by driving a Type S screw through each flange and into the strap. Screw both sides of the track. Turn over the bottom track, then set the top track on top and match its shape. Tape and screw the top track.

Fasten the bottom track to the floor, using 1¼" drywall screws. Mark the stud layout onto both tracks. Cut the studs to length. Install the studs one at a time, using a level to plumb each along its narrow edge, then driving a 1¼" screw through the flange or strap and into the stud on both sides.

Fit the top track over the studs and align them with the layout marks. Fasten the studs to the top track with one screw on each side, checking the wall for level and height as you work. Set the level on top of the track, both parallel and perpendicular to the track, before fastening each stud.

Installing Drywall on Curves

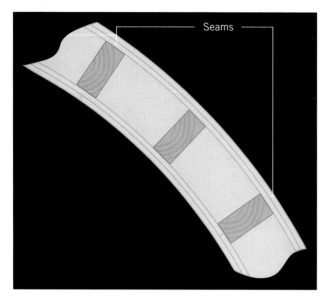

Use two layers of ¼" flexible drywall for curved walls and arches. If there are butted seams, stagger the seams between layers.

Install corner bead with adhesive and staples or drywall nails. Do not use screws to attach corner bead; they will cause the bead material to kink and distort.

Hanging Flexible Drywall

Start at the center for concave curves. Cut the first panel a little long and position it lengthwise along the wall. Carefully bend the panel toward the midpoint of the curve and fasten it to the center stud. Work toward the ends to fasten the rest of the panel. Install the second panel over the first, then trim along the top of the wall with a drywall saw.

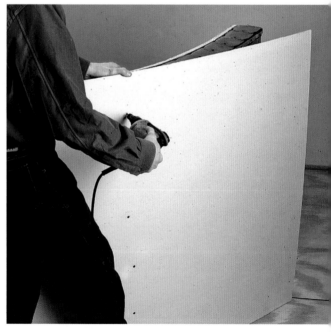

Start at one end for convex curves. Cut the panel long and fasten it lengthwise along the wall, bending the panel as you work. Add the second layer, then trim both to the framing. To cover the top of a curved wall, set a ½" panel on the wall and scribe it from below.

Hanging Drywall in Archways

Cut ¼" flexible drywall to width and a few inches longer than needed. Fasten to the arch with 1¼" drywall screws, working from the center out to the ends. Trim the ends of the piece, and install a second to match the thickness of the surrounding drywall.

VARIATION: Score the backside of ½" drywall every inch (or more for tighter curves) along the length of the piece. Starting at one end, fasten the piece along the arch; the scored drywall will conform to the arch.

WET-BENDING

Drywall is relatively easy to conform to surfaces that curve in just one direction, as long as you wet the tensioned surface of the drywall and don't try to bend it farther than it will go. When wetted and rested for an hour, ½" drywall will bend to a 4 foot radius, ⅜" to a 3 foot radius, and ¼" to a 2 foot radius. Special flexible ¼" drywall does not require wetting for radii greater than 32".

Set framing members closer together for curved surfaces to avoid flat spots. Radii less than 5 feet require 12" frame spacing, less than 4 feet require 8" spacing, and less than 3 feet require 6" spacing. Hang the factory edge of panels perpendicular to the framing so the panels bend longwise. ¼" panels should be doubled up; stagger the panels so no joints line up.

Wet the side of the panel that will be stretched by the bend with about 1 quart of water using a paint roller. Cover the panel with plastic or face the wet sides of two sheets of drywall toward each other, and let sit for 1 hour before application.

Architectural Details

Drywall can be installed in layers or in conjunction with a 2× framework to bring a wide variety of architectural detail to a room. From a simple series of tiers wrapping the perimeter of a room (shown here) to curved soffits or raised panels on walls, you can replicate designs you've seen in high-end homes or bring your own creation to life.

The same basic technique used to hang drywall in multiple layers applies to adding built-up drywall detail. Use a sharp utility knife and a rasp for cutting as panel edges must be clean for finishing. The use of adhesive is highly recommended to create strong bonds between layers so the pieces hold together tightly. Use Type G screws to hold panels together while the adhesive sets up. Use L-bead to create sharp, clean panel ends. Finish all seams and beads with joint tape and at least three coats of compound, following standard finishing techniques.

See pages 108 to 109 for more information on installing drywall in multiple layers.

Add architectural detail to walls and ceilings by building up decorative layers of drywall.

TOOLS & MATERIALS

Work gloves	T-square	Screwgun or ⅜" drill	L-bead
Eye protection	Utility knife	Drywall	Adhesive
Tape measure	Chalk line	Drywall screws	Joint compound

CREATING BUILT-UP DRYWALL DETAILS

For a more substantial step soffit, build a 2× framework as a base for the drywall. As you lay out the placement of the new framing, make sure to account for the thickness of the drywall in all final dimensions.

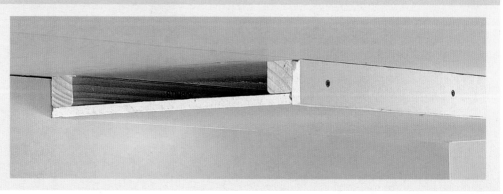

How to Add Decorative Tiers to a Ceiling

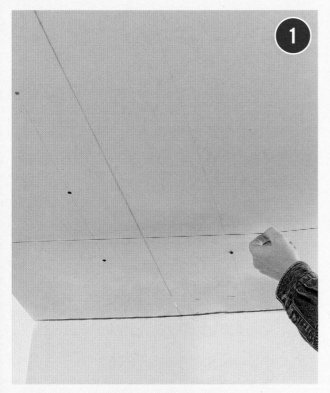

Measure and mark the width of the first tier on the ceiling along each wall, then snap chalk lines to mark the perimeter.

Cut pieces of drywall to size, apply ⅜" beads of adhesive to the backside, and install with drywall screws, following the spacing chart on page 73.

Snap chalk lines for the second tier, then cut and install the drywall as described in step 2. Stagger all seams at corners and along tiera runs.

Install L-bead on all exposed edges of each tier, then finish with three coats of joint compound. Edges can also be finished with flexible corner tape.

Archways

While an arch may be framed and drywalled on site, polyurethane inserts create a symmetrical arch in the style of your choosing much more easily, making them popular among pros and DIYers alike. This arch was ordered to fit, so no further cutting or fitting was needed. Note that polyurethane products carve and sand like wood, so it's better to run thicker rather than thinner when attempting to match your wall thickness.

WHERE TO CUT IN?

If you are simply adding an arch to an existing passageway, use a hacksaw and utility knife to cut free corner bead in the area that will receive the arch inserts. Prying out bead will leave an indent for tape and mud. Leave enough corner bead at the sides so arch overlaps bead by about ¾".

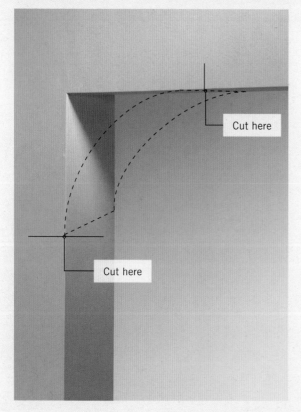

A framed and drywalled archway divides a large space into smaller, more intimate space and makes a dramatic design statement in the process.

TOOLS & MATERIALS

Work gloves	Drywall screws
Eye protection	Arch inserts
Framing lumber	Panel adhesive
Hammer and nails	Corner bead
Drywall panels	Finishing materials
Screwgun	

How to Build an Archway

Frame a partition wall with the alcove opening roughed in as a rectangle. Secure the frame so it is plumb and square to the ceiling joists, the adjacent wall studs (if possible), and to the floor.

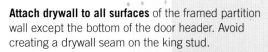

Attach drywall to all surfaces of the framed partition wall except the bottom of the door header. Avoid creating a drywall seam on the king stud.

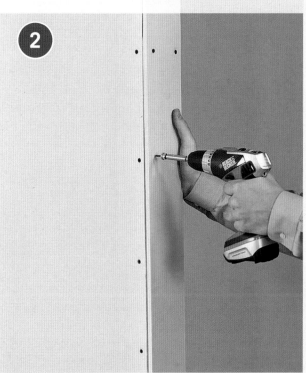

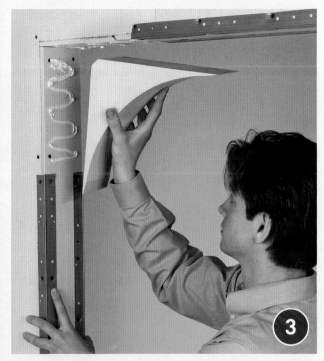

Install corner beads and arches so the arch inserts will overlap the bead by ¾". Typically, arches are secured with panel adhesive and screws.

Tape, fill, and finish all seams, exposed fastener heads, and corners of the partition wall. Trim and finish the arched partition wall to match existing walls.

Preformed Domes

Work gloves
Eye protection
Compass
Straightedge
Screwgun
Drywall screws
Framing lumber
Spiral saw
Insulation (if necessary)
Light fixture
Caulk
Finishing materials

Domes and other three-dimensional features may be ordered preformed. The one we installed here is made of polyurethane. The most difficult and critical steps in dome installation involve the modifications you must make to the ceiling framing. Joists under a roof and the bottom chords of roof trusses are often under tension since the split-leg action of roof rafters pushes out against the walls on which they rest. Joists lower in the building may be supporting tremendous loads that aren't obvious. Therefore, before you cut through structural members, you must have a framing-modification plan drawn up by a qualified structural engineer. In most localities, these drawings need to be approved by a building inspector in order to get a building permit to do the work.

A simple domed shape transforms an ordinary ceiling into a grand design statement, especially when the dome is appointed with an attractive ceiling light or chandelier. This Fypon dome (see Resources, page 267) is fabricated from urethane foam and installed as one piece.

Preformed Dome Styles

A plain round dome is hard to beat for versatility and ease of installation. This fabricated dome does require that you either remove sections of ceiling joist or create a lower ceiling with a furred-out framework.

Ornate domes add high drama, especially when they include a chandelier or an intricate medallion.

How to Install a Preformed Dome

Trace the dome onto cardboard in an upside-down position, and transfer four alignment lines onto the outline. Since this outline includes the flange, it's larger than the hole you need to cut in the ceiling.

Scribe a second, smaller circle inside the outline by setting a compass or scribe slightly less than the width of the flange and following along the outline. Use a straightedge and marker to connect the opposite alignment marks, forming a cross. Cut out the inside circle to make your template.

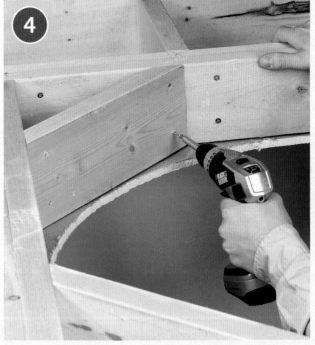

Screw the cardboard template to the ceiling. The alignment cross may be used to center a round dome or to make an oval dome parallel with a wall. Transfer the alignment marks to the ceiling with a pencil to guide positioning of the domes that are oval or imperfectly round.

Cut through the drywall and framing at the edge of the template. Add re-enforcement framing as specified by a qualified structural engineer. Add trimmers and blocking to the dome edges at screw locations. Add insulation if necessary, above the dome.

Cut a hole for the light fixture wiring in the center of the dome. A hole saw that's slightly bigger than the round electrical fixture box works. For larger or more challenging openings, use a spiral saw to cut the outline of the fixture box in the dome.

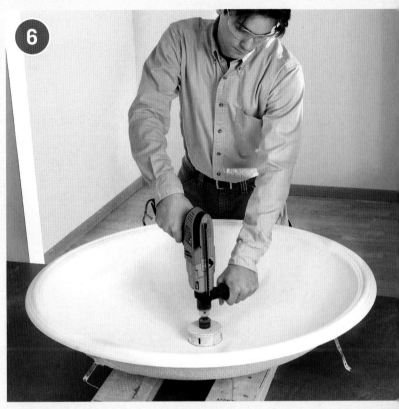

Prepare for a fixture box if a light fixture or fan will be hung in the dome. Drill a 1" hole in the center of the dome. Raise framing above the ceiling opening to secure an electric fixture box above the center of the opening. Dome specifications will determine how far to recess the fixture box from the face of the ceiling. Typically, the face of the fixture box should be flush with the finished (visible) face of the dome. You may temporarily attach the dome to help position the fixture box.

Hang your light or fan and caulk all air gaps through and around the fixture box. Caulk the seam where the dome flange meets the ceiling. Cover the fastener heads with joint compound. Finish the dome with ceiling paint.

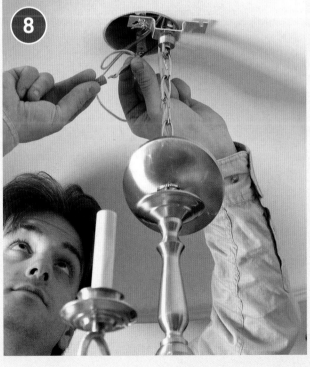

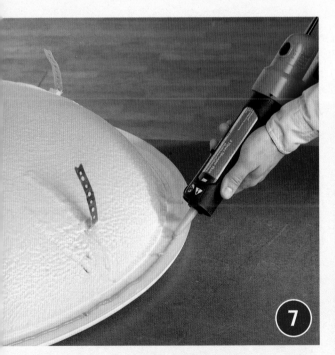

Apply polyurethane construction adhesive to the back of the dome flange. Lift the dome into place with helpers, aligning the ceiling and dome alignment marks and fitting the dome around the electrical box. Attach the flange of the dome to the blocking through the ceiling with drywall screws. Countersink the screw heads slightly.

Garage Drywall

Whether or not to install finished interior walls on your garage is mostly a matter of preference. The only time wall surfaces are required is when your garage shares a wall with your house (an attached garage) or if one of the walls in your detached garage runs parallel to the house and is constructed within 3 feet of the house. In both cases, only the shared or closest walls need to be finished to block the spreading of fire. Typically, a wallcovering of ½-inch-thick (minimum) drywall with taped seams is required. Some circumstances may demand that you install fire-rated, Type X drywall or a double layer of drywall. The seams between drywall panels on fireblocking walls must be finished with tape embedded in joint compound or with adhesive-backed fireblocking tape.

If the area above the garage is occupied by a habitable room, the garage walls should be covered with ½-inch drywall to provide rigidity and structure and the ceiling should be finished with ⅝-inch-thick Type X drywall. Ceiling seams should be covered with tape and compound. Fastener heads do not need to be covered with compound except for visual reasons.

If your goal is to create a garage with walls that are finished to interior standards or serve to prevent fire spreading, then drywall is an excellent wallcovering. Although the price and availability of diverse building materials fluctuates rather dramatically, drywall is typically one of the more economical choices. But because drywall is relatively susceptible to damage from impact (for example, from tools or bicycles) and doesn't withstand exposure to moisture well, many homeowners choose other wallcoverings for their garage. Exterior siding panels are thick enough to hold fasteners and withstand moisture well, but are relatively costly and most have a rougher texture that can be bothersome on interior spaces. Interior paneling has only minimal structural value, but it may be more visually pleasing to you and some styles are fairly inexpensive.

Plywood and oriented strand-board are popular products for garage walls. Thicker panels (½ to ¾-inch-thick) give excellent rigidity to the walls and are suitable for holding some fasteners. They can be left unfinished, clear-coated for protection with polyurethane finish (or comparable), or you may choose to paint them. A lighter colored wall paint in semi-gloss or gloss is a good choice. Sheet goods that have a pleasing color or woodgrain may be finished with either a clear coating or a protective deck/siding stain. Lauan plywood underlayment, for example, has a natural mahogany color that can be pleasing when treated with a reddish exterior stain or clear coat. It is also inexpensive, but it is thin (roughly ¼") and can only support very light-duty fasteners with little load, such as a stickpin holding a wall calendar.

Finishing your garage walls with drywall or other panel products improves the appearance of your garage and also can serve practical functions such as forming a fireblock or concealing wiring or plumbing.

How to Hang Drywall in a Garage

Begin installing drywall panels in a corner. You can install the panels vertically or horizontally, depending on the wall height and how much cutting is involved. Unlike interior walls, garage walls are seldom a standard 8 ft. If you are finishing a ceiling with drywall, cover the ceiling first so you can press the tops of the wall panels up against the ceiling panels. This helps support the ends of the ceiling panels. Drive coarse 1¼" drywall screws every 16".

Cut drywall pieces to fit around doors and windows. Take special care if you are covering a firewall since any gaps will need to be filled with joint compound and taped over. Make straight cuts that run full width or length by scoring through the face paper with a utility knife and then snapping along the scored line. Finish the cut by slicing through the paper of the back face.

Mark and make cutouts for electrical and utility boxes. Use a drywall saw, keyhole saw, or spiral saw to make the cutouts. Make sure the front edges of the boxes are flush with the face of the drywall (move the boxes or add mud rings, if necessary). Finish installing all panels.

Cover seams between drywall panels with joint compound; use drywall tape on walls that serve as firewalls. Cover tape with two layers of feathered-out joint compound, and then cover all fastener heads if you will be painting the walls. Give the panels a coat of drywall primer before painting.

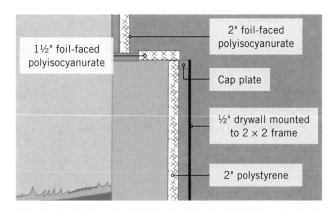

1½" foil-faced polyisocyanurate

2" foil-faced polyisocyanurate

Cap plate

½" drywall mounted to 2 × 2 frame

2" polystyrene

Basement Prep: Solution 1

A s a general rule, avoid insulating the interior side of your basement walls. It is best to leave breathing space for the concrete or block so moisture that enters through the walls is not trapped. If your basement walls stay dry and show no signs of dampness, however, adding some interior insulation can increase the comfort level in your basement. If you are building a stud wall for hanging wallcovering materials, you can insulate between the studs with rigid foam; do not use fiberglass batts, and do not install a vapor barrier. If you are building a stud wall, it's a good idea to keep the wall away from the basement wall so there is an air channel between the two.

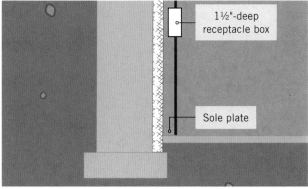

1½"-deep receptacle box

Sole plate

Interior insulation can be installed in the basement if your foundation walls are dry. It is important to keep the framed wall isolated from the basement wall with a seamless layer of rigid insulation board.

How to Insulate an Interior Basement Wall

1

Begin on the exterior wall by digging a trench and installing a 2"-thick rigid foam insulation board up to the bottom of the siding and down at least 6" below grade. The main purpose of this insulation is to inhibit convection and air transfer in the wall above grade.

2

Insulate the rim joist with strips of 2"-thick isocyanurate rigid insulation with foil facing. Be sure the insulation you purchase is rated for interior exposure (exterior products can produce bad vapors). Use adhesive to bond the insulation to the rim joist, and then caulk around all the edges with acoustic sealant.

Attach sheets of 2"-thick extruded polystyrene insulation to the wall from the floor to the top of the wall. Make sure to clean the wall thoroughly and let it dry completely before installing the insulation.

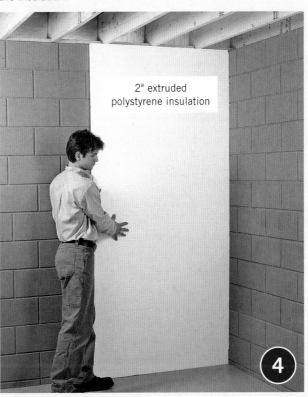

2" extruded polystyrene insulation

④

③

Seal and insulate the top of the foundation wall, if it is exposed, with strips of 1½"-thick, foil-faced isocyanurate insulation. Install the strips using the same type of adhesive and caulk you used for the rim joist insulation.

Install a stud wall by fastening the cap plate to the ceiling joists and the sole plate to the floor. If you have space, allow an air channel between the studs and the insulation. Do not install a vapor barrier on the interior side of the wall.

Vapor barrier tape

⑤

⑥

Seal the gaps between the insulation boards with insulation vapor barrier tape. Do not caulk gaps between the insulation boards and the floor.

Basement Prep: Solution 2

Wall framing members can be attached directly to a concrete foundation wall to provide a support for wall coverings and to house wires and pipes. Because they have no significant structural purpose, they are usually made with smaller stock called furring strips, which can be 2 × 2 or 2 × 3 wood. Do not install furring strips in conjunction with a vapor barrier or insulation, and do not attach them to walls that are not dry walls, with insulation on the exterior side. For an insulated basement wall installation, see page 34.

Furring strips serve primarily to create nailing surfaces for drywall. Attach them to dry basement walls at web locations of block wall where possible.

How to Attach Furring Strips to Dry Foundation Walls

Cut a 2 × 2 top plate to span the length of the wall. Mark the furring-strip layout onto the bottom edge of the plate using 16" O.C. spacing. Attach the plate to the bottom of the joists with 2½" drywall screws. The back edge of the plate should line up with the front of the blocks.

If the joists run parallel to the wall, you'll need to install backers between the outer joist and the sill plate to provide support for ceiling drywall. Make T-shaped backers from short 2 × 4s and 2 × 2s. Install each so the bottom face of the 2 × 4 is flush with the bottom edge of the joists. Attach the top plate to the foundation wall with its top edge flush with the top of the blocks.

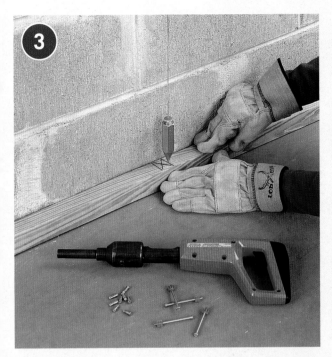

Install a bottom plate cut from pressure-treated 2 × 2 lumber so the plate spans the length of the wall. Apply construction adhesive to the back and bottom of the plate, then attach it to the floor with a nailer. Use a plumb bob to transfer the furring-strip layout marks from the top plate to the bottom plate.

Cut 2 × 2 furring strips to fit between the top and bottom plates. Apply construction adhesive to the back of each furring strip, and position it on the layout marks on the plates. Nail along the length of each strip at 16" intervals.

OPTION: Leave a channel for the installation of wires or supply pipes by installing pairs of vertically aligned furring strips with a 2" gap between each pair.

NOTE: Consult local codes to ensure proper installation of electrical or plumbing materials.

ISOLATE THE WALL

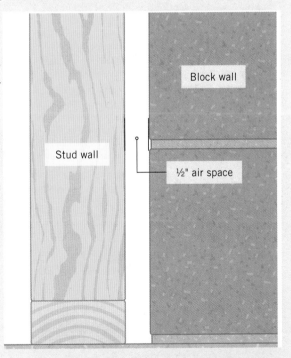

Block wall

Stud wall

½" air space

It consumes more floorspace, but a good alternative to a furred-out wall is to build a 2 × 4 stud wall parallel to the foundation wall, but ½" away from it. This eliminates any contact between the wall-framing members and the foundation wall. See page 34.

Soundproofing

In making homes quieter, building professionals add soundproofing elements to combat everything from the hum of appliances to the roar of airliners. Many of the techniques they use are simple improvements involving common products and materials. What will work best in your home depends upon a few factors, including the types of noises involved, your home's construction, and how much remodeling you have planned. For starters, it helps to know a little of the science behind sound control.

Sound is created by vibrations traveling through air. Consequently, the best ways to reduce sound transmission are by limiting airflow and blocking or absorbing vibrations. Effective soundproofing typically involves a combination of methods.

Stopping airflow—through walls, ceilings, floors, windows, and doors—is essential to any soundproofing effort. (Even a 2-ft.-thick brick wall would not be very soundproof if it had cracks in the mortar.) It's also the simplest way to make minor improvements. Because you're dealing with air, this kind of soundproofing is a lot like weatherizing your home: Add weatherstripping and door sweeps, seal air leaks with caulk, install storm doors and windows, etc. The same techniques that keep out the cold also block exterior noise and prevent sound from traveling between rooms.

After reducing airflow, the next level of soundproofing is to improve the sound-blocking qualities of your walls and ceilings. Engineers

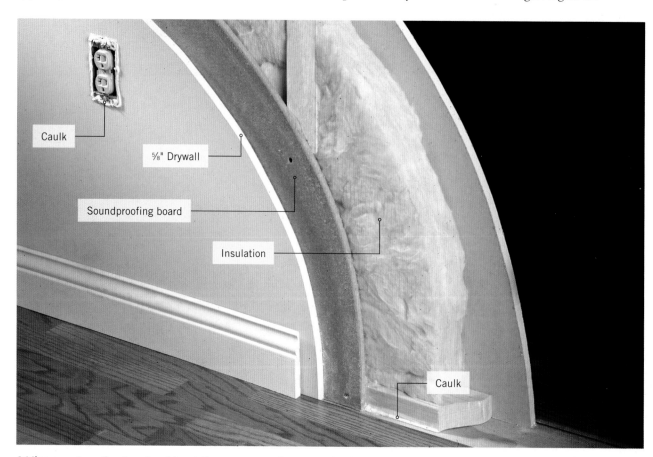

Caulk

⅝" Drywall

Soundproofing board

Insulation

Caulk

Adding soundproofing board and insulation are among the many simple ways you can reduce noise in your home.

STC RATINGS FOR VARIOUS WALL & CEILING CONSTRUCTIONS*

ASSEMBLY	STC RATING
Wood-frame Walls	
2 × 4 wall; ½" drywall on both sides; no caulk	30
2 × 4 wall; ½" drywall on both sides; caulked	35
2 × 4 wall; ½" drywall on both sides; additional layer of ⅝" fire-resistant drywall on one side	38
2 × 4 wall; ½" drywall on both sides; additional layer of ⅝" fire-resistant drywall on both sides	40
2 × 4 wall; ½" drywall on both sides; insulated	39
Staggered-stud 2 × 4 wall; ⅝" fire-resistant drywall on each side; insulated	50
2 × 4 wall, soundproofing board (base layer) and ⅝" fire-resistant drywall on each side; insulated	50
2 × 4 wall with resilient steel channels on one side; ⅝" fire-resistant drywall on both sides; insulated	52
Steel-frame Walls	
3⅝" metal studs, spaced 24" on-center; ⅝" fire-resistant drywall on both sides	40
3⅝" metal studs, spaced 24" on-center, ½" fire-resistant drywall single layer on one side, doubled on other side; insulated	48
2½" metal studs, spaced 24" on-center; soundproofing board (base layer) and ½" fire-resistant drywall on both sides; insulated	50
Wood-frame Floor/Ceiling	
Drywall below; subfloor and resilient (vinyl) flooring above	32
⅝" fire-resistant drywall attached to resilient steel channels below; subfloor, pad, and carpet above	48
Double layer ⅝" fire-resistant drywall attached to resilient steel channels below; subfloor, pad, and carpet above	Up to 60

*All assemblies are sealed with caulk, except where noted. Ratings are approximate.

rate soundproofing performance of wall and ceiling assemblies using a system called Sound Transmission Class, or STC. The higher the STC rating, the more sound is blocked by the assembly. For example, if a wall is rated at 30 to 35 STC, loud speech can be understood through the wall. At 42 STC, loud speech is reduced to a murmur. At 50 STC, loud speech cannot be heard through the wall.

Standard construction methods typically result in a 28 to 32 STC rating, while soundproofed walls and ceilings can carry ratings near 50. To give you an idea of how much soundproofing you need, a sleeping room at 40 to 50 STC is quiet enough for most people; a reading room is comfortable at 35 to 40 STC. For another gauge, consider the fact that increasing the STC rating of an assembly by 10 reduces the perceived sound levels by 50 percent. The chart above lists the STC ratings of several wall and ceiling assemblies.

Improvements to walls and ceilings usually involve increasing the mass, absorbancy, or resiliency of the assembly; often, a combination is best. Adding layers of drywall increases mass, helping a wall resist the vibrational force of sound (⅝-inch fire-resistant drywall works best because of its greater weight and density). Insulation and soundproofing board absorb sound. Soundproofing board is available through drywall suppliers and manufacturers (see page 273). Some board products are gypsum-based; others are lightweight fiberboard. Installing resilient steel channels over the framing or old surface and adding a new layer of drywall increases mass, while the channels allow the surface to move slightly and absorb vibrations. New walls built with staggered studs and insulation are highly effective at reducing vibration.

In addition to these permanent improvements, you can reduce noise by decorating with soft materials that absorb sound. Rugs and carpet, drapery, fabric wall hangings, and soft furniture help reduce atmospheric noise within a room. Acoustical ceiling tiles effectively absorb and help contain sound within a room but do little to prevent sound from entering the room.

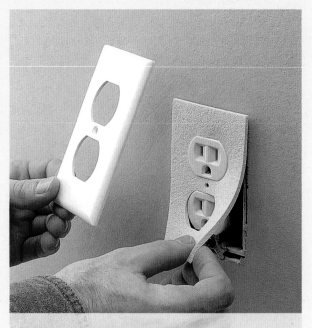

Stop airflow between rooms by sealing the joints where walls meet floors. With finished walls, remove the shoe molding and spray insulating foam, acoustic sealant, or non-hardening caulk under the baseboards. Also seal around door casings. With new walls, seal along the top and bottom plates.

Cover switch and receptacle boxes with foam gaskets to prevent air leaks. Otherwise, seal around the box perimeter with acoustic sealant or caulk, and seal around the knockout where the cables enter the box.

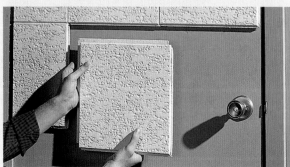

Soundproof doors between rooms by adding a sweep at the bottom and weatherstripping along the stops. If doors are hollow-core, replacing them with solid-core units will increase soundproofing performance. Soundproof workshop and utility room doors with a layer of acoustical tiles.

Relocate loud ductwork. If a duct supplying a quiet room has a takeoff point close to that of a noisy room, move one or both ducts so their takeoff points are as distant from each other as possible.

Installing Resilient Steel Channels

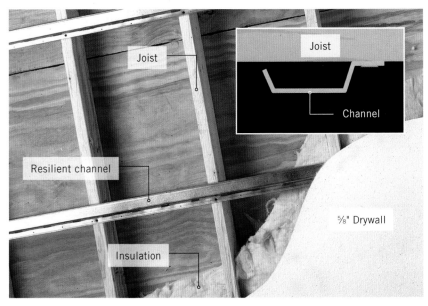

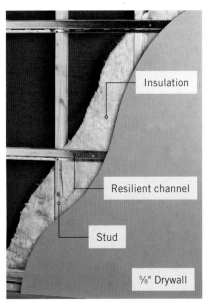

On ceilings, install channels perpendicular to the joists, spaced 24" on-center. Fasten at each joist with 1¼" Type W drywall screws, driven through the channel flange. Stop the channels 1" short of all walls. Join pieces on long runs by overlapping the ends and fastening through both pieces. Insulate the joist bays with unfaced fiberglass or other insulation, and install ⅝" fire-resistant drywall perpendicular to the channels. For double-layer application, install the second layer of drywall perpendicular to the first.

On walls, use the same installation techniques as with the ceiling application, installing the channels horizontally. Position the bottom channel 2" from the floor and the top channel within 6" of the ceiling. Insulate the stud cavities and install the drywall vertically.

How to Build Staggered-stud Partition Walls

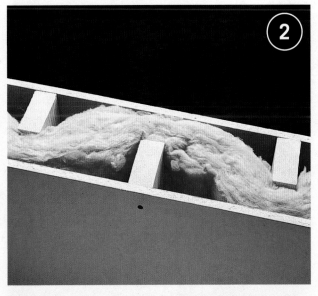

Frame new partition walls using 2 × 6 plates. Space the studs 12" apart, staggering them so alternate studs are aligned with opposite sides of the plates. Seal under and above the plates with acoustic sealant.

Weave R-11 unfaced fiberglass blanket insulation horizontally between the studs. Cover each side with one or more layers of ⅝" fire-resistant drywall.

Multiple Drywall Layers

Installing drywall in multiple layers is an effective means of soundproofing and also increases the fire-rating of walls and ceilings. Drywall can be heavy, especially when installed in layers, so it's important to install panels correctly to prevent sagging, cracks, and popped fasteners. Always fasten both the base layer (which can be standard drywall or a soundproofing board) and the face layer with the correct number of screws (see page 73). Panels can be secured with fasteners alone, though many manufacturers recommend the use of panel adhesive. It's best to install the base layer vertically and the face layer horizontally, staggering the joints. If panels must be hung in the same direction, stagger parallel seams between layers by at least 10 inches.

See pages 104 to 107 for more on soundproofing walls and ceilings.

Specialty materials can help eliminate sound transmission better than drywall alone. High-density gypsum and cellulose fiber soundproofing board (A) provides excellent noise attenuation. MLV (mass-loaded vinyl) sheeting (B) can double a wall's soundproofing value. Type G drywall screws (C) have coarse threads to hold drywall panels together as the panel adhesive (D) sets to create a strong bond. Acoustical caulk (E) seals gaps to absorb noise vibrations. And for added protection, install closed cell foam gaskets (F) behind electrical coverplates.

TOOLS & MATERIALS

Tape measure	Caulk gun	Type G drywall screws	Panel Adhesive
Screwgun or ⅜" drill	Drywall panels	Acoustical caulk	

Building code requires that the front face of electrical boxes be flush with the finished wall surface. In new construction, attach boxes so they extend past the framing of the combined thickness of the drywall layers. If you're covering an old surface, use extension rings to bring existing boxes flush.

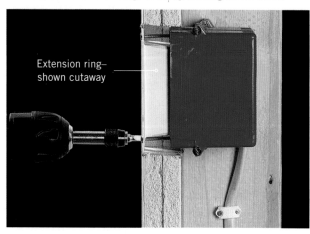

Extension ring– shown cutaway

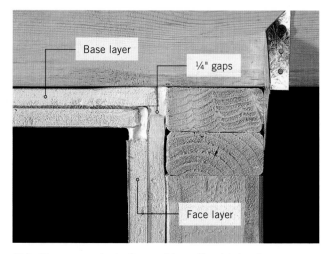

Base layer

¼" gaps

Face layer

At inside corners, including wall-to-ceiling joints, stagger the joints between the layers, leaving a ¼" gap between panels. Seal all gaps with acoustical caulk to help absorb sound vibration.

How to Hang Multiple Layers of Drywall

Install the base layer of drywall or soundproofing board parallel to the framing, using the screws and spacing found on page 73. Leave a ¼" gap around the perimeter of each surface (at corners, ceilings, and along floors). After panels are installed, seal the perimeter gaps with acoustical caulk.

To install the face layer, use adhesive to ensure a strong bond to the base. Apply ⅜" beads of adhesive every 16" across the backside of the panels.

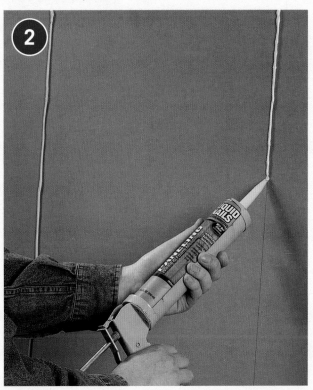

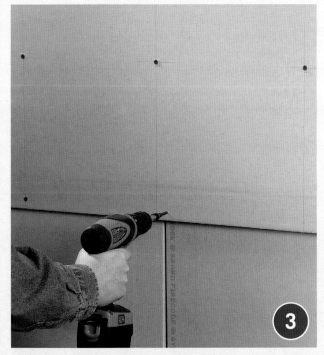

Install the face layer of drywall perpendicular to the framing and joints of the base layer, spacing screws as recommended on page 73. Make sure to stagger the seams between layers. Use Type G screws to temporarily hold panels together as the adhesive sets up.

Seal the perimeter gaps at corners, ceiling, and along floors with acoustical caulk. Also seal around electrical boxes and HVAC ducts.

Soundproof Room

Home theaters are quickly becoming a common feature in many homes. And while finding an affordable yet impressive multimedia system is no longer a problem, finding a space within your home to enjoy it may not be so easy. The walls of the average house are not designed to contain extreme sound levels. To combat this issue, there are numerous soundproofing products and materials available to help keep those on both sides of a home theater wall happy.

As discussed on page 105, engineers rate the soundproofing performance of wall and ceiling assemblies using a system called Sound Transmission Class (STC). Standard partition walls carry STC ratings of 28 to 32. Determining an appropriate STC rating for your home theater is dependent on a number of factors, such as the power of your multimedia system and the type of room opposite the wall. But a minimum of 60 STC is adequate for most. Remember: The higher the STC rating, the more sound is blocked.

But blocking sound is not the only consideration. The low frequencies generated by subwoofers cause vibrations, which in turn create unwanted noise within the room. The most effective approach for soundproofing a home theater is to install both sound barriers to minimize sound escaping and sound absorbers to reduce noise within the room.

Adding mass to walls and ceilings is an effective way to block sound. In new construction, staggered-stud partitions (page 107) or double stud partitions (two adjacent rows of studs) are possibilities. Hanging soundproofing board, sound-rated drywall, or multiple layers of drywall can increase STC ratings significantly. Two of the most effective systems are resilient channels (page 107) and mass loaded vinyl (MLV) underlayment, a heavy vinyl sheeting that many manufacturers claim can more than double a wall's STC rating.

For sound absorption, closed-cell acoustical foam matting can be used to insulate between drywall panels and framing. Similarly, padded tape minimizes transmission of sound vibration between wall panels and framing, and can be used to line resilient channels for added insulation. Sound isolation mounting clips contain molded neoprene to provide added insulation between resilient channels and framing. Vibration pads made of cork and closed-cell acoustical foam or neoprene isolate sound vibration to reduce transmission between objects.

When fastening soundproofing and drywall panels to resilient channels, leave a ¼-inch gap between all panels at corners and fill the gaps with acoustical caulk. In fact, all gaps, seams, and cracks should be filled with acoustical caulk. The more airtight a home theater, the more soundproof it is.

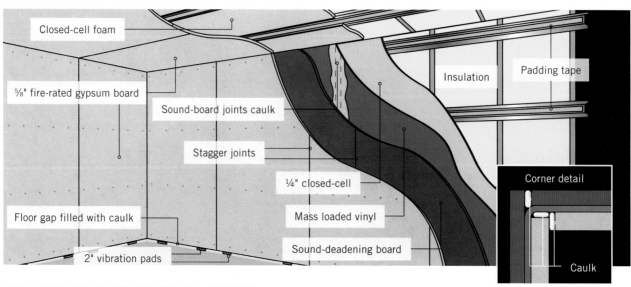

Closed-cell foam

⅝" fire-rated gypsum board

Sound-board joints caulk

Stagger joints

¼" closed-cell

Floor gap filled with caulk

Mass loaded vinyl

2" vibration pads

Sound-deadening board

Insulation

Padding tape

Corner detail

Caulk

Soundproofing a Room

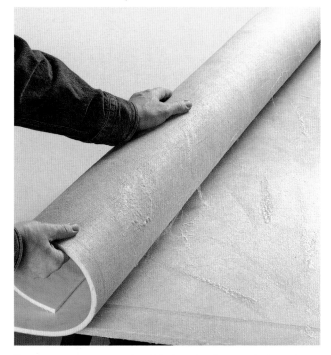

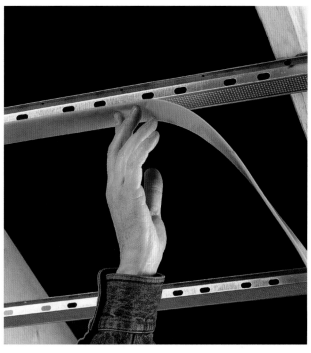

Use contact cement to glue ¼" closed-cell acoustical matting directly to existing wall and ceiling surfaces or to the backside of drywall panels in new construction.

Apply self-adhesive padded tape to resilient channels or directly to the edges of framing members.

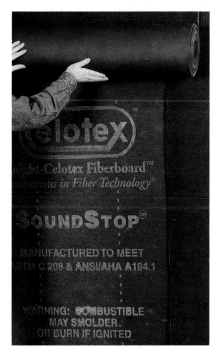

Install 2" vibration pads every 2 ft. between flooring and installed drywall panels. Fasten baseboard into framing only, not into vibration pads.

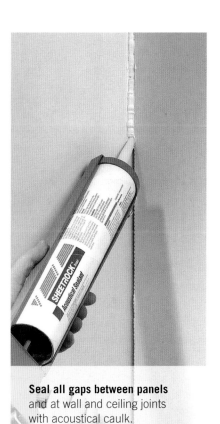

Staple MLV (mass loaded vinyl) underlayment directly to framing members, between layers of drywall and soundproofing board, or directly to existing wall and ceiling surfaces. Overlap seams by at least 6".

Seal all gaps between panels and at wall and ceiling joints with acoustical caulk.

Finishing Drywall

The process of finishing drywall involves distinct steps: Tape seams; cover fastener heads; install corner bead; apply a second coat of joint compound; apply a third coat of joint compound; sand (if necessary); apply a skim coat or finished texture (optional); prime and paint.

The process is not as complicated or time-consuming as the list of tasks may make it sound. By simply doing careful work when applying finishing materials you can eliminate most of the sanding (which happens to be the messiest part). The most important part of the job—and the area where most people take ill-advised shortcuts—is in the three rounds of joint compound application. The key here is to use taping knives of increasingly larger size, ending with a knife that has a blade at least 12 inches wide. By feathering out the joint compound on each side of the seam with a 12-inch knife, you will create a smooth compound layer that's a full 24 inches wide and virtually impossible to detect after the wall is primed and painted.

Once the wall is mudded, a light sanding and a coat of drywall primer are all that's needed to prepare for a fine painted finish. If you wish, you can apply a texture or a skim coat to the wall or ceiling before painting to create an interesting surface.

In this chapter:
- Recommended Levels of Drywall Finish
- Installing Corner Bead
- Taping Drywall Seams
- Fixing Problems & Final Inspection
- Sanding Drywall
- Textures & Skim Coats
- Priming & Painting Drywall

Recommended Levels of Drywall Finish

The main purpose of finishing drywall is to create an acceptable base surface for the desired decorative finish. For example, walls and ceilings that will be illuminated by bright light or finished with gloss paint or thin wallcovering require a smooth, consistent surface to prevent taped seams, covered fasteners, and minor imperfections from showing through—a condition called *photographing*. On the other hand, surfaces that will be sprayed with a texture don't need as polished a drywall finish, and areas that only need to meet fire codes may be acceptable with a single tape coat.

For years, there were no universal guidelines for what was considered an "acceptable" drywall finish, which often left contractors and homeowners at odds over what "industry standard finish" actually meant. But recently four major trade associations devised a set of guidelines that have been accepted industry-wide. Below are their recommendations for finishing drywall.

Level 0

"No taping, finishing, or accessories required."

This level of finish may be useful in temporary construction or whenever the final decoration has not been determined.

Level 1

"All joints and interior angles shall have tape set in joint compound. Surface shall be free of excess joint compound. Tool marks and ridges are acceptable."

Frequently specified in plenum areas above ceilings, in attics, in areas where the assembly would generally be concealed or in building service corridors, and other areas not normally open to public view. Accessories (beads, trims, or moldings) are optional at specifier discretion in corridors and other areas with pedestrian traffic.

Some degree of sound and smoke control is provided; in some geographic areas this level is referred to as "firetaping." Where a fire-resistance rating is required for the gypsum board assembly, details of construction shall be in accordance with reports of fire tests of assemblies that have met the fire-rating requirement. Tape and fastener heads need not be covered with joint compound.

Level 2

"All joints and interior angles shall have tape embedded in joint compound and wiped with a joint knife leaving a thin coating of joint compound over all joints and interior angles. Fastener heads and accessories shall be covered with a coat of joint

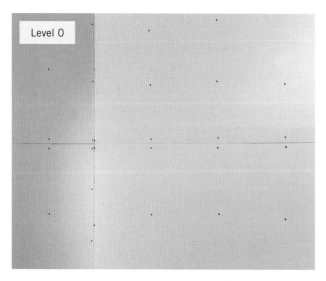

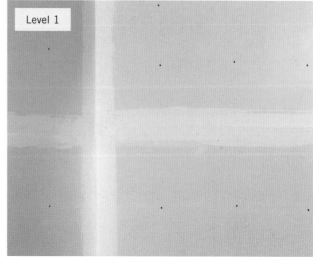

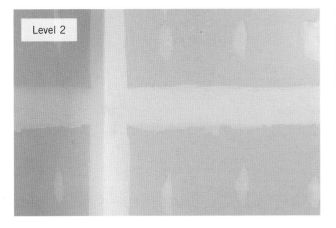

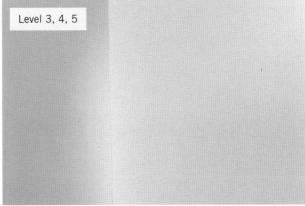

compound. Surface shall be free of excess joint compound. Tool marks and ridges are acceptable. Joint compound applied over the body of the tape at the time of tape embedment shall be considered a separate coat of joint compound and shall satisfy the conditions of this level."

This level is specified where water-resistant gypsum backing board (ASTM C 630) is used as a substrate for tile; may be specified in garages, warehouse storage, or other similar areas where surface appearance is not of primary concern.

Level 3

"All joints and interior angles shall have tape embedded in joint compound and one additional coat of joint compound applied over all joints and interior angles. Fastener heads and accessories shall be covered with two separate coats of joint compound. All joint compound shall be smooth and free of tool marks and ridges. *Note: It is recommended that the prepared surface be coated with a drywall primer prior to the application of final finishes. See painting/wallcovering specification in this regard.*"

Typically specified in appearance areas that are to receive heavy- or medium-texture (spray or hand applied) finishes before final painting, or where heavy-grade wallcoverings are to be applied as the final decoration, this level of finish is not recommended where smooth, painted surfaces or light-to-medium wallcoverings are specified.

Level 4

"All joints and interior angles shall have tape embedded in joint compound and two separate coats of joint compound applied over all flat joints and one separate coat of joint compound applied over interior angles. Fastener heads and accessories shall be covered with three separate coats of joint compound. All joint compound shall be smooth and free of tool

marks and ridges. *Note: It is recommended that the prepared surface be coated with a drywall primer prior to the application of final finishes. See painting/wallcovering specification in this regard.*"

This level should be specified where flat paints, light textures, or wallcoverings are to be applied. In critical lighting areas, flat paints applied over light textures tend to reduce joint photographing. Gloss, semi-gloss, and enamel paints are not recommended over this level of finish.

The weight, texture, and sheen level of wallcoverings applied over this level of finish should be carefully evaluated. Joints and fasteners must be adequately concealed if the wallcovering material is lightweight, contains limited pattern, has a gloss finish, or any combination of these finishes is present. Unbacked vinyl wallcoverings are not recommended over this level of finish.

Level 5

"All joints and interior angles shall have tape embedded in joint compound and two separate coats of joint compound applied over all flat joints and one separate coat of joint compound applied over interior angles. Fastener heads and accessories shall be covered with three separate coats of joint compound. A thin skim coat of joint compound or a material manufactured especially for this purpose, shall be applied to the entire surface. The surface shall be smooth and free of tool marks and ridges. *Note: It is recommended that the prepared surface be coated with a drywall primer prior to the application of finish paint. See painting specification in this regard.*"

This level of finish is highly recommended where gloss, semi-gloss, enamel, or non-textured flat paints are specified or where severe lighting conditions occur. This highest quality finish is the most effective method to provide a uniform surface and minimize the possibility of joint photographing and of fasteners showing through the final decoration.

Installing Corner Bead

After the drywall is hung, the next step is to install corner bead to protect outside corners, soffits, drywall-finished openings, and any other outside angles. Corner bead provides a clean, solid-edge wall corner that can withstand moderate abuse. It is available in a variety of styles for a variety of applications (see page 49). The three most common types are metal, vinyl, and paper-faced beads.

Metal beads can be fastened with nails, screws, or a crimper tool. Vinyl beads are easily installed with spray adhesive and staples, or can be embedded in compound, similar to paper-faced beads.

A number of specialty beads are also available, including flexible archway beads for curved corners and J-bead for covering panel ends that meet finished surfaces. Decorative bullnose beads and caps for 2- and 3-way corners are easy ways to add interesting detail to a room.

Metal corner bead installed over steel framing can be fastened using a crimper tool. Cut the bead to size and position in the corner (see step 1 below), then crimp every 4 to 6".

TOOLS & MATERIALS

Work gloves	Screwgun or drill	Corner bead	1½" ring-shank drywall nails	Archway bead
Eye protection	Stapler	Spray adhesive		Metal file
Aviation snips	Hammer	1¼" drywall screws	½" staples	

How to Install Metal Corner Bead

Cut metal corner bead to length using aviation snips, leaving a ½" gap at the floor. Position the bead so the raised spine is centered over the corner and the flanges are flat against both walls.

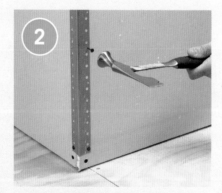

Starting at the top, fasten the bead flanges with drywall nails, driven every 9" and about ¼" from the edge. Alternate sides with each nail to keep the bead centered. The nails must not project beyond the raised spine.

Use full lengths of corner bead where possible. If you must join two lengths, cut the two pieces to size, then butt together the finished ends. Make sure the ends are perfectly aligned and the spine is straight along the length of the corner. File ends, if necessary.

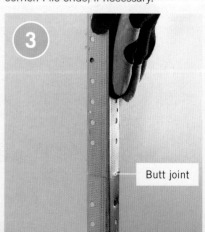

Butt joint

How to Install Vinyl Corner Bead

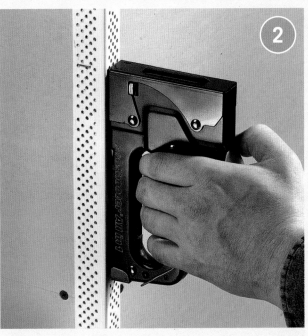

Cut vinyl bead to length and test fit over corner. Spray vinyl adhesive evenly along the entire length of the corner, then along the bead.

Quickly install the bead, pressing the flanges into the adhesive. Fasten the bead in place with ½" staples every 8".

 # How to Install Corner Bead at Three-way Corners

Fasten the first bead in place, then test fit each subsequent piece, trimming any overlapping flanges. Align the tips of the two pieces and fasten in place. Install additional beads in the same way.

FILE EDGES

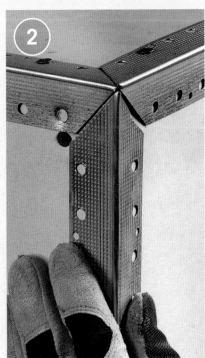

Where two or more outside corners meet, trim back the overlapping flanges of each bead to 45° mitered ends using aviation snips. The ends don't have to match perfectly, but they should not overlap.

Blunt any sharp edges or points created by metal bead at three-way corners using a metal file.

How to Install Flexible Bead for an Archway

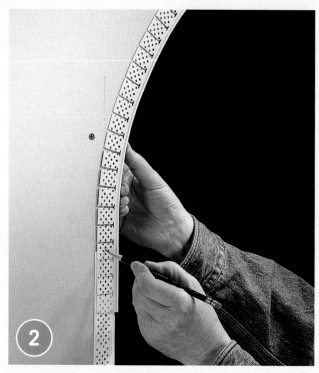

Install standard corner bead on the straight lengths of the corners (see pages 116 to 117) so it is ½" from the floor and 2" from the start of the arch.

Flatten flexible vinyl bead along the archway to determine the length needed, then add 3". Cut two pieces of bead to this length, one for each side of the archway.

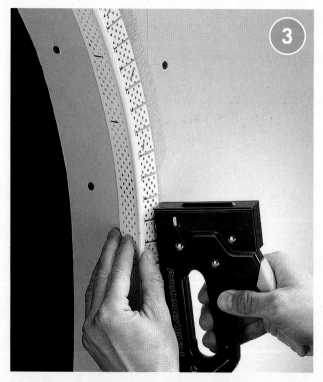

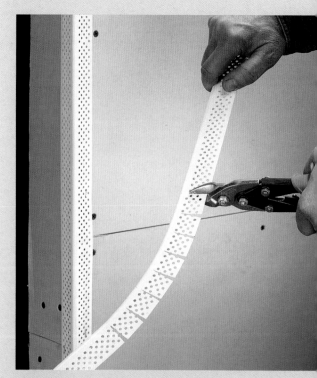

Spray one side of the archway with vinyl adhesive, then spray the bead. Immediately install the bead; work from one end, pushing the bead tight into the corner along the arch. Secure with ½" staples every 2". Trim the overlapping end so it meets the end of the straight length of corner bead.

VARIATION: To substitute for flexible bead, snip one flange of standard vinyl bead at 1" intervals. Be careful not to cut into or through the spine.

How to Install L-Bead

L-bead caps the ends of drywall panels that abut finished surfaces such as paneling or wood trim, providing a finished edge. The drywall is installed ⅛" from the finished surface, then the L-bead is positioned tight against the panel, so its finished edge covers the edge of the adjacent surface.

Fasten L-bead to the drywall with ½" staples or drywall screws every 6", then finish with a minimum of three coats of compound (see pages 121 to 127). After final sanding, peel back the protective strip to expose the finished edge of the L-bead.

INSTALLING VINYL BULLNOSE CORNER BEAD

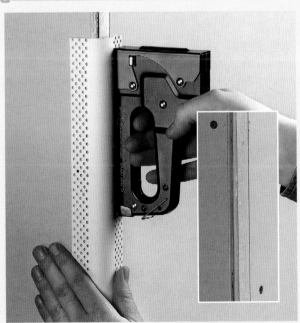

Vinyl bullnose corner bead is installed with vinyl adhesive and ½" staples, just like standard vinyl bead (see page 117). However, bullnose beads that have shallow curves may require that the ends of drywall panels be cut back (inset).

Drywall manufacturers offer a variety of corner caps to ease the process of finishing soffits and other openings trimmed out with bullnose corner bead.

Taping Drywall Seams

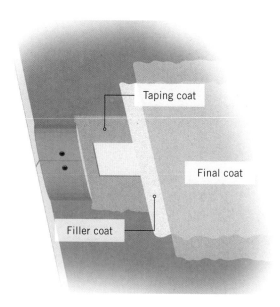

Taping coat

Final coat

Filler coat

Finishing newly installed drywall is satisfying work that requires patience and some basic skill, but it's easier than most people think. Beginners make their biggest, and most lasting, mistakes by rushing the job and applying too much compound in an attempt to eliminate coats. But even for professionals, drywall finishing involves three steps, and sometimes more, plus the final sanding.

The first step is the taping coat, when you tape the seams between the drywall panels. The taping is critical to the success of the entire job, so take your time here, and make sure the tape is smooth and fully adhered before it's allowed to dry. If you're using standard metal corner bead on the outside corners, install it before starting the taping coat; paper-faced beads go on after the tape. The screw heads get covered with compound at the beginning of each coat.

After the taping comes the second, or filler, coat. This is when you leave the most compound on the wall, filling in the majority of each depression. With the filler coat, the walls start to look good, but they don't have to be perfect; the third coat will take care of minor imperfections. Lightly scrape the second coat with a taping knife, then apply the final coat. If you still see imperfections, add more compound before sanding.

For best results, especially with fiberglass tape, use a setting-type compound for the taping coat. It creates a strong bond and shrinks very little. Because setting-type compound hardens by chemical reaction, once it begins to set up the process cannot be slowed or stopped, rendering excess compound unusable. Make sure to prepare only as much as you can use in the amount of work time specified by the manufacturer. Use lightweight setting-type compound because it is easier to sand.

For the other two coats, use an all-purpose compound. These drying-type compounds are available premixed and can be thinned with water if setup begins prematurely. Add small amounts of water to avoid over-thinning and mix using a hand masher. If compound is too thin, add thicker compound from another container. Remix periodically if the liquid begins to separate and rise to the top. If pre-mixed compound is moldy or foul-smelling, it is unusable and must be discarded.

Allow each coat of compound to set up and dry thoroughly before applying the next coat. Setting time is dependent on a number of factors, such as size of project and type of compound used, but for most finishing projects, count on one day per coat—a total of three days. Refer to the manufacturer's instructions for product specifications. To speed up the process, compound accelerants are available, or use a fan.

As you work, keep your compound smooth and workable by mixing it in the mud pan frequently, folding it over with the drywall knife. Try to remove dried chunks, and throw away any mud that gets dirty or has been added to and scraped off the wall too many times. Always let your compound dry completely between coats. If you have a large ceiling area to finish, it may be practical to rent a pair of drywall stilts.

TOOLS & MATERIALS

Work gloves	Inside corner taping knife
Eye protection	Mud pan
Screwdriver	Setting-type joint compound (for tape coat)
Utility knife	
5-gal. bucket	All-purpose compound (for filler and finish coat)
½" electric drill with mixing paddle	Cool potable water
Hand masher	Paper joint tape
4, 6, 10, and 12" taping knives	Self-adhesive fiberglass mesh tape

Preparing Joint Compound

Mix powdered setting-type compound with cool, potable water in a clean 5-gal. bucket, following the manufacturer's directions. All tools and materials must be clean; dirty water, old compound, and other contaminants will affect compound set time and quality.

Use a heavy-duty drill with a mixing paddle to thoroughly mix compound to a stiff, yet workable consistency (see below). Use a low speed to avoid whipping air into the compound. Do not overwork setting-type compound, as it will begin setup. For powdered drying-type compound, remix after 15 minutes. Clean tools thoroughly immediately after use.

Joint compound should appear smooth in consistency and stiff enough so as not to slide off a trowel or taping knife.

Use a hand masher to loosen premixed compound. If the compound has been around awhile and is stiff, add a little water and mix to an even consistency.

How to Apply the Taping Coat

Inspect the entire drywall installation and fill any gaps wider than ¼" with setting-type compound. Smooth off excess so it's flush with the panel face. Also remove any loose paper and fill in with compound.

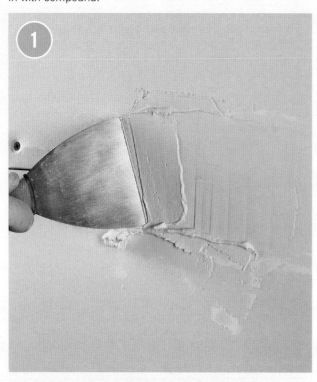

On tapered seams, apply an even bed layer of setting-type compound over the seam, about ⅛" thick and 6" wide using a 6" taping knife.

NOTE: With paper tape, you can use premixed taping or all-purpose compound instead.

Center the tape over the seam and lightly embed it in the compound, making sure the tape is smooth and straight. At the end of the seam, tear off the tape so it extends all the way into inside corners and up to the corner bead at outside corners.

Using a 4 or 6" taping knife, smear compound over each screw head, forcing it into the depression. Firmly drag the knife in the opposite direction, removing excess compound from the panel surface.

VARIATION: Cover an entire row of screw heads in the field of a panel with one steady, even pass of compound. Use a 6" taping knife and apply a thin coat.

(5)

Smooth the tape with the taping knife, working out from the center. Apply enough pressure to force compound from underneath the tape, so the tape is flat and has a thin layer beneath it.

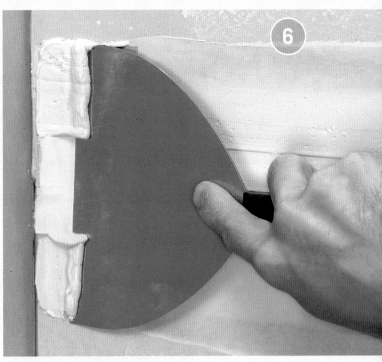

(6)

At inside corners, smooth the final bit of tape by reversing the knife and carefully pushing it toward the corner. Carefully remove excess compound along the edges of the bed layer with the taping knife.

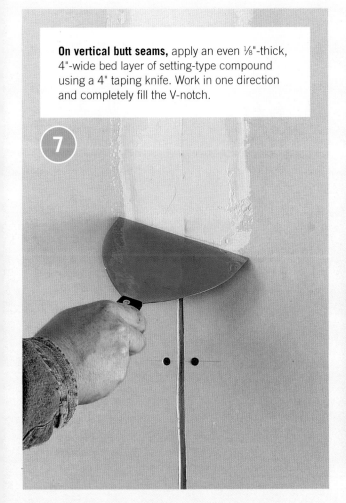

On vertical butt seams, apply an even ⅛"-thick, 4"-wide bed layer of setting-type compound using a 4" taping knife. Work in one direction and completely fill the V-notch.

(7)

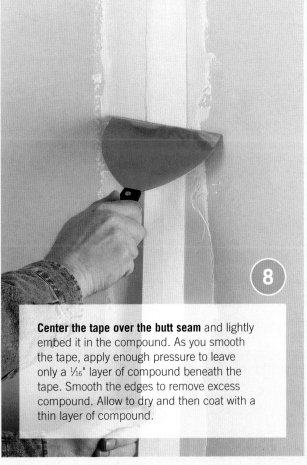

(8)

Center the tape over the butt seam and lightly embed it in the compound. As you smooth the tape, apply enough pressure to leave only a ¹⁄₁₆" layer of compound beneath the tape. Smooth the edges to remove excess compound. Allow to dry and then coat with a thin layer of compound.

(continued)

Tape inside corners by folding precreased paper tape in half to create a 90° angle.

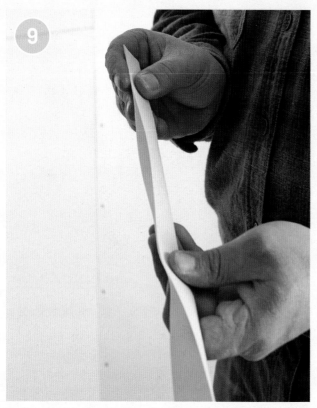

9

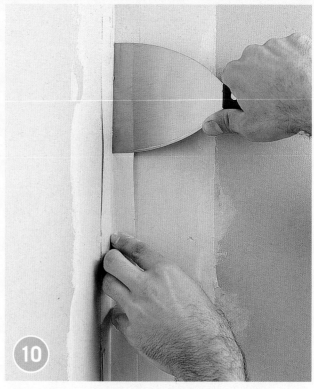

10

Apply an even layer of compound, about ⅛" thick and 3" wide, to both sides of the corner using a 4" taping knife. Embed the tape into the compound using a taping knife.

Carefully smooth and flatten both sides of the tape, removing excess compound to leave only a thin layer beneath. Make sure the center of the tape is aligned straight with the corner.

11

TOOL TIP

An inside corner knife can embed both sides of the tape in one pass; draw the knife along the tape, applying enough pressure to leave a thin layer of compound beneath. Feather each side using a straight 6" taping knife, if necessary.

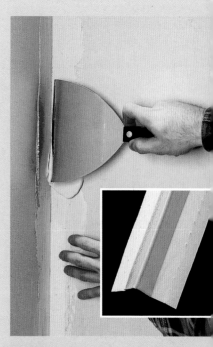

VARIATION: Paper-faced metal inside corner bead produces straight, durable corners with little fuss. To install the bead, embed it into a thin layer of compound, then smooth the paper, as with a paper-tape inside corner.

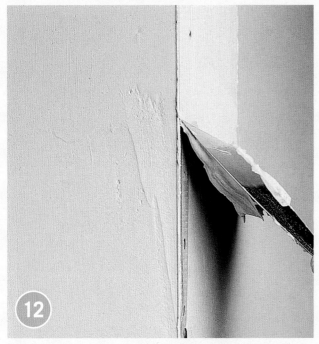

 Finish outside corner bead with a 6" knife. Apply the compound while dragging the knife along the raised spine of the bead. Make a second pass to feather the outside edge of the compound, then a third dragging along the bead again. Smooth any areas where the corner bead meets taped corners or seams.

VARIATION: To install paper-faced outside corner bead, spread an even layer of compound on each side of the corner using a 6" taping knife. Press the bead into the compound and smooth the paper flanges with the knife.

How to Apply Mesh Tape

To use self-adhesive mesh tape on seams, apply the tape over the seam center so it's straight and flat. Run mesh tape to corners, then cut using a sharp utility knife.

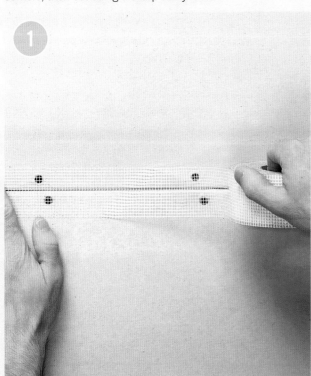

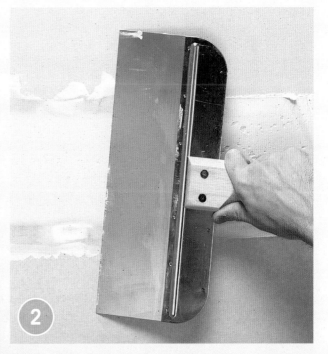

Coat the mesh with an even layer of compound, about ⅛" thick using a 6" taping knife. Smooth the joint with a 10" or 12" knife, removing excess compound.

NOTE: Use setting-type compound for the first coat.

How to Apply the Filler Coat

After the taping coat has dried completely, scrape off any ridges and chunks. Begin second-coating at the screw heads using a 6" taping knife and all-purpose compound (see page 122).

NOTE: Setting-type compound and drying-type topping compound are also acceptable.

Apply an even layer of compound to both sides of each inside corner using a 6" taping knife. Smooth one side at a time, holding the blade about 15° from horizontal and lightly dragging the point along the corner. Make a second pass to remove excess compound along the outer edges. Repeat, if necessary.

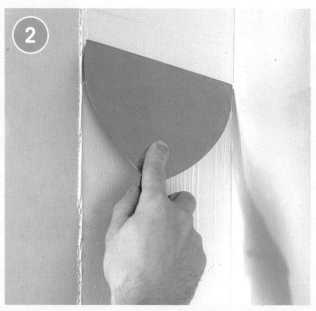

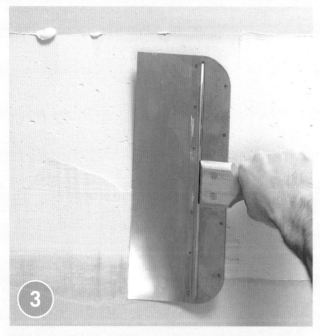

Coat tapered seams with an even layer of compound using a 12" taping knife. Whenever possible, apply the coat in one direction and smooth it in the opposite. Feather the sides of the compound first, holding the blade almost flat and applying pressure to the outside of the blade, so the blade just skims over the center of the seam.

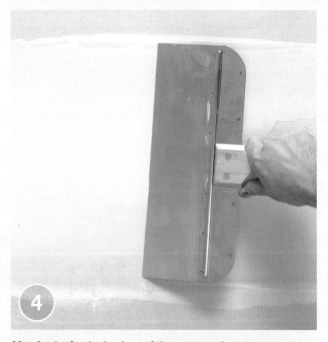

After feathering both edges of the compound, make a pass down the center of the seam, applying even pressure to the blade. This pass should leave the seam smooth and even, with the edges feathered out to nothing. The joint tape should be completely covered.

For butt seams, use the same technique as for tapered seams, however, feather the edges out 8 to 10" on each side to help mask the seam. Apply compound in thin layers and smooth out as needed.

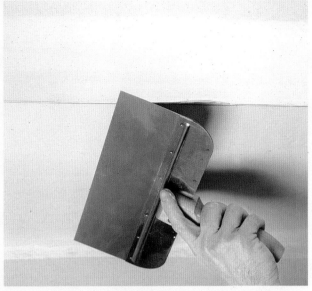

Second-coat the outside corners, one side at a time using a 12" knife. Apply an even layer of compound, then feather the outside edge by applying pressure to the outside of the knife—enough so that the blade flexes and removes most of the compound along the edge but leaves the corner intact. Make a second pass with the blade riding along the raised spine, applying even pressure.

 # How to Apply the Final Coat

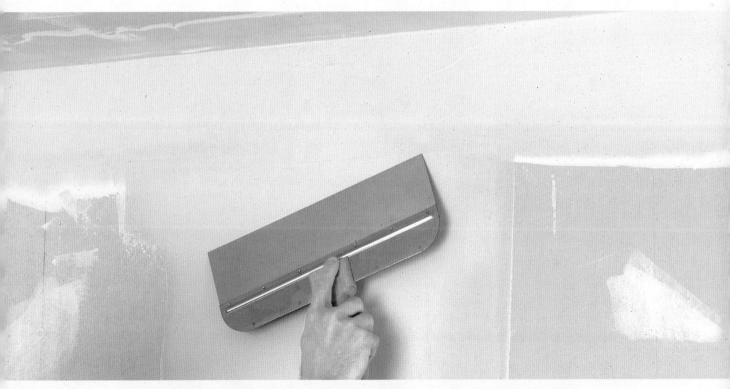

After the filler coat has dried, lightly scrape all of the joints, then third-coat the screws. Apply the final coat, following the same steps used for the filler coat—but do the seams first, then the outside corners, followed by the inside corners. Use a 12" knife and spread the compound a few inches wider than the joints in the filler coat. Remove most of the wet compound, filling scratches and low spots but leaving only traces elsewhere. Make several passes, if necessary, until the surface is smooth and there are no knife tracks or other imperfections. Carefully blend intersecting joints so there's no visible transition.

How to Flat-tape

Trim any loose paper along the drywall edge with a utility knife. If the gap between the drywall and the object is wider than ¼", fill it with joint compound and let it dry. Cover the joint with self-adhesive mesh joint tape, butting the tape's edge against the object without overlapping the object.

Cover the tape with a 4"-wide layer of setting-type taping compound. Smooth the joint, leaving just enough compound to conceal the tape. Let the first coat dry completely, then add two more thin coats using a 6" taping knife. Feather the outside edge of the joint to nothing.

 # How to Round Inside Corners

Lightly drag the knife across the seam, perpendicular to the corner, to sculpt a rounded base for the filler coat. Work in the same direction along the entire length of the seam, then make a second pass, pulling the knife across in the opposite direction.

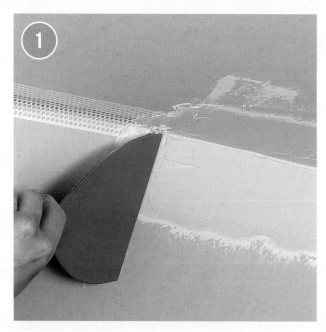

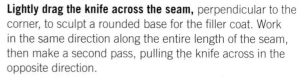

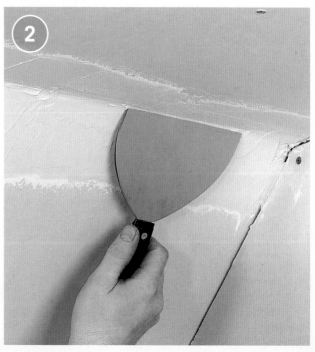

To soften off-angle inside corners, round them off. Center self-adhesive fiberglass mesh tape over the seam, and smooth it flat. Apply a ⅛"-thick layer of compound 4" wide along each side of the mesh using a 6" taping knife.

NOTE: Use setting-type compound to prevent significant shrinkage.

Once the tape is completely covered, smooth out any ridges and feather the edges of the compound along the length of the seam.

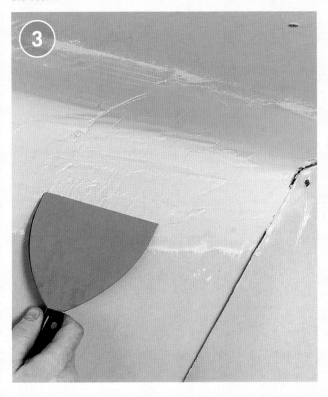

After the tape coat is dry, apply another ⅛" layer of setting-type compound along the seam, then use a 12" taping knife to create the rounded corner, following the same technique as in step 2.

After the fill coat has dried, lightly scrape ridges and high spots, then apply a thin layer of all-purpose or topping compound for the final coat, following the same technique as for the previous two coats.

VARIATION: Flexible corner beads are available for off-angle joints that are prone to cracking, such as those between pitched ceilings and flat kneewalls. The vinyl center crease flexes along with normal structural shifts. Install flexible bead with adhesive or embed it in compound; keep the center crease free of compound.

Fixing Problems & Final Inspection

After the final coat of joint compound has dried but before you begin sanding, inspect the entire finish job for flaws. If you discover scrapes, pitting, or other imperfections, add another coat of joint compound. Repair any damaged or overlooked areas such as cracked seams and over-cut holes for electrical boxes prior to sanding.

During your inspection, make sure to check that all seams are acceptably feathered out. To check seams, hold a level or 12-inch taping knife perpendicularly across the seam; fill concave areas with extra layers of compound and correct any convex seams that crown more than ¹⁄₁₆ inch.

Scratches, dents, and other minor imperfections can be smoothed over with a thin coat of all-purpose compound.

TOOLS & MATERIALS

Work gloves	Sanding block or pole sander	Utility knife	220-grit sanding screen or 150-grit sandpaper
Eye protection		Self-adhesive fiberglass mesh tape	
6 and 12" taping knives	All-purpose joint compound		

Common Taping Problems

Pitting occurs when compound is overmixed or applied with too little pressure to force out trapped air bubbles. Pitting can be fixed with a thin coat of compound. If trapped air bubbles are present, scrape lightly before covering with compound.

Mis-cut holes for electrical boxes can be flat taped. Cover the gap with self-adhesive mesh tape, and cover with three coats of all-purpose compound. Precut repair patches are also available (shown).

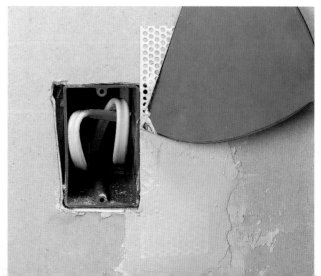

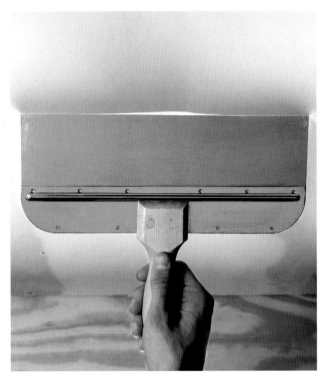

Concave seams can be filled with an extra layer or two of all-purpose compound, repeating the filler and final coats (see pages 126 to 127).

For seams crowned more than 1/16", carefully sand along the center (see pages 133 to 135), but do not expose the tape. Check the seam with a level. If it's still crowned, add a layer of compound with a 12" knife, removing all of it along the seam's center and feathering it out toward the outside edges. After it dries, apply a final coat, if necessary.

Bubbled or loose tape occurs when the bed layer is too thin, which causes a faulty bond between the tape and compound. Cut out small, soft areas with a utility knife and retape. Large runs of loose tape will have to be fully removed before retaping.

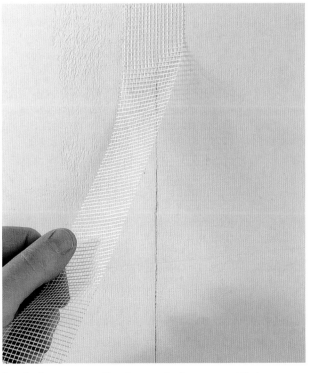

Cracked seams are often the result of compound that has dried too quickly or shrunk. Re-tape the seam if the existing tape and compound is intact; otherwise, cut out any loose material. In either case, make sure to fill the crack with compound.

Sanding Drywall

Sanding is the final step in finishing drywall. The goal is to remove excess joint compound and crowned seams, smooth out tool and lap marks, and feather the edges so they blend into the panel surface. How much sanding is required depends on the quality of the taping job and the level of finish you need for the final decoration (see pages 114 to 115).

Sanding drywall is a two-step process: pole sanding to remove excess compound and feather edges, and hand sanding to take care of the final smoothing work.

Pole sanders have a flat head on a swivel that holds sandpaper or sanding screen. The length of the pole keeps you distanced from dust and brings ceiling seams within reach. You don't have to apply much pressure to get results; simply push the head along the seam and let the weight of the tool do the work. You can use a 120-grit sanding screen or sandpaper for joints finished with all-purpose compound, or you can use 150-grit on lightweight or topping compounds, which are softer.

Hand sanding can be done with a block sander or dry sanding sponge. The object of this step is to smooth all the joints and create a uniform surface, so again you need not apply much pressure to get the job done. Use 150- to 220-grit sanding screen or sandpaper for final sanding.

As you work, make sure to sand only the compound rather than the panels. Face paper can scuff easily, necessitating a thin coat of compound to repair. Do not use power sanders on drywall; they are too difficult to control. Even brief lingering can remove too much compound or mar panels.

Sanding drywall is a messy job. The fine dust generated will easily find its way into all areas of the home if the work area is not contained. Sealing all doorways and cracks with sheet plastic and masking tape will help prevent dust from leaving the work zone. However, wet sanding may be more practical in some instances. With wet sanding, or sponging, the abrasive papers and screens are replaced by a damp sponge that is used to smooth the water-soluble compound and blend it with the surface. Very little dust becomes airborne.

But if your goal is to eradicate dust, your best bet is to use a dust-free sanding system. Available at most rental centers, dust-free systems contain hoses with sanding attachments that connect to a wet/dry vacuum to cut dust by nearly 95 percent. A water filter can be added to the system to capture most of the dust and spare your vacuum's filter.

TOOLS & MATERIALS

Work gloves	Broom or towel
Eye protection	N95-rated dust mask
Swivel-joint pole sander	Eye goggles
Hand-sander block	Sheet plastic
Work light	2" painter's tape
Dry sanding sponge	120-, 150-, and 220-grit sandpaper or sanding screens
Wet sanding sponge	
Wet/dry shop vacuum	6" taping knife

MARK LOW SPOTS

As you work, if you oversand or discover low spots that require another coat of compound, mark the area with a piece of painter's tape for repair after you finish sanding. Make sure to wipe away dust so the tape sticks to the surface.

Minimizing Dust

Use sheet plastic and 2" masking tape to help confine dust to the work area. Cover all doorways, cabinets, built-ins, and any gaps or other openings with plastic, sealing all four edges with tape. The fine dust produced by sanding can find its way through the smallest cracks.

Prop a fan in an open window so it blows outside to help pull dust out of the work area during sanding. Open only one window in the space to prevent a cross-breeze.

How to Sand Drywall

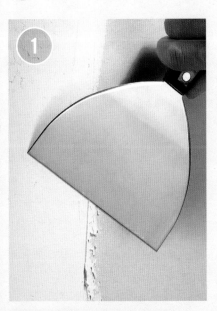

Prior to sanding, knock down any ridges, chunks, or tool marks using a 6" taping knife. Do not apply too much pressure; you don't want to dig into the compound, only remove the excess.

Lightly sand all seams and outside corners using a pole sander with 220-grit sanding screen or 150-grit sandpaper. Work in the direction of the joints, applying even pressure to smooth transitions and high areas. Don't sand out depressions; fill them with compound and resand. Be careful not to over-sand or expose joint tape.

(continued)

Inside corners often are finished with only one or two thin coats of compound over the tape. Sand the inside edge of joints only lightly and smooth the outside edge carefully; inside corners will be sanded by hand later.

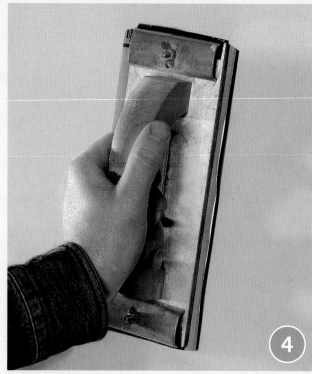

Fine-sand the seams, outside corners, and fastener heads using a sanding block with 150- to 220-grit sanding screen or sandpaper. As you work, use your hand to feel for defects along the compound. A bright work light angled to highlight seams can help reveal problem areas.

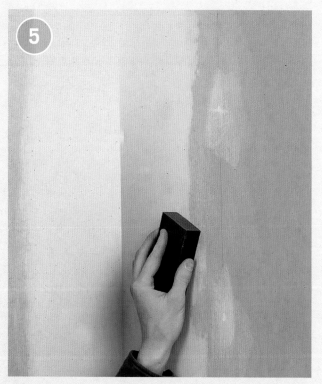

To avoid damage from over-sanding, use a 150-grit dry sanding sponge to sand inside corners. The sides of sanding sponges also contain grit, allowing you to sand both sides of a corner at once to help prevent over-sanding.

For tight or hard-to-reach corners, fold a piece of sanding screen or sandpaper in thirds and sand the area carefully. Rather than using just your fingertips, try to flatten your hand as much as possible to spread out the pressure to avoid sanding too deep.

Repair depressions, scratches, or exposed tape due to over-sanding after final sanding is complete. Wipe the area with a dry cloth to remove dust, then apply a thin coat of all-purpose compound. Allow to dry thoroughly, then resand.

7

8

With sanding complete, remove dust from the panels with a dry towel or soft broom. Use a wet-dry vacuum to clean out all electrical boxes and around floors, windows, and doors, then carefully roll up sheet plastic and discard. Finally, damp mop the floor to remove any remaining dust.

Dust-free Drywall Sanding

Dust-free sanding systems come with both pole and hand-sanding attachments that connect directly to your wet/dry vacuum or to a water filter that captures the bulk of the dust, keeping your vacuum filter clean.

Wet sanding is a dust-free alternative to dry sanding. Use a high-density sponge made for wet sanding. Saturate it with cool, clean water and wring it out just enough so it doesn't drip. Wipe joints and corners in the direction they run, and rinse the sponge frequently. Sponge sparingly, to avoid streaking.

Textures & Skim Coats

The most common texture on walls and ceilings is no texture at all. Smooth surfaces are easy to clean, are non-abrasive and are less likely to accumulate moisture, dirt, and mold. And when the time comes, smooth surfaces are easy to repair and repaint. A coat of high-quality drywall primer, tinted to the color of the topcoat and sanded lightly with fine sandpaper, makes an adequate base for flat wall paint.

For a custom appearance, you can apply a skim coat of joint compound, which will make your wall resemble traditional plaster. Or, you can apply one of many textured finishes. For a basic skim coat, roll or spray a thinned drywall topping compound onto a properly taped and filled drywall surface, and then scrape the surface smooth with a 12" trowel. A skim-coated surface is consistently smooth, and differences between the drywall paper and the dried joint compound are eliminated. This prevents taped joints and fastener patches from showing through paint. Skim coating is especially important under gloss paints and on surfaces that will be harshly lit.

Textured coatings have the advantage of being more forgiving of surface imperfections than paint alone. Most textures start with joint compound or, better, a joint-compound-like substance specially formulated for texturing. This "mud" may be thinned with water to a pancake-batter consistency for sprayer or roller application. Aggregates like sand or perlite may be included in the compound to create a gravelly texture. Applied mud may be left to dry or tooled to achieve a particular look.

Ceilings sprayed with popcorn texture contain vermiculite or polystyrene aggregates. Popcorn textures should not be used in contact areas, where aggregates may be scraped off. Aggregated textures may be left unpainted or spray-painted if desired (rollers tend to lift off the aggregate). If a somewhat washable aggregate surface is desired from the start, paints mixed with aggregates are available. Acoustical-rated ceiling textures have the best sound-deadening qualities.

Interesting textures involving swirls, patterns, or ridges add yet increased visual dimension to the surface of walls and ceilings. Thick and sharp textures should not be used where people may scrape against them, since peaks of plaster and sharp aggregates can cut through skin and catch clothing. Deep textures are also difficult to clean. Smooth, low textures such as orange-peel and knock-down are most appropriate for walls, since they are non-abrasive and are easy to paint and clean.

Ceiling and wall textures may be added to paint and rolled on or applied with a sprayer as a base coat for paint.

Applying a Skim Coat

Joint compound and drywall face paper have different porosities, which cause each to absorb paint and other decorative finishes differently. If taped walls and ceilings are not properly primed, seams and fastener heads can show through the finished paint job. This is called photographing and is readily apparent on surfaces that are under bright light or that are covered with high-gloss paint.

To combat photographing, apply a skim coat of thinned-down joint compound. A skim coat evens out surface textures to create a smooth, perfectly primed surface. Use all-purpose compound or drying-type topping compound for skim coating. Avoid setting-type compounds; if they dry too quickly, they may not properly bond with the surface.

TOOLS & MATERIALS

Work gloves	Paint roller
Eye protection	Paint screen or roller pan
Particle mask	12 to 14" taping knife
Heavy-duty drill with paddle mixer	Premixed all-purpose or drying-type topping compound
5-gal. bucket	Clean potable water

Thin compound with cool water to a paint-like consistency, using a drill and mixing paddle. Pour compound into a roller tray. Note: Use all-purpose compound or drying-type topping compound.

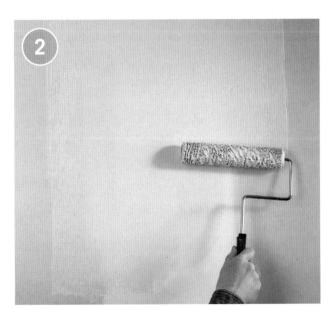

Apply a thin coat of compound to the taped surface using a paint roller with a thin nap. Work in small sections so compound doesn't dry before you can smooth it.

Once a section is covered with compound, smooth the surface using a 12 to 14" taping knife. Work from the top down, applying enough pressure to leave a thin film of compound over the surface and remove ridges.

Priming & Painting Drywall

Paints are either latex (water-based) or alkyd (oil-based). Latex paint is easy to apply and clean up, and the improved chemistry of today's latexes makes them suitable for nearly every application. Some painters feel that alkyd paint provides a smoother finish, but local regulations may restrict the use of alkyd products.

Paints come in various sheens, from high-gloss to flat. Gloss enamels dry to a shiny finish and are used for surfaces that need to be washed often, such as walls in bathrooms and kitchens and woodwork. Flat paints are used for most wall and ceiling applications.

Paint prices are typically an accurate reflection of quality. As a general rule, buy the best paint your budget can afford. High-quality paints are easier to use, look better, last longer, cover better, and because they often require fewer coats they are usually less expensive in the long run.

Before applying the finish paint, prime all of the surfaces with a good-quality primer. Primer bonds well to all surfaces and provides a durable base that keeps the paint from cracking and peeling. Priming is particularly important when using a high-gloss paint on walls and ceilings, because the paint alone might not completely hide finished drywall joints and other variations in the surface. To avoid the need for additional coats of expensive finish paint, tint the primer to match the new color.

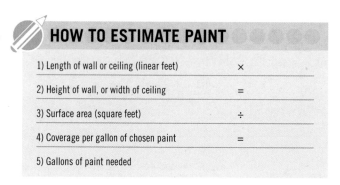

HOW TO ESTIMATE PAINT

1) Length of wall or ceiling (linear feet)	×
2) Height of wall, or width of ceiling	=
3) Surface area (square feet)	÷
4) Coverage per gallon of chosen paint	=
5) Gallons of paint needed	

For large jobs, mix paint together (called "boxing") in a large pail to eliminate slight color variations between cans. Stir the paint thoroughly with a wooden stick or power drill attachment.

Latex-based drywall primer and sealer equalizes the absorption rates between the dried joint compound and the drywall paper facing, allowing the paint to go on evenly with no blotching.

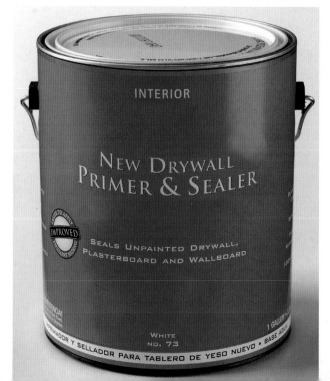

Selecting a Quality Paint

Paint coverage (listed on can labels) of quality paint should be about 400 sq. ft. per gallon. Bargain paints (left) may require two or even three coats to cover the same area as quality paints (right).

High washability is a feature of quality paint. The pigments in bargain paints (right) may "chalk" and wash away with mild scrubbing.

Paint Sheens

Paint comes in a variety of surface finishes, or sheens. Gloss enamel (A) provides a highly reflective finish for areas where high washability is important. All gloss paints tend to show surface flaws. Alkyd-base enamels have the highest gloss. Medium-gloss (or "satin") latex enamel (B) creates a highly washable surface with a slightly less reflective finish. Like gloss enamels, medium-gloss paints tend to show surface flaws. Eggshell enamel (C) combines a soft finish with the washability of enamel. Flat latex (D) is an all-purpose paint with a matte finish that hides surface irregularities.

Painting Tools

Most painting jobs can be completed with a few quality tools. Purchase two or three premium brushes, a sturdy paint pan that can be attached to a stepladder, and one or two good rollers. With proper cleanup, these tools will last for years. See pages 142 to 143 for tips on how to use paintbrushes and rollers.

Choosing a Paintbrush

A quality brush (left), has a shaped hardwood handle and a sturdy, reinforced ferrule made of noncorrosive metal. Multiple spacer plugs separate the bristles. A quality brush has flagged (split) bristles and a chiseled end for precise edging. A cheaper brush (right) will have a blunt end, unflagged bristles, and a cardboard spacer plug that may soften when wet.

There's a proper brush for every job. A 4" straight-edged brush (bottom) is good for cutting in along ceilings and corners. For woodwork, a 2" trim brush (middle) works well. A tapered sash brush (top) helps with corners. Use brushes made of natural bristles only with alkyd paints. All-purpose brushes, suitable for all paints, are made with a blend of polyester, nylon, and sometimes natural bristles.

Choosing Paint Rollers

Choose a sturdy roller with a wire cage construction. Nylon bearings should roll smoothly and easily when you spin the cage. The handle end should be threaded for attaching an extension handle.

Select the proper roller cover for the surface you intend to paint. A ¼"-nap cover is used for enamel paints and very flat surfaces. A ⅜"-nap cover will hide the small flaws found in most flat walls and ceilings. A 1"-nap cover is for rough surfaces like concrete blocks or stucco. Foam rollers fit into small spaces and work well when painting furniture or doing touch-ups. Corner rollers have nap on the ends and make it easy to paint corners without cutting in the edges. Synthetic covers are good with most paints, especially latexes. Wool or mohair roller covers give an even finish with alkyd products. Always choose good-quality roller covers, which will be less likely to shed lint.

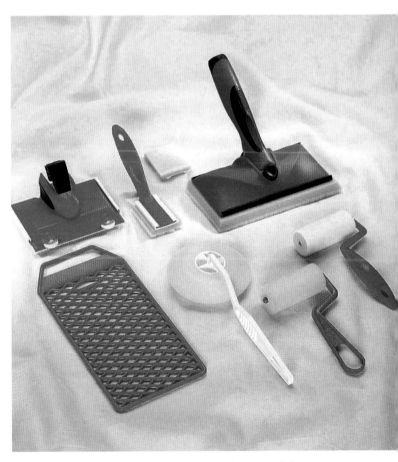

Paint pads and specialty rollers come in a wide range of sizes and shapes to fit different painting needs.

How to Use a Paint Roller

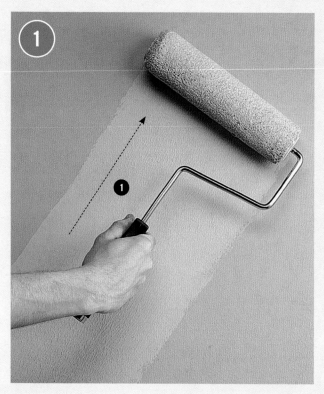

Draw the roller straight down (2) from the top of the diagonal sweep made in step 1. Lift and move the roller to the beginning of the diagonal sweep and roll up (3) to complete the unloading of the roller.

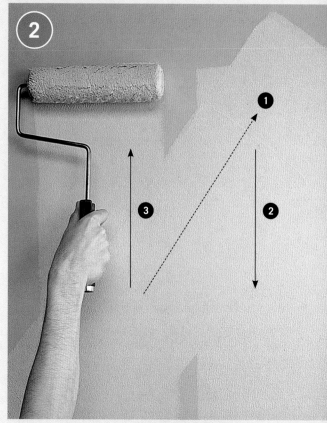

Wet the roller cover with water (for latex paint) or mineral spirits (for alkyd enamel), to remove lint and prime the cover. Squeeze out excess liquid. Dip the roller fully into the paint pan reservoir and roll it over the textured ramp to distribute the paint evenly. The roller should be full, but not dripping. Make an upward diagonal sweep about 4 ft. long on the surface, using a slow stroke to avoid splattering.

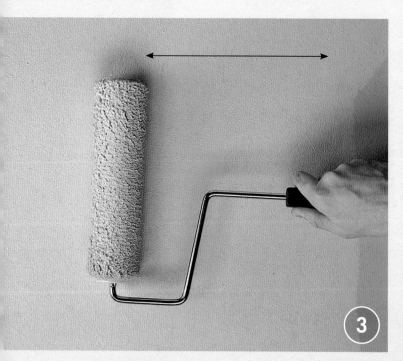

Distribute the paint over the rest of the section with horizontal and diagonal back-and-forth strokes.

Smooth the area by lightly drawing the roller vertically from the top to the bottom of the painted area. Lift the roller and return it to the top of the area after each stroke.

How to Use a Paintbrush

1

Dip the brush into the paint, loading one-third of its bristle length. Tap the bristles against the side of the can to remove excess paint, but do not drag the bristles against the lip of the can.

Paint along the edges (called "cutting in") using the narrow edge of the brush, pressing just enough to flex the bristles. Keep an eye on the paint edge, and paint with long, slow strokes. Always paint from a dry area back into wet paint to avoid lap marks.

2

3

Brush wall corners using the wide edge of the brush. Paint open areas with a brush or roller before the brushed paint dries.

To paint large areas with a brush, apply the paint with 2 or 3 diagonal strokes. Hold the brush at a 45° angle to the work surface, pressing just enough to flex the bristles. Distribute the paint evenly with horizontal strokes.

4

Smooth the surface by drawing the brush vertically from the top to the bottom of the painted area. Use light strokes and lift the brush from the surface at the end of each stroke. This method is best for slow-drying alkyd enamels.

5

Painting Walls & Ceilings

For a smooth finish on large wall and ceiling areas, paint in small sections. First use a paintbrush to cut in the edges, then immediately roll the section before moving on. If brushed edges are left to dry before the large surfaces are rolled, visible lap marks will be left on the finished wall. Working in natural light makes it easier to see missed areas.

Spread the paint evenly onto the work surface without letting it run, drip, or lap onto other areas. Excess paint will run on the surface and can drip onto woodwork and floors. Conversely, stretching paint too far leaves lap marks and results in patchy coverage.

For fast, mess-free painting, shield any surfaces that could get splattered. If you are painting only the ceiling, drape the walls and woodwork to prevent splatters. When painting walls, mask the baseboards and the window and door casings. (See top of opposite page.)

While the tried-and-true method of aligning painter's tape with the edge of moldings and casings is perfectly adequate, the job goes much faster and smoother with a tape applicator. Similarly, painter's tape can be used to cover door hinges and window glass, but hinge masks and corner masks simplify the job enormously. Evaluate the available choices and the project at hand: there are many new, easy-to-use options available.

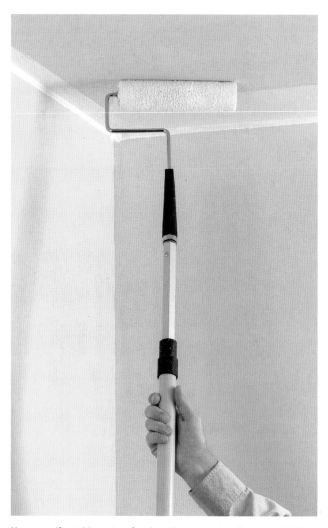

Use an adjustable extension handle to paint ceilings and tall walls easily without a ladder.

Cut in around doors and window casing with a paintbrush and then finish painting the wall with a roller.

How to Tape and Drape for Walls and Ceilings

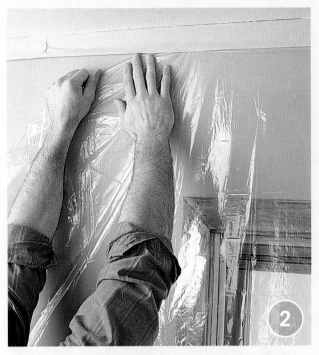

Align wide masking tape with the inside edge of the molding; press in place. Run the tip of a putty knife along the inside edge of the tape to seal it against seeping paint. After painting, remove the tape as soon as the paint is too dry to run.

Press the top half of 2" masking tape along the joint between the ceiling and the wall, leaving the bottom half of the tape loose. Hang sheet plastic under the tape, draping the walls and baseboards. After painting, remove the tape as soon as the paint is too dry to run.

SPECIALIZED ROLLER TECHNIQUES

Using a corner roller makes it unnecessary to cut in inside corners. It also matches the rolled texture of the rest of the wall better than most paint brushes.

Minimize brush marks. Slide the roller cover slightly off of the roller cage when rolling near wall corners or a ceiling line. Brushed areas dry to a different finish than rolled paint.

How to Paint Ceilings

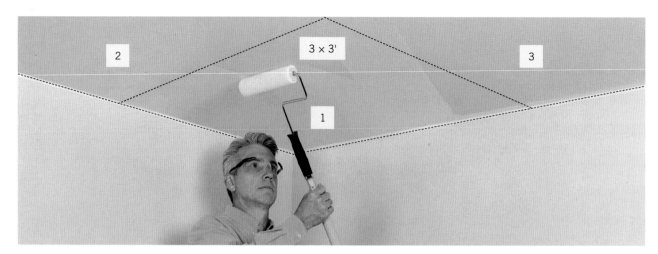

Paint ceilings with a roller handle extension. Use eye protection while painting overhead. Start at the corner farthest from the entry door. Paint the ceiling along the narrow end in 3 × 3-ft. sections, cutting in the edges with a brush before rolling. Apply the paint with a diagonal stroke. Distribute the paint evenly with back-and-forth strokes. For the final smoothing strokes, roll each section toward the wall containing the entry door, lifting the roller at the end of each sweep.

 # How to Paint Walls

Paint walls in 2 × 4-ft. sections. Start in an upper corner, cutting in the ceiling and wall corners with a brush, then rolling the section. Make the initial diagonal roller stroke from the bottom of the section upward, to avoid dripping paint. Distribute the paint evenly with horizontal strokes, then finish with downward sweeps of the roller. Next, cut in and roll the section directly underneath. Continue with adjacent areas, cutting in and rolling the top sections before the bottom sections. Roll all finish strokes toward the floor.

Cleaning Up

At the end of a paint job you may choose to throw away the roller covers (especially if you used oil), but the paint pans, roller handles, and brushes can be cleaned for future use. Always follow the manufacturer's guidelines for disposing of paint waste.

The easiest way to clean brushes and roller covers you'd like to use again is to use a spinner tool. Wash the roller cover or brush with water (or solvent), then attach it to the spinner. Pumping the handle throws liquids out of the roller cover or brush. Hold the spinner inside a cardboard box or 5-gallon bucket to catch paint and avoid splatters. Once clean, store brushes in their original wrappers, or fold the bristles inside brown wrapping paper. Store washed roller covers on end to avoid flattening the nap.

Stray paint drips can be wiped away if they are still wet. A putty knife or razor will remove many dried paint spots on hardwood or glass. You can use a chemical cleaner to remove stubborn paint from most surfaces, though make sure to test the product on an inconspicuous area to make sure the surface is colorfast.

Cleaning products include (from left): chemical cleaner for dried paint drips, spinner tool, cleaner tool for brushes and roller covers.

Using a Cleaner Tool

Comb brush bristles with the spiked side of a cleaner tool. This aligns the bristles so they dry properly.

Scrape paint from a roller cover with the curved side of cleaner tool. Remove as much paint as possible before washing.

Installing Trim on Walls & Ceilings

Trim moldings are installed primarily to decorate our houses by adding rich wood tones and creating ornamental effects that often feature light and shadow. Moldings do perform minor structural jobs, too, mainly to conceal gaps between walls, floor, and ceilings, and around doors and windows.

Before beginning your trim project, do plenty of planning and get to know your tools. Safety is paramount when working with any power tools. Make sure you use the correct tools for the project and that the tools are well maintained. Always use proper techniques and safety practices.

In this chapter:
- Victorian Trim Style
- Arts & Crafts Trim Style
- Neoclassical Trim Style
- Modern Trim Style

Victorian Trim Style

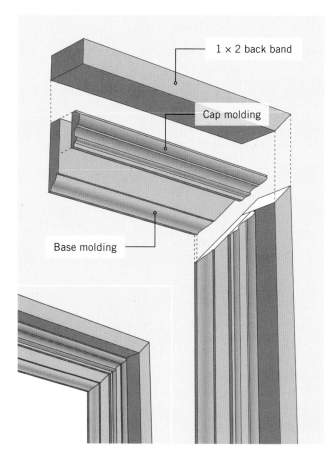

1 × 2 back band

Cap molding

Base molding

Victorian style began in the mid-nineteenth century and lasted approximately 60 years. Trimwork of this style is generally very ornate with large elaborate casings that emphasize curves and decoration rather than material. Moldings were built by stacking layers multiple times, rather than using a single piece.

Victorian style is generally seen in houses with higher ceilings. Due to the sheer size and nature of these moldings, they may tend to crowd a standard 8-foot-tall room, especially if all types of trim elements are included from the floor up. However, the term "Victorian" encompasses many different variations and can be successfully installed in smaller homes by sizing down the scale of the trimwork.

This Victorian door casing is not made up of casing at all but actually a combination of baseboard and cap molding with 1 × 2 as a back band. The overall width of the casing is 4", creating a strong statement when compared to a single-piece stock molding.

Victorian frame-and-panel walls were often so elaborate that they were constructed outside the home and brought in to be installed.

Baseboards were commonly 7" tall or greater, with plinth blocks at door openings rather than a straight casing to the floor.

Victorian style cornice moldings were often very large and elaborate. Made up of multiple pieces of material, the decoration can sometimes be seen as out of proportion with current construction standards.

Arts & Crafts Trim Style

Arts & Crafts style originated near the turn of the twentieth century. Trim components of this style generally emphasize wood grain, function, and simplicity in design. Typical Arts & Crafts furnishings and trim are made from quartersawn white oak, but painted trim work is a less expensive alternative that still maintains the style.

There are many variations of Arts & Crafts style. The projects provided in this book illustrate only a few common trim techniques. Research the movement if you like the idea of wider, straight-line casing, but don't see exactly what you want. The installation techniques are the same, with variations in joinery and style elements.

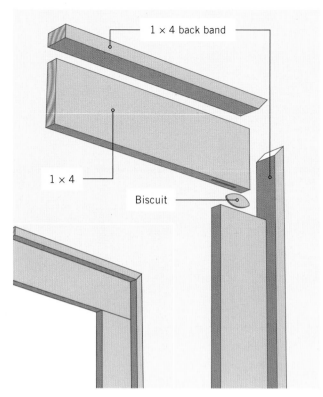

Use biscuits to join butted joints of an Arts & Crafts window or door treatment. Mitered corner molding wraps around the perimeter of the solid stock, to add depth to the casing.

Decorative elements from these Arts & Crafts cabinets are repeated in the window frame and throughout the room to an impressive visual effect.

Arts & Crafts plate rail doubles as wainscot cap, which is usually higher than wainscot in other decorating vernaculars. In a typical Arts & Crafts installation, the wainscot is between 48 and 54" high. Corbels located above frame-and-panel stiles are a common motif.

White oak is the preferred Arts & Crafts wood type. The window apron above is from quartersawn white oak, the preferred cut. The wainscot panels are plainsawn white oak veneer plywood.

Fancy Arts & Crafts embellishments, like the newel post (above) and the wraparound window header (left), still feature relatively plain wood treatments with a very linear appearance.

Neoclassical Trim Style

The term "Neoclassical" refers to any style derived from classic Roman or Greek architecture. Specific Neoclassical styles include Federal and Georgian styles. Traditional Greek buildings had structural components such as columns and pedestals, which, in modern time, have been replaced with interior trim elements such as door casings and baseboard. An example of a Neoclassical door trim would be a fluted casing with plinth blocks at the floor. This style is a direct, but flatter, version of classic Greek architecture.

Neoclassical style is also represented in many of the buildings of the U.S. Federal Government. Many national monuments have Neoclassical elements in their window and door treatments as well as the obvious exterior trim components such as columns.

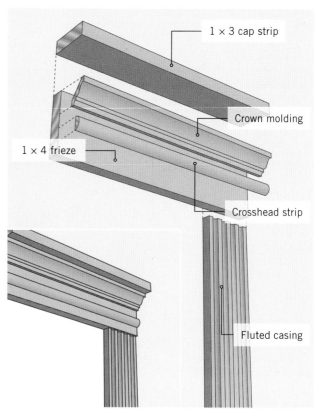

This illustrated Neoclassical fluted casing (right) is capped off with a 4-piece decorative head including: half-round cross-head strip, 1 × 4 frieze board, crown molding, and 1 × 3 cap strip.

Neoclassical is a very broad trim category that includes many styles and interpretations. Basically, it boils down to "Formal and Fancy."

In this Neoclassical doorway, decorative "keystones" highlight the archway over the door and are repeated in the cornice molding as well.

Not all Neoclassical trim is extremely ornate. The clean lines of this door casing and plinth blocks are crisp and graceful, an effect that is enhanced by the white painted finish.

Neoclassical moldings often are, again, ornate, like this Federal-style exterior door head molding.

Dentil moldings are also common in crown moldings, mantels, and frieze boards.

Modern Trim Style

Modern style is relatively plain, downplaying decorative carving or complex profiles. Where Victorian trim pieces are elaborate multiple-piece moldings high on decoration, Modern trim can be as basic as plywood cut to a uniform width with clean lines and butted joints. Hardware on Modern cabinetry, doors, and windows is generally sleek, with chrome or black oxide coating. Six-panel doors are replaced with slab doors, and industrial materials are incorporated into the design whenever possible, including revealing the internal systems of a home such as heating ducts and electrical lines.

More so than the styles of the past, Modern style represents a complete change in how we view trim and architecture. Traditional ideas about what materials should be used and where and how they are installed are challenged. The focus of Modern style is function, never purely decoration.

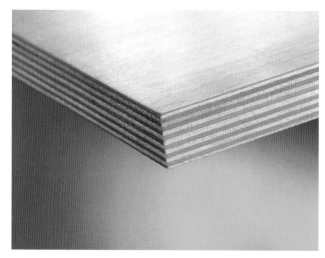

Birch plywood, commonly known as Baltic Birch, is frequently used to make Modern style trim. The plywood is ripped to strips of desired width and installed with an exposed plywood edge.

Modern trim isn't defined by any specific profiles or shapes; it simply is trim that has a clean, simple, and open appearance that's unlike the fanciness of the tradional styles.

Plain Colonial or ranch casings are mitered at the header of the door in the typical Modern home. Matching base moldings are butted against the door casings without a plinth block.

Clean lines and hard shadows are the hallmarks of Modern trim. White semi-gloss paint is the finish of choice.

Glass block is a Modern-style material that allows light into a room without sacrificing safety. The window trim shown is made of ceramic tile rather than wood.

Dining Room Trim

36 lin. ft. - 3" door casing - oak.

18 lin. ft. - 2 ¼" window casing - oak.

6 - 3×3" plinth blocks

50 lin. ft. - 4" base - oak

50 lin. ft. - ¾" cap - oak

50 lin. ft. - ¾" shoe - oak

Preparing for a Trim Project

Like other types of home improvement work, successful trim carpentry requires a good deal of careful preparation. However, where preparation for installing flooring or painting walls requires time with brushes and levelers and primers and such, preparing for trim installation is mostly a matter of thinking and making good choices. After all, the point of trim is often to conceal problems that resulted from inadequate preparation or poor execution.

The fundamental questions you need to answer during the preparation process are "What should I install?" and "How should I attach it?" Then, you need to choose a trim profile and material. Finally, you'll have to specify a finish.

Choosing a method of attachment is usually rather obvious. In almost all cases, pneumatic nails are the best choice. But not all walls will accept nails, and some heavier trim material may require the holding strength of screws. Other lighter trims should be attached with adhesives only. There is a lot to think about. But once you've answered the basic questions, devising a plan of attack is relatively simple.

In this chapter:
- Choosing a Style
- Tools & Materials
- Molding Profiles
- Glues & Adhesives
- Screws & Nails
- Abrasives
- Wood Fillers
- Job Site Preparation
- Estimating Material
- Planning a Deadline
- Planning a Trim Layout
- Removing Old Trim

Choosing a Style

When you begin to design your new trim project, you will want to make choices about the style and the types of moldings that are most appropriate for your home. Balance and scale, existing furnishings, and the applied finish will all change the effect your project has on the room as well as the overall house.

Choosing a specific style for your trim project can be as difficult as the actual installation. Architectural styles evoke different feelings from each individual. To help you choose a style, start with the feeling that you are trying to achieve in the room. The simplistic nature of Arts & Crafts may be relaxing to you, or maybe you find it boorish and unappealing.

Neoclassical style may create a formal appearance for a dining room or den. It is possible that maintaining the existing style of your home is important to you. Or perhaps you would prefer to change the style in an individual room to make it more relaxed than the rest of your home. Whatever the case is, keep in mind there are no rules written in stone that state what you can and cannot do.

When adding trim, it generally is best to stay within the same period or style as already exists in your house. Mixing periods of trim, when not handled thoughtfully, can be awkward and confusing to the eye.

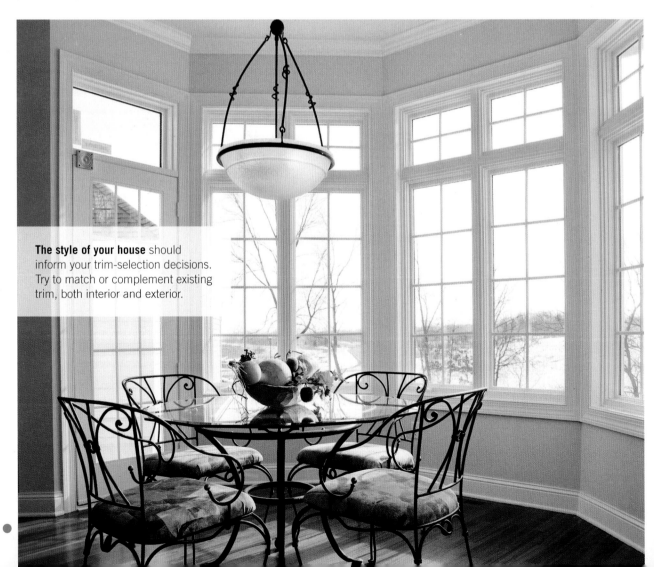

The style of your house should inform your trim-selection decisions. Try to match or complement existing trim, both interior and exterior.

Balance & Scale

Scale can be defined as the size of a particular object in relation to its surroundings. When considering a trim style, scale is very important because moldings that are too large or small might not have an impact on a room the way you had planned.

Moldings that are well-balanced create a sense of comfort and stability in a room and are well proportioned to each other; that is, they are scaled proportionally. For example, if you originally wanted to install very tall base molding, the crown or cornice treatment should be similar in scale or the room may be thrown out of balance.

The Ancient Greeks used a scale of proportion that mimics that of a column. The general rule of thumb for a room with an 8-foot ceiling is that the base should be a minimum of 5 inches wide, the chair rail a minimum of 3 inches wide (set at a height between 32 and 36 inches up from the floor), and the crown a minimum of 5 inches wide. The wall represents the column shaft, the base molding represents the base, and the crown represents the capital.

When choosing trim elements for your project, keep in mind the existing moldings of the room so that the new trim will have the effect you desire. It is a good idea to maintain balance and scale.

While our eye, in general, does not like surprises when it comes to scale, it is possible to create effective illusions by violating the normal rules of proportional scale. For example, by trimming a small room with an elaborate built-up crown, you can make the room appear taller. But use caution; if not handled gracefully, the trick can backfire and simply make your room look small and cluttered.

Scale can be used to your advantage. With an elaborate, built-up crown detail, this standard-height room looks like it has a taller ceiling than it actually does.

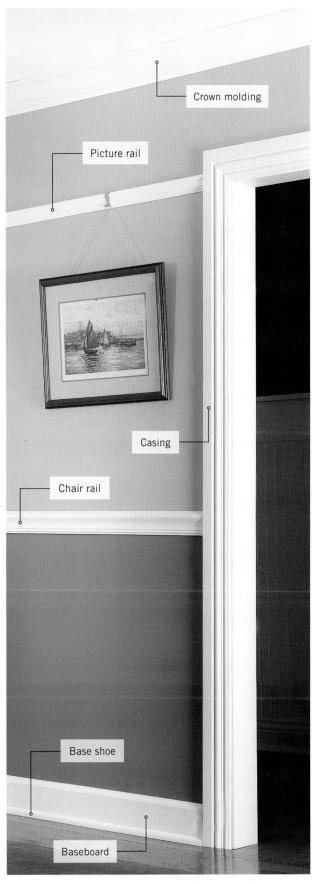

Crown molding

Picture rail

Casing

Chair rail

Base shoe

Baseboard

The style of the trim in this room is well balanced. The individual elements are similar in color and molding profile and do not overpower each other with strong differences in size.

Tools & Materials

Installing finish trim and casings is a challenging job that requires patience, attention to detail, and the right tool for each task. Without these requirements, the result will suffer. Start off right by using high-quality tools. Be sure to read and follow all safety instructions, and become familiar with the tool and its operation prior to using it for your project. Good tools last longer and are generally more accurate than cheaper versions.

Many people buy tools only as they are needed to avoid purchases they will not use. This rationale should only apply to power tools and higher-priced specialty items. A high-quality basic tool set is important for every do-it-yourselfer to have on hand and ready when you need to use it. Doing so avoids improper tool usage and makes your job easier, with improved results.

Purchase the highest-quality layout tools you can afford. They are crucial for accurate measuring and marking of trim, and help you avoid costly mistakes with expensive stock.

Layout Tools

Layout tools help you measure, mark, and cut materials and surfaces with accuracy. Many layout tools are inexpensive and simply provide a means of measuring for level, square, and plumb lines. However, recent technologies have incorporated lasers into levels, stud finders, and tape measures, making them more accurate than ever before, at a slightly higher price. Although these new tools are handy in specific applications, their higher price is not always warranted and the average do-it-yourselfer can produce quality results without them.

- **A tape measure** with a thicker, reinforced tape will allow you to take longer measurements—up to 11 feet without the tape buckling. The thicker tapes are also more durable. The constant extending and reeling in of the tape will put strain on the end, causing thinner tapes to rip and expose sharp edges.

Hand Tools

The hand tools you will need for most finish carpentry jobs can be broken down into two types: layout tools and construction tools. It is common for most people to own construction tools yet lack necessary layout tools for basic trim jobs.

Tape measure

Combination square

Levels

- **A framing square,** also known as a carpenter's square, is commonly used to mark sheet goods and check recently installed pieces for position. Framing squares are also used as an initial check for wall squareness and plumb in relation to a floor or ceiling.

- **Chalk lines** are used to make temporary straight lines anywhere they are needed. The case of a chalk line, or the "box," is tear shaped so the tool doubles as a plumb bob. Use a chalk line to mark sheet goods for cutting or to establish a level line in a room. Keep in mind that chalk can be difficult to remove from porous surfaces.

- **A stud finder** is used to locate the framing members in a wall or ceiling. Higher-priced versions also find plumbing, electrical, or other mechanicals in the wall. Although a stud finder is not completely necessary, it is convenient when installing a larger job.

- **Levels** are available in a variety of lengths and price ranges. The longer and more accurate the level, the higher the price. The two most commonly used sizes are 2-foot and 4-foot lengths. The 2-foot levels are handy for tighter spaces, while the 4-foot variety serves as a better all-purpose level. Laser levels are handy for creating a level line around the perimeter of a room or for level lines along longer lengths. They provide a wide range of line or spot placement, depending on the model.

- **A T-bevel** is a specialized tool for finding and transferring precise angles. T-bevels are generally used in conjunction with a power miter saw to gauge angled miters of nonsquare corners. This tool is especially handy in older homes where the concepts of square, plumb, and level do not necessarily apply.

- **A profile gauge** uses a series of pins to recreate the profile of any object so that you may transfer it to a work piece. Profile gauges are especially useful when dealing with irregular obstructions.

- **A combination square** is a multifunction square that provides an easy reference for 45- and 90-degree angles, as well as marking reveal lines or a constant specific distance from the edge of a work piece.

Framing square

Chalk lines

Stud finder

Laser Level

T-bevel

Profile gauge

Construction Tools

- **A good quality hammer** is a must for every trim carpentry project. A 16-oz. curved claw hammer, otherwise known as a finish hammer, is a good all-purpose choice.

- **Utility knives** are available in fixed, retracting, and retractable blades. This tool is used for a wide variety of cutting tasks from pencil sharpening to back-beveling miter joints. Always have additional blades readily available.

- **A set of chisels** is necessary for installing door hardware as well as notching trim around obstacles and final fitting of difficult pieces.

- **Block planes** are used to fit doors into openings and remove fine amounts of material from trim. A finely tuned block plane can even be used to clean up a sloppy miter joint.

- **A coping saw** has a thin, flexible blade designed to cut curves and is essential for making professional trim joints on inside corners. Coping-saw blades should be fine-toothed, between 16 and 24 teeth per inch for most hardwoods, and set to cut on the pull stroke of the saw to offer you more blade control.

- **A sharp handsaw** is convenient for quick cut-offs and in some instances where power saws are difficult to control. Purchase a cross-cut saw for general-purpose cutting.

- **Protective wear,** including safety glasses and ear protection, is required any time you are working with tools. Dust masks are necessary when sanding.

- **Pry bars** come in a variety of sizes and shapes. A quality forged high-carbon steel flat bar is the most common choice for trim projects. Wrecking bars make lighter work of trim and door removal due to their added weight.

- **Side cutters and end nippers** are useful for cutting off and pulling out bent nails. The added handle length and curved head of end nippers makes them ideal for larger casing nails. Pneumatic brad nails and smaller pins will pull out easier with side cutters. Purchase a nail set for countersinking nail heads. Three-piece sets are available for different nail sizes.

- **A rasp and a metal file set** are important for fitting coped joints precisely. The variety of shapes, sizes, and mills allows faster, rougher removal of material or smoother, slower removal, depending on the file.

- **Use a putty knife** to fill nail holes with putty and for light scraping tasks.

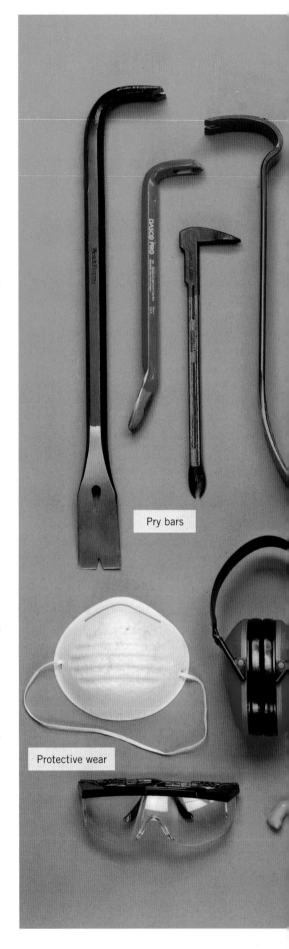

Pry bars

Protective wear

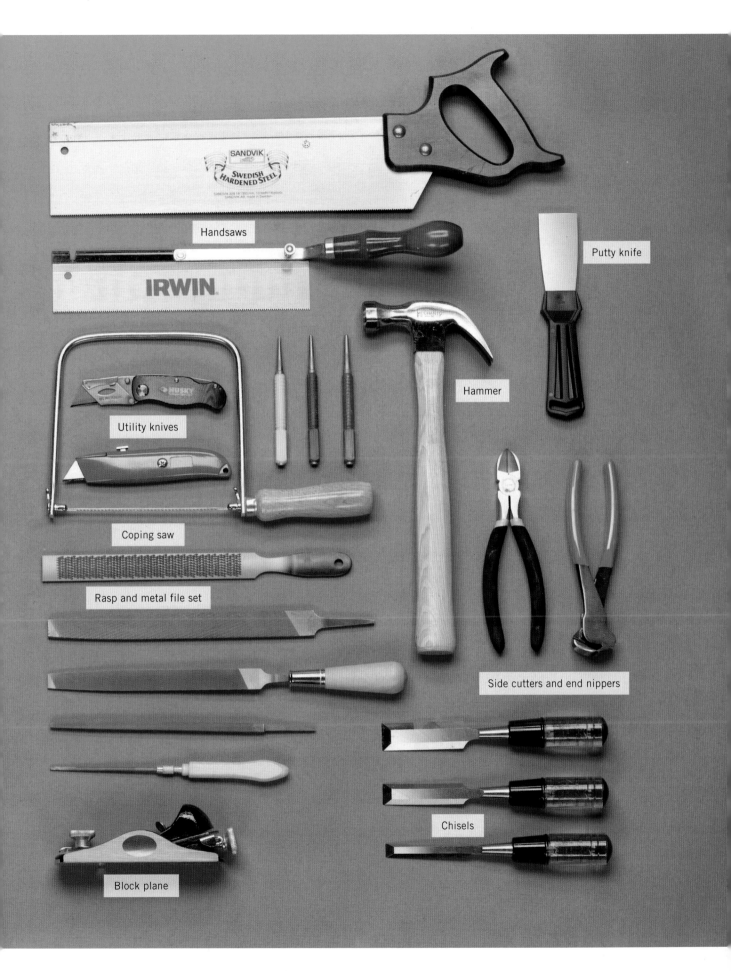

Handsaws

IRWIN.

Putty knife

Utility knives

Hammer

Coping saw

Rasp and metal file set

Side cutters and end nippers

Chisels

Block plane

Power Tools

Despite the higher price as compared to hand tools, power tools are a great value. They allow you to do work more quickly and accurately than with hand tools and make repetitive tasks like sanding, drilling, and sawing more enjoyable. Basic trim jobs do not require every power tool shown here, but some tools, such as a power miter box, are crucial for professional results. Purchase power tools on an as-needed basis, keeping in mind that while the cheapest tool is not always your best option, the most expensive and powerful is probably not necessary, either. Cheaper tools generally sacrifice precision, while the most expensive tools are made for people who use them every day, not just for occasional use. Power tools that are midrange in price are a good choice for the do-it-yourselfer.

- **A cordless drill** is one of the handiest tools available. Although drills are not normally used to install trim, they make quick work of installing wood backing for wainscoting and other trim features. Occasionally, trim head screws are used rather than nails to install trim. This situation is most common with steel-stud walls and necessitates a drill.

- **A circular saw** is ideal for straight cuts in plywood and quick cut-offs of solid material. Purchase a plywood blade to make smooth cuts in plywood and a general-purpose blade for other cuts.

- **A jigsaw** is the perfect tool for cutting curves, or notching out trim around obstructions. Jigsaw blades

Corded reciprocating saw

Circular saw

Cordless reciprocating saw

Cordless drill/driver

Jigsaw

Router

Random-orbit sander

Biscuit, or plate, joiner

Finish, or detail, sander

Power planer

Belt sander

Tablesaw

come in an array of designs for different styles of cuts and different types and thicknesses of materials. Always use the right type of blade, and do not force the saw during the cut or it may bend or break.

- **A biscuit joiner** is a specialty tool used to make strong joints between two square pieces of stock.

- **A reciprocating saw** is used for removal and tear-down applications for trim projects. This tool is especially handy to remove door jambs.

- **A power miter saw,** or chop saw, will yield professional trim results. Most have a 10- or 12-inch diameter blade. A compound power miter saw has a head that pivots to cut bevels and miters at the same time. Sliding miter saws have more cutting capacity but are less portable. A fine-tooth carbide-tipped blade is best for trim projects.

- **A belt sander** is not essential but is a handy tool for quick removal of material.

- **Random-orbit sanders** are a good choice for smoothing flat areas, such as plywood, quickly. Random-orbit sanders leave no circular markings, like a disc sander, and can sand in any direction regardless of wood grain.

- **Finish sanders** are available in a variety of sizes and shapes for different light sanding applications.

- **A power planer** is used to trim doors to fit openings and flatten or straighten out materials. Power planes are faster to use than manual hand planes, but results are more difficult to control.

- **A tablesaw** is the best tool for ripping stock to width, and larger models can be fitted with a molding head for cutting profiles.

- **A router** (plunge router is shown here) has many uses in trim carpentry, especially for cutting edge profiles to make your own custom wood trim.

Pneumatic Tools

Portable compressor

Brad nailer

Stapler

Pin nailer

Angled finish nailer

Along with a good power miter saw, pneumatic tools are the key to timely, professional trim results. Pneumatic tools save time and energy over traditional hammer-and-nail installation. Not only do they drive fasteners quickly, but they countersink at the same time, avoiding multiple strikes to the trim, which could throw joints out of alignment. Predrilled holes are not necessary with pneumatic tools. Splitting occurs infrequently if the work piece is held firmly in place and the nails are positioned at least 1 inch from trim ends. Nail guns also allow you to concentrate on the placement of the work piece with one hand and fasten it with the other. You needn't fumble around with single fasteners because they are already loaded in the gun.

Cost of pneumatic tools, compressors, and fasteners has decreased over the years, making them not only the professional's choice, but a great option for the do-it-yourselfer as well. Pneumatic kits are available at home centers with two different guns and a compressor at a value price. For smaller trim jobs, consider renting pneumatics.

Portable compressors are available in different styles, including pancake and tumbler styles. Any compressor with air pressure of 90 psi or greater will work for a finish gun or brad nailer. Consider options like tank size, weight of the unit, and noise levels while the compressor is running. Talk to a home center specialist about what your specific compressor needs are, and keep in mind any future pneumatic tools you might want.

The two basic pneumatic tools used in trim carpentry are a finish nailer and a brad nailer. A finish nailer drives 15-gauge nails ranging from 1 to 2½ inches. These nails work for a variety of moldings, door-and-window trim, and general-purpose fastening. Angled finish nailers are easier to maneuver in tight corners than straight guns, but either option will work. Brad nailers drive smaller 18-gauge fasteners ranging in length from ½ to 2 inches. Some brad nailers' maximum length is 1¼ inches. Because the fasteners are smaller, it is no surprise that the gun is lighter and smaller than a finish gun. Brad nailers are used to attach thinner stock, with less tendency of splitting the trim. Headless pinners drive fasteners similar to brad nailers without the head. These nails have less holding power but are normally used to hold small moldings in place until the glue dries. Be sure to load headless pins with the points down, taking note of the label on the magazine. The ⅜-inch crown staplers are used to attach backing to trim pieces and in situations where maximum holding power is needed but the fastener head will not be visible. Because staples have two legs and a crown that connects them, their holding power is excellent. However, the hole left by the staple's crown is large and can be difficult to fill.

Pneumatic Fasteners

The 15-gauge finish nails and angled finish nails range in length up to 2½ inches. The angled variety are exactly the same as the straight nails but come in angled clips. These nails are also available galvanized for exterior applications. Use finish nails to attach larger moldings and trim casings. Drive fasteners at regular intervals along the moldings, and keep the position of the nails at least 1 inch from the molding ends. Fastener length is dependent upon the size of molding installed and what the backing is. Typical stock moldings are approximately ¾ inch thick. The fastener must pass through the molding and wallboard and into the stud behind. Generally, half the fastener should be embedded in the backing or stud, so in standard trim applications,

2-inch fasteners should suffice. 18-gauge brad nails range in length up to 2 inches for some guns and leave smaller holes to fill than finish guns. Brad nails are commonly used for thinner casings that are nailed directly to a solid backer. A specific example of this is along the inner edge of a door or window casing. The outer edge of the trim is nailed with a finish gun through the wallboard, while the inside edge rests against the door jamb so it can be fastened with a brad nailer. Headless pins leave almost no nail hole to fill but are limited in length to 1 inch. Their holding power is greatly diminished due to the lack of head, but they are generally used in conjunction with wood glue. Use ⅜-inch crown staples only when the fastener head will not be visible.

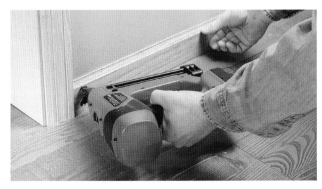

Cordless nailers offer the advantages of pneumatic nailers but without the trailing hose and the compressor. A battery-operated model, such as the 12-volt, 18-gauge brad nailer, is good for small jobs. Heavy-duty models powered by fuel cells can handle larger jobs but cost quite a bit more.

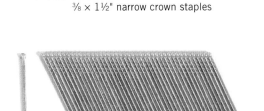

⅜ × 1½" narrow crown staples

15 ga. × 2½" finish nails

18 ga. × 1¼" brads

15 ga. × 2" finish nails

1¼ × ¾" narrow crown staples

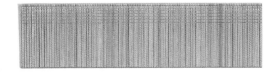

18 ga. × 1¼" brads

⅜ × 1" narrow crown staples

18 ga. × ⅝" brads

Molding Profiles

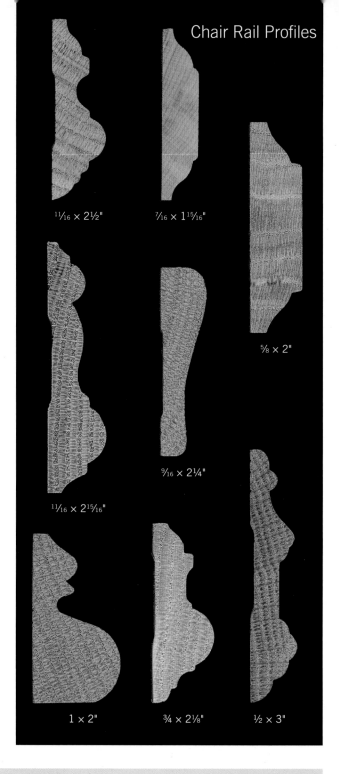

$^{11}/_{16} \times 2^{1}/_{2}"$ $^{7}/_{16} \times 1^{15}/_{16}"$

$^{5}/_{8} \times 2"$

$^{9}/_{16} \times 2^{1}/_{4}"$

$^{11}/_{16} \times 2^{15}/_{16}"$

$1 \times 2"$ $^{3}/_{4} \times 2^{1}/_{8}"$ $^{1}/_{2} \times 3"$

Trim moldings in stock profiles are available off the shelf at most home centers. Most molding manufacturers assign codes such as "WM166" or "HWM127" to every profile and size. However, you will find that the codes are not applied uniformly, making them virtually worthless if you're trying to track down specific molding profiles. The best way to order molding is to obtain a catalog from your molding supplier and use its labeling conventions.

There are a few conventions that are fairly consistently applied. In general, moldings labeled with a code starting with "WM" are paint-grade or softwood moldings. "HWM" designates the trim piece as a hardwood molding. If you like the style of a softwood molding but would prefer to buy the piece in a hardwood species, ask for the equivalent in a hardwood species, ask for the equivalent in hardwood from the lumber yard sales associate.

Even though moldings are commonly found under categories such as "baseboard" or "cove," these categories relate to the style of the trim piece, not necessarily where it should be used. In fact, even among seasoned trim carpenters you'll frequently encounter arguments over which type a particular size or profile belongs to. The similarities are especially apparent when comparing base molding to case molding, as the following photos will confirm.

MINI-GLOSSARY OF MOLDING SHAPES & PROFILES

Bead—a rounded profile

Chamfer—a 45° beveled edge profile

Dentil—a series of rectangular blocks spaced close together to form a border pattern

Flute—a shallow groove with a round profile, usually running longitudinally on the workpiece in groups of at least three

Frieze—horizontal banding on the wall at the wall-ceiling joint

Ogee—an S-shape or reverse curve profile

Rosette—a square block with concentric circular carving, usually placed at the intersection of head and side casing

Case Molding Profiles

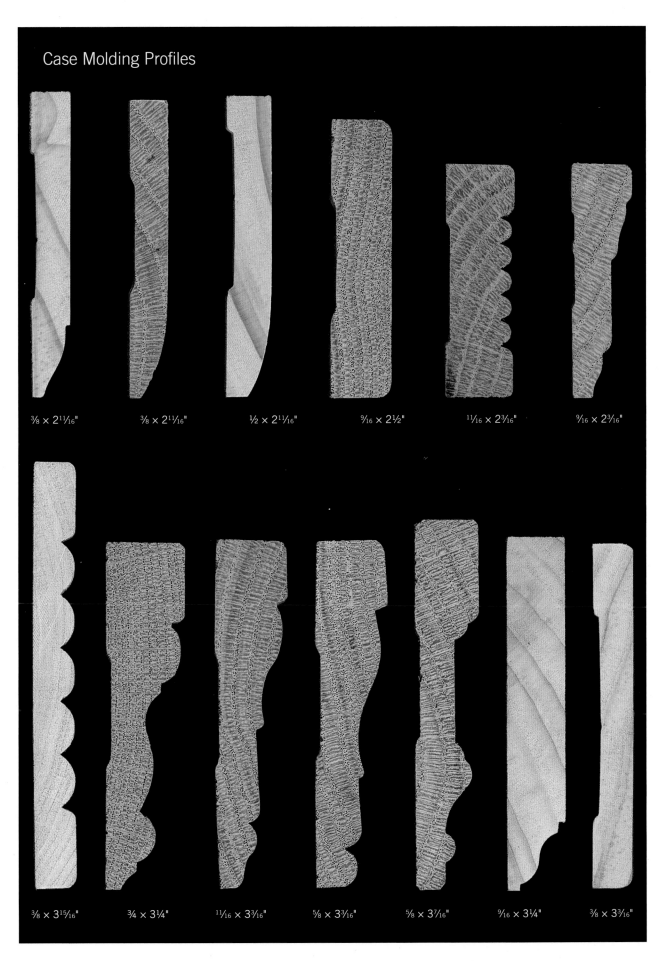

³⁄₈ × 2¹¹⁄₁₆"   ³⁄₈ × 2¹¹⁄₁₆"   ½ × 2¹¹⁄₁₆"   ⁹⁄₁₆ × 2½"   ¹¹⁄₁₆ × 2³⁄₁₆"   ⁹⁄₁₆ × 2³⁄₁₆"

³⁄₈ × 3¹⁵⁄₁₆"   ¾ × 3¼"   ¹¹⁄₁₆ × 3³⁄₁₆"   ⅝ × 3³⁄₁₆"   ⅝ × 3⁷⁄₁₆"   ⁹⁄₁₆ × 3¼"   ³⁄₈ × 3³⁄₁₆"

Base Molding

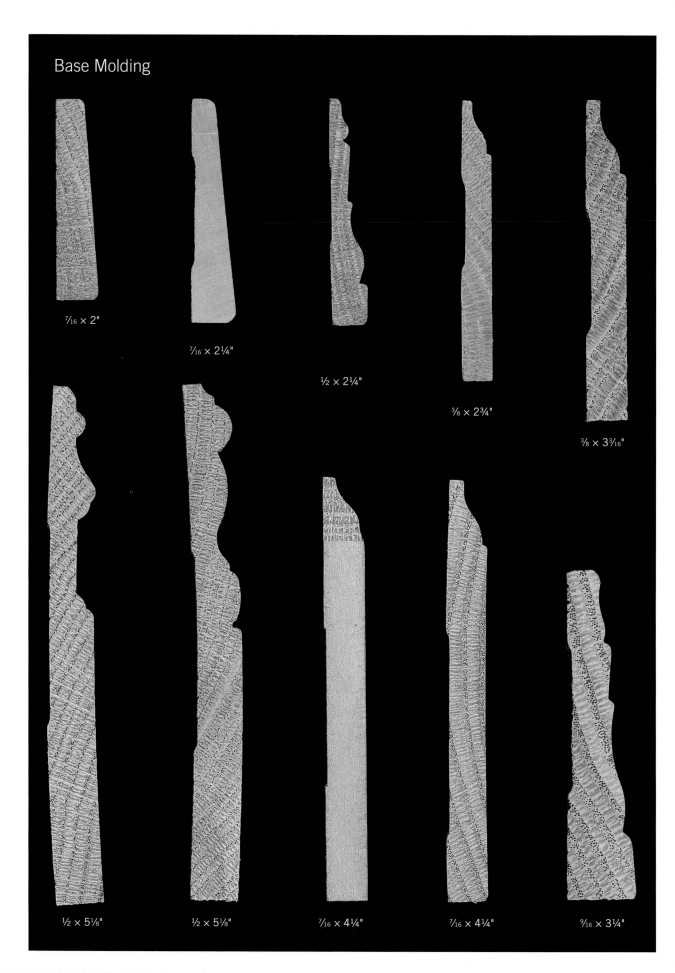

7⁄16 × 2"

7⁄16 × 2¼"

½ × 2¼"

3⁄8 × 2¾"

3⁄8 × 3³⁄16"

½ × 5⅛"

½ × 5⅛"

7⁄16 × 4¼"

7⁄16 × 4¼"

9⁄16 × 3¼"

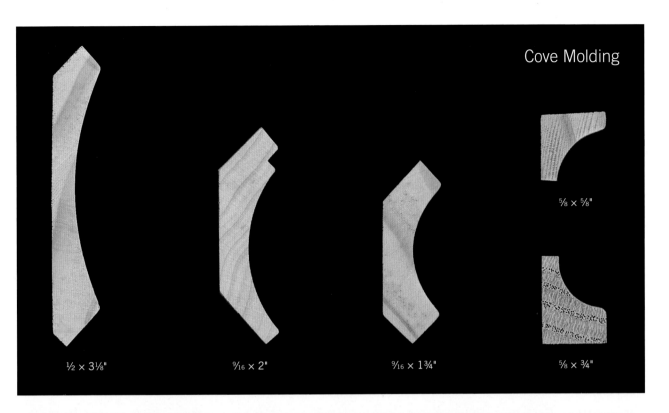

Cove Molding

½ × 3⅛"

⁹⁄₁₆ × 2"

⁹⁄₁₆ × 1¾"

⅝ × ⅝"

⅝ × ¾"

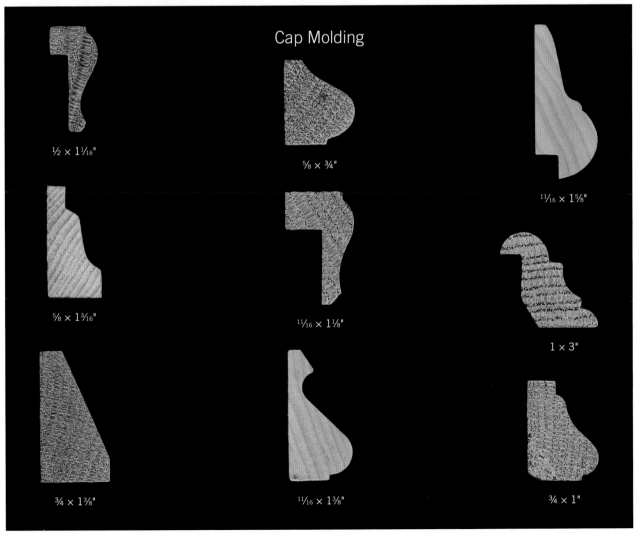

Cap Molding

½ × 1¹⁄₁₆"

⅝ × ¾"

¹¹⁄₁₆ × 1⅝"

⅝ × 1³⁄₁₆"

¹¹⁄₁₆ × 1⅛"

1 × 3"

¾ × 1⅜"

¹¹⁄₁₆ × 1⅜"

¾ × 1"

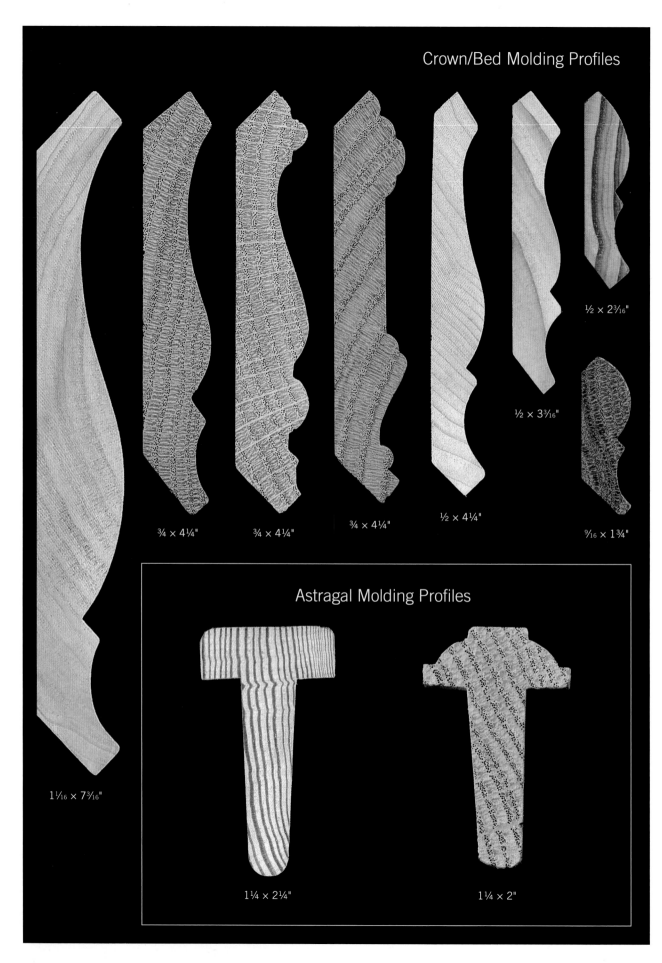

½ × 2³⁄₁₆"

½ × 3³⁄₁₆"

¾ × 4¼"

¾ × 4¼"

¾ × 4¼"

½ × 4¼"

⁹⁄₁₆ × 1¾"

Astragal Molding Profiles

1¹⁄₁₆ × 7³⁄₁₆"

1¼ × 2¼"

1¼ × 2"

Quarter-Round

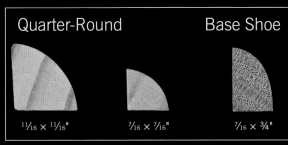

$^{11}/_{16} \times {}^{11}/_{16}$" $^{7}/_{16} \times {}^{7}/_{16}$"

Base Shoe

$^{7}/_{16} \times {}^{3}/_{4}$"

Stool Molding

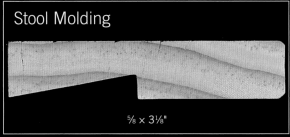

$^{5}/_{8} \times 3{}^{1}/_{8}$"

Stop Molding Profiles

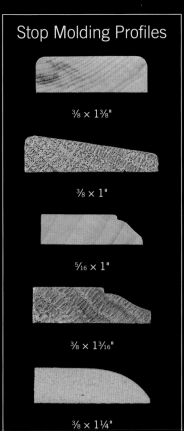

$^{3}/_{8} \times 1{}^{3}/_{8}$"

$^{3}/_{8} \times 1$"

$^{5}/_{16} \times 1$"

$^{3}/_{8} \times 1{}^{3}/_{16}$"

$^{3}/_{8} \times 1{}^{1}/_{4}$"

Corner Moldings

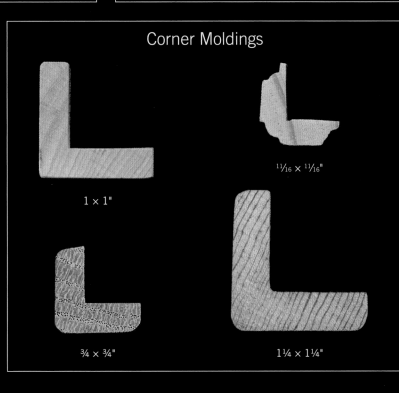

1×1"

$^{11}/_{16} \times {}^{11}/_{16}$"

$^{3}/_{4} \times {}^{3}/_{4}$"

$1{}^{1}/_{4} \times 1{}^{1}/_{4}$"

Picture Rail Molding

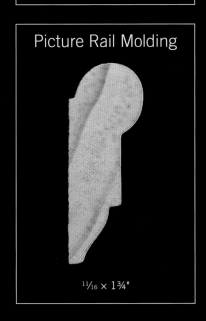

$^{11}/_{16} \times 1{}^{3}/_{4}$"

Screen Retainer Profiles

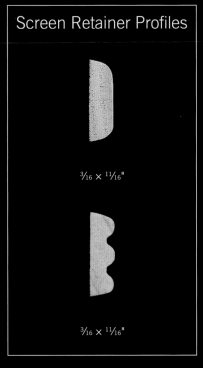

$^{3}/_{16} \times {}^{11}/_{16}$"

$^{3}/_{16} \times {}^{11}/_{16}$"

Shelf Edge Profiles

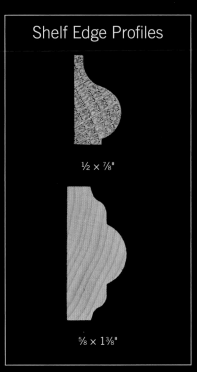

$^{1}/_{2} \times {}^{7}/_{8}$"

$^{5}/_{8} \times 1{}^{3}/_{8}$"

Glues & Adhesives

Glues and adhesives are available at any hardware store or home center in many different specialty forms, depending upon the type of application. Use hot glue for lightweight trim projects, carpenter's glue for wood joints, and adhesive for strong bonds between panels or lumber.

Panel adhesive is used to install paneling, wainscot, or other tongue-and-groove materials. Most adhesives are applied with a caulk gun, but some types are available in squeeze tubes for smaller applications. Caulks are designed to permanently close joints, fill gaps in woodwork, and hide subtle imperfections. Different caulks are made of different compounds and vary greatly in durability and workability. Latex caulks clean up with water and are paintable but don't last as long as silicone-based products. Read the product label for adhesion quality to specific materials, and ask a store representative for more information if you are uncertain which will work best for you.

If you are installing a trim project with a darker wood, such as walnut, or your trim has a dark finish applied, consider purchasing dark carpenter's glue for joint application. Dark glue dries at the same rate and with the same strength as regular carpenter's glue, but squeeze-out from the joints will be less visible with a dark background. Exterior wood glue has a longer shelf life than regular glue and is a better multipurpose choice.

Polyurethane glue provides a high-strength bond between almost any materials; however, do not overapply. The dried product is difficult to remove from finished surfaces.

Carpentry adhesives include carpenter's wood glue, exterior carpenter's glue, liquid hide glue, polyurethane glue, panel adhesive, construction adhesive, latex caulk, silicone caulk, and a hot glue gun with glue sticks.

Screws & Nails

Screws and nails are the fasteners of choice for trim carpentry projects. Nails are the most common way of fastening trim in place, but screws are used for installing blocking, building up backing material, and installing trim in instances where nails don't have the holding power. Use box nails or long wallboard screws for rough framing of blocking or backing for panels. For exterior trim projects and fastening door jambs, use casing nails. Finish nails are used for most trim installation because they have a slight head that is easy to countersink and conceal. To install smaller or thinner trim pieces that are prone to splitting, use brad nails. Brad nails are shorter and have a smaller gauge than finish nails for light trim work.

No matter what you are fastening, make sure the fasteners you choose are appropriate for your installation. Approximately half of the fastener should be embedded in the backing material when driven in place. It is a good idea to drill pilot holes in all materials before fastening them. Driving a fastener

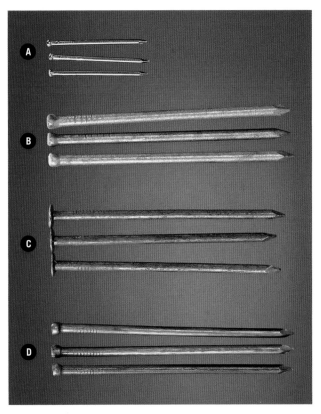

"Hand" nails for trim projects include brad nails (A), casing nails rated for exterior use (B), box nails (C), and finish nails (D).

through wood without a pilot hole can split the wood fibers. These splits may not be visible when you are finished, but the integrity of your trim will be affected. Predrilling eliminates this splitting and creates stronger joints that last longer.

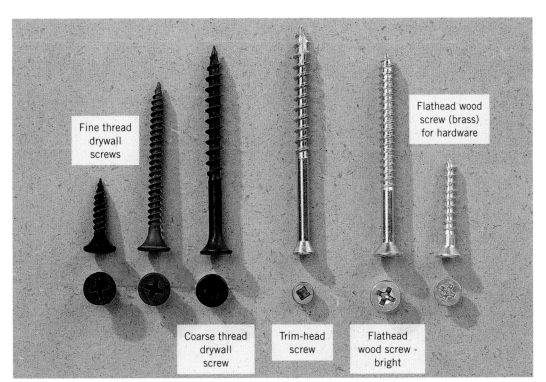

Use deck and drywall screws for general-purpose, convenient fastening. Driving options include Phillips drive and square drive. Use trimhead screws to fasten trim to walls.

Fine thread drywall screws

Coarse thread drywall screw

Trim-head screw

Flathead wood screw - bright

Flathead wood screw (brass) for hardware

Abrasives

Sandpaper is readily available from any hardware store or home center in a variety of styles, shapes, and sizes for just about any sanding task. Sandpaper is generally available in grits from 60 to 220, but finer and coarser grits are also offered at some locations.

The 60-grit sandpaper is used to grind down badly scratched surfaces and is rarely needed for trim carpentry applications. A 100-grit sandpaper is used for initial smoothing of wood. Stock moldings purchased from a home center or lumberyard may need a light initial sanding with 100-grit paper. Use 150-grit sandpaper to put a smooth finish on wood surfaces before painting or staining material. And 220-grit sandpaper is useful for light sanding between coats of varnish or to remove sanding marks left from power sanders.

No matter what you are sanding, begin with a lower-grit paper and work your way up the grit levels until you reach the desired smoothness for your project. Do not skip grit levels, especially 100-grit paper. Doing so will make it very difficult to remove scratches from previous sanding and will leave some hardwoods with deep grain marks that will be visible through your finish.

RANDOM-ORBIT SANDERS

Random-orbit sanders are great for trim carpentry work. Their random, circular motion leaves a very smooth finish that is free from uniform sanding marks. When working with a random-orbital sander, keep light pressure on the sander and move with the grain of the material. Leaving the sander in one place may cause an uneven finish and can possibly wear through a thin veneer. It is important to use sandpaper with the correct hole orientation. The holes (either five or eight) in the sandpaper allow particles to be drawn through the sanding pad and into dust-collection ports. When adhering the sheets (some are self-adhesive and some use hook-and-loop fabric), be sure that the holes align with the holes in the sander.

Detail sander being used on a piece of trim.

Always wear a dust mask when sanding, particularly when using power sanders. The airborne particles created while sanding can cause serious health problems. The dust from some hardwoods, such as walnut, is known to cause serious allergic reactions in some people.

Sandpaper is available in a variety of styles for various applications: basic sheet sandpaper for general use, sponge sanding blocks for materials with light curves, and foam-backed paper for sanding tight curves and intricate details. Precut papers for power sanders include Velcro or adhesive backing.

Sanding block

Precut papers for power sanders

Sheet sandpaper

Foam backed sandpaper

Wood Fillers

No matter what type of finish you choose, painted or clear, wood fillers provide a convenient way to fill fastener holes quickly and effectively with minimal sanding or cleanup. Each product differs in some way, including varying drying times, hardness when dry, and adhesion to specific materials. Read the packaging carefully to determine which product will best suit your needs.

Clear finishes require a filler that will either match the final finish color or stain similarly to the trim material. If you will be staining and varnishing your trim after it is installed, consider purchasing filler that will match when stained. Available in solvent and solvent-free form, these fillers apply easily with a putty knife, dry in a very brief amount of time, and sand with ease. Before applying stain-matching filler, use a scrap piece of trim to test the color.

If your trim will be finished prior to installation, use oil-based finishing putty to fill holes. This putty is available in numerous colors that can be mixed to achieve a nearly indistinguishable fill. Finish putty will never harden completely, so it's a good idea to apply one coat of varnish over the top to match the sheen of the finish.

Fastener holes in painted finishes can be filled with two main types of filling material. One is a premixed filler that is normally solvent based, such as plastic wood. The other requires mixing.

Solvent-based premixed fillers generally dry faster and harder than their water-based counterparts. Although premixed fillers are convenient to use, they have a shorter shelf life and are more expensive.

Fillers that require mixing are available in powder form for water-based products and two-part resin and hardener mixes for solvent-based products. Both work equally well in most circumstances; however, two-part resin and hardener mixes may emit dangerous fumes and should be handled with caution.

Wood fillers are available for two finish types: painted and clear finish. Based on the type of finish you choose and the fastener-hole size to fill, these products provide many options for your filling needs.

Grain filler is available to brush on open-grained woods before finishing. These products fill in wood grain so that it does not mirror through the finish, creating a smoother appearance.

Job Site Preparation

Whether you are installing base trim in an entire house or just improving the appearance of window with an additional molding, preparing the job site is an important step of your project. Remove as much furniture from the rooms you will be working in as possible so that you won't worry about getting sawdust on a nice upholstered chair or damaging an antique furnishing with a scratch. Cover any items you cannot remove with plastic sheeting. You may also want to cover finished floors with cardboard or plastic as well to protect them from scratches or just to make cleanup easier.

Organize your tools and avoid a bulky work belt by setting up a dedicated tool table where all of your project tools and materials can be staged.

The Work Area

Set up tools such as a power miter saw at a central workstation to avoid walking long distances between where you are installing and where you are cutting material. This central location is key to professional results because measurements are easier to remember and quick trimming is possible without the added time of exiting and entering the house.

Make sure the work area is well lit. If you don't already own one, purchase a portable light (trouble light) to make viewing the workpieces easier. Keep your tools sharp and clean. Accidents are more likely when blades are dull and tools are covered in dust and dirt.

Keep the work area clean and organized. A dedicated tool table for staging your tools is a great organizational aid. Tool tables also make it possible to conveniently keep tools from disappearing. If you only use the tools that you need and set them on the tool table when you aren't using them, tools stay off the floor and out of other rooms. Add a set of clamps to the table, and you have a convenient space for fine-tuning the fit of each trim piece.

In some trimwork projects, the most efficient way to accomplish the work is to convert the installation room into a temporary workshop.

Project Safety

Personal safety should be a priority when working on any project. Power tools and hand tools can cause serious injuries that require immediate attention. Be prepared for such situations with a properly stocked first aid kit. Equip your kit with a variety of bandage sizes and other necessary items such as antiseptic wipes, cotton swabs, tweezers, sterile gauze, and a first aid handbook.

To help you avoid using the first aid kit, read the owner's manuals of all power tools before operating them, and follow all outlined precautions. Protect yourself with safety glasses, ear protection, and dust masks and respirators when necessary.

Keep your work environment clean and free of clutter. Clean your tools and put them away after each work session, sweep up dust and any leftover fasteners, and collect scraps of cutoff trim in a work bucket. These scraps may come in handy before the end of the project, so keep them around until you are finished.

Maintain safety throughout your project, and remember that being safe is a priority. Everyone needs to use ear protection when operating loud tools. If you don't, you will lose your hearing. People don't just get used to loud noise. They lose their hearing and the noise doesn't seem as loud. The concept that safety applies to everyone but you is foolish. Take the necessary precautions to prevent injury to yourself and those around you.

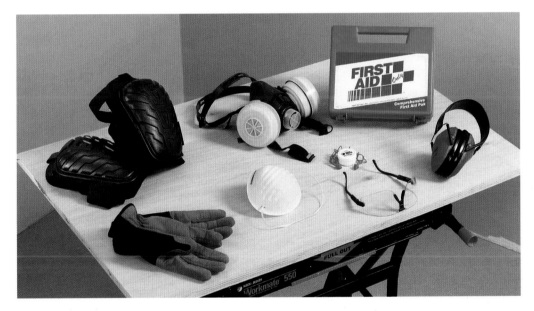

Always wear safety glasses and ear protection when operating power tools. Use dust masks when necessary, and protect yourself from chemicals with a respirator. Work gloves save your hands when moving or handling large amounts of material. Knee pads are useful when working on floor-level projects such as baseboard.

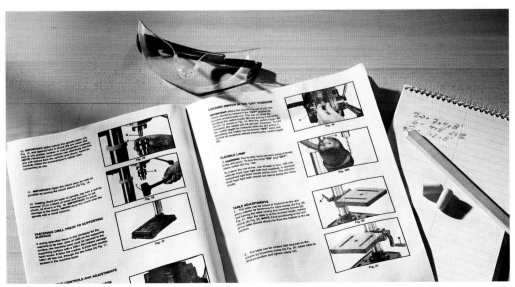

Read the owner's manual before operating any power tool. Your tools may differ in many ways from those described in this book, so it's best to familiarize yourself with the features and capabilities of the tools you own. Always wear eye and ear protection when operating a power tool. Wear a dust mask when the project will produce dust.

Estimating Material

Estimating material is an important part of any trim project. Taking the time to do a quality estimation of your needs will pay off with fewer trips to the lumberyard and little excess material. Estimating materials also helps keep your project in budget as you only buy what you need to get the job done.

Begin by measuring the precise length needed for each piece of molding and marking the dimensions in your scale drawings. When all dimensions are measured, add the total lineal feet together. This number represents the minimum number of feet you need to purchase to complete the job.

To save yourself the difficulty of splicing in materials over every length, you may need to call the lumberyard or home center you are purchasing from to find out what dimensions the moldings are available in. Some moldings are sold in random lengths ranging from 1 to 16 feet Others are only available in 8- or 10-foot lengths. When you know the availability of the moldings you want, take the time to write out a detailed list, optimizing the lengths of material with the fewest number of joints.

Similar methods should be used to estimate paint, paneling, and plywood. Make a separate list for every trim element, molding, or sheet good needed. Separate lists help avoid confusion when ordering materials or picking the stock off the shelf. Consider purchasing a project calculator for easier estimating. Project calculators are preprogrammed with formulas for everything including estimating paint coverage, lineal feet for moldings, and calculating to the nearest $\frac{1}{16}$ inch or better.

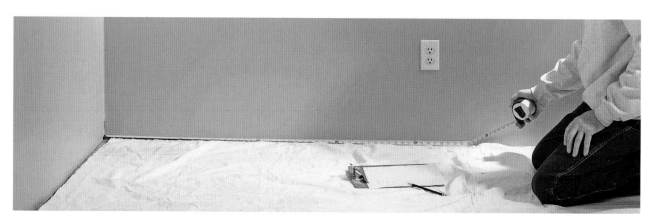

Calculating the lineal, or running, length of molding you need is one of the first steps in estimating your material needs. Take precise measurements, then add 10 percent to account for waste and improperly cut materials.

Project calculators simplify the math of square-foot coverage for paint, panel coverage for wainscoting, and lineal feet for trim components. The model shown calculates in fractions as well, making precise measurement addition simple.

Make a detailed list for each trim component, listing which lengths can be cut from a stock dimension. Label the list clearly with the wood molding number and a description of the piece at the top of the page.

Planning a Deadline

Planning a deadline is just as important as buying the material for a trim project. Without a deadline, the other people around you don't know what to expect from the project. Because trim components are cosmetic and not necessary for function of a home, trim projects have a tendency to become drawn out like no other. Planning a deadline gives you a specific point for completion as well as an overall goal to shoot for.

Do not sacrifice the quality of your installation to meet a deadline. Instead, choose a realistic timeline for certain components to be completed, altering the schedule as necessary. Remember that although the project may be exciting and fun now, there may come a time when it begins to feel like too much work. It is at this point that your schedule becomes your friend. No one wants to leave a project incomplete, but you need to make it a priority or other things will pop up that sound more appealing—and your living room will look like a construction project for too long.

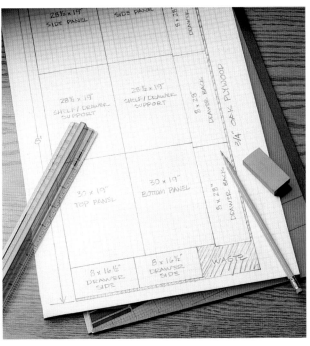

Draw cutting diagrams to help you make efficient use of materials. Make scale drawings of sheet goods on graph paper, and sketch cutting lines for each part of your project. When laying out cutting lines, remember that the cutting path (kerf) of a saw blade consumes up to ⅛" of material.

Laying out your project with scale drawings helps you anticipate what tools will be necessary and what the overall impact of your project will be as well as how it will affect your living space.

ESTABLISHING LEVEL, PLUMB & SQUARE

Good carpenters strive to achieve three basic ideals in their work: plumb, level, and square. Go into any home, however, and you are bound to find walls that bow, floors that slope, and corners that don't form right angles. This doesn't always mean the carpenter did a poor job, but rather reflects the fact that wood and many building materials are natural products that expand, contract, and settle with the seasons. These natural movements do not always occur at the same rate, however, causing fluctuations that sometimes become permanent. That's why it's no surprise that older homes more commonly have larger fluctuations.

These movements can make installing a new trim project challenging. Level and plumb are hard concepts to apply to a wainscot project where the floor slopes heavily and corners float in or out. Compounding the problem further is that power tools are made to cut and shape wood precisely. Preset angles on a compound miter saw don't include angles such as 47 degrees.

In most cases, your installation of chair rail, picture rail, or cornice molding will require compromises. Keep in mind the overall appearance of your project and remember that the concepts of plumb and level are only concepts. Strive to achieve them for quality joints, but don't insist on them when they affect the overall appearance of your project negatively.

A plumb bob is hung to establish a plumb (exactly vertical) line. Plumb can be difficult to visualize. Most chalk boxes can double as plumb bobs for rough use.

Window and door jambs are normally installed level and plumb, but if they aren't, your casing should still follow an even reveal of ³⁄₁₆ to ¼" (about the thickness of a nickel) around the inside edge. Set the blade on a combination square to the depth of the reveal. Then use the square as a guide for your pencil when marking. Install the casings flush with the mark.

Use a spacer block as a guide to install moldings near a ceiling. The spacer will allow you to easily follow any ups and downs of an uneven ceiling, making the trim run parallel to it rather than exactly level.

Install baseboard as close to level as possible, paying attention to areas where a floor dips or slopes over a longer length. In these instances, "cheat" the baseboard as close to level as you can, leaving a gap below it. You can only cheat the molding to less than the height of your base shoe, or quarter round. These trim pieces will cover the gap because they are thinner and easier to flex to the contour of your floor. Cheating the molding will also make cutting miters easier because they will require less of a bevel.

Use a T-bevel to measure for miter-cutting trim on out-of-square corners. Use a piece of scrap 1 × 4 to trace lines parallel to the corner walls. Place the T-bevel so the blade runs from the corner of the wall to the point where the lines intersect. Transfer this angle to your miter saw to cut your moldings.

Planning a Trim Layout

Planning the order, layout, and type of joint at each end of trim you will be installing is an important step before you actually start nailing things down. A good layout plan like the one shown below helps avoid frustration and errors during installation.

Generally, trim installations begin at the opposing wall to the entry to the room. The numbers in the sample layout plan below represent the order in which each piece is installed. Here, the first piece installed is butted at both ends, tight to the finished walls. Trim pieces are added to the installation, working back and forth around the room in both directions back toward the entry. The added trim is coped at all inside corners and mitered at outside corners. All window and door casings should be installed before any horizontal molding that will butt into it. When running cope joints, install all the butt-to-butt walls first and then the cope-to-outside-

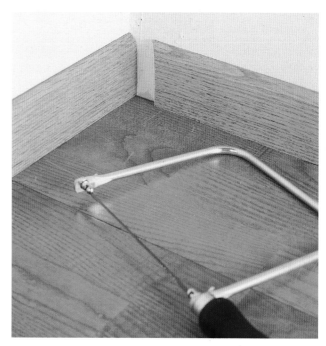

For professional results, contoured molding is coped at inside corners with a coping saw. Fine-tune the cut with a metal file or rasp.

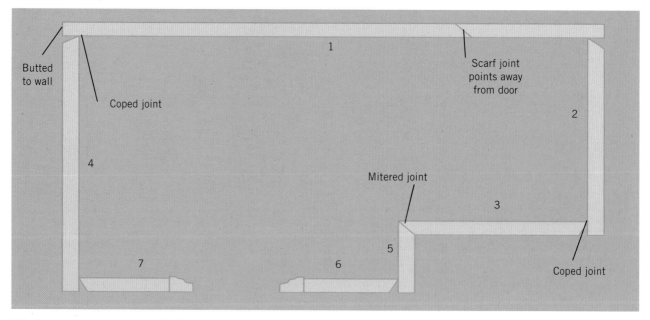

Butted to wall

Coped joint

Scarf joint points away from door

Mitered joint

Coped joint

1   2   3   4   5   6   7

Plan the order of your trim installation to minimize the number of difficult cuts on individual pieces. Use the longest pieces of molding for the most visible walls, saving the shorter ones for less conspicuous areas. When possible, place the joints so they point away from the direct line of sight from the room's entrance. If a piece will be coped on one end and mitered on the other, such as no. 3 above, cut and fit the coped end first. Also keep in mind the nailing points; mark all framing members you'll be nailing into before starting the installation. At a minimum, all trim should be nailed at every wall stud and every ceiling joist, if applicable. Install door and window casing before installing horizontal molding that will butt into it.

Standard Trim Joints

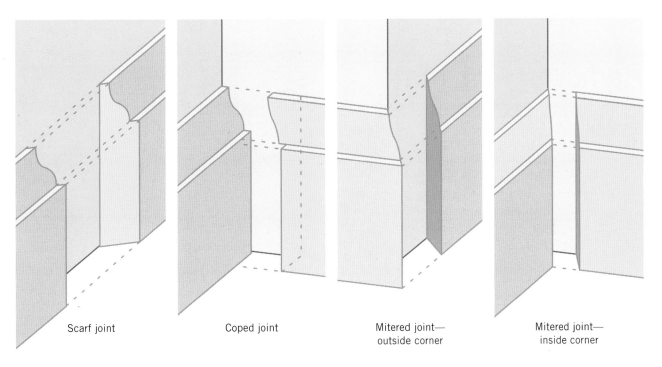

Scarf joint   Coped joint   Mitered joint— outside corner   Mitered joint— inside corner

The basic joints for installing most trim are shown here. A scarf joint joins two pieces along a length of wall. Coped joints join contoured molding at inside corners: The first piece is butted into the corner; the second piece is cut and fitted against the face of the first. Coped joints are less likely than mitered joints to show gaps if the wood shrinks. Mitered joints are used at outside and inside corners. They're typically made with two pieces cut at a 45° angle, but the angle may vary depending on the shape of the corner. Uncontoured moldings can also be butted together at inside corners.

corners. On occasion, a cope-to-cope may need to be cut and installed. If the molding has any significant thickness at the top, measure from the face of the moldings rather than the face of the wall.

Minimize the number of joints necessary on each wall by using the longest pieces available. Keep in mind that the most visible spaces should have fewer joints whenever possible. Cut all joints so they face away from the direct line of sight from the room's entrance. If a piece will be coped on one end and mitered on the other, cut and fit the coped end first. All nailing points should be clearly labeled before you begin. At a minimum, every piece of trim should be nailed at each wall stud and at every ceiling joist, if installing cornice molding.

If you have never installed trim before or if it is likely that you won't be able to complete the project all at once, consider making a layout plan like the one shown on page 186. There is no absolutely right or wrong order for most tasks, but the chapters ahead dealing with the specific type of installation you'll be doing provide some helpful suggestions about sequencing your project. If you get confused about what to do next or can't remember where you left off, the layout plan will guide you through the installation.

Miter outside corners, cutting each piece at 45°. Use a pattern with mitered ends to help position your workpieces. Fasten the first piece of each joint to within 2 ft. of the corner, leaving some flexibility for making adjustments when you install the adjoining piece.

Removing Old Trim

Damaged trim moldings are an eyesore and a potentially dangerous splinter waiting to happen. There is no reason not to remove damaged moldings and replace them. Home centers and lumberyards sell many styles of moldings, but they may not stock the one you need, especially if you live in an older home. If you have trouble finding the trim you need, consider looking at home salvage stores in your area. They sometimes carry styles no longer manufactured.

Removing existing trim so that it can be reused is not always easy, especially if you live in a home with intricate moldings. Age of the trim and the nailing sequence used to install it greatly affect your ability to remove it without cracks or splits. Some moldings may be reusable in other areas of the home as well.

Whether you intend to reuse the trim or not, take your time and work patiently. It is always a good idea to remove trim carefully so you don't damage the finished walls, floor, or ceiling surrounding it.

Even trim that's been damaged should be removed carefully to avoid inflicting harm on innocent bystanders, like the baseboard behind the splintered base shoe above.

TOOLS & MATERIALS

Utility knife	Side cutters or end nippers
Flat pry bars (2)	Scrap plywood
Nail set	or dimensional lumber
Hammer	Eye protection
Metal file	Gloves

How to Remove Painted Moldings

Before removing painted trim, cut along the top seam of the molding and the wall with a new, sharp blade in a utility knife. Cut completely through the paint and caulk between the molding and the wall. If you wish to salvage the material, cut with the knife blade at a slight angle to avoid slipping and cutting across the face.

Work the molding away from the wall from one end to the other, prying at the nail locations. Apply pressure to the molding with your other hand to help draw it away from the wall. A wide joint compound or putty knife makes a good guard to insert between the tool and the wall.

How to Remove Clear-finish Moldings

Use large flat scraps of wood to protect finished surfaces from damage. Insert one bar beneath the trim and work the other between the base and wall. Force the pry bars in opposing directions to draw the molding away from the wall.

Remove the molding starting with the base shoe or the thinnest piece of trim. Pry off the trim with a flat bar using leverage rather than brute force and working from one end to the other. Tap the end of the bar with a hammer if necessary to free the trim.

How to Remove Nails

OPTION 1: Extraction. Use an end nippers or a side cutters to pull the nails from the moldings. Take advantage of the rounded head of the end nippers, "rolling" the nail out of the molding rather than pulling it straight out.

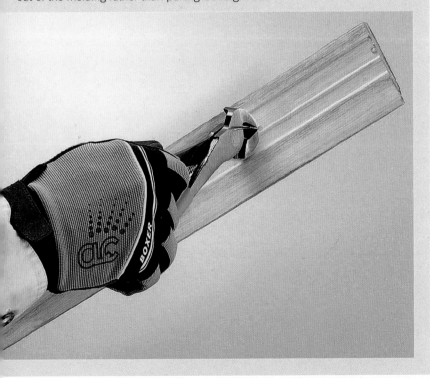

OPTION 2: Reversing course. Secure the workpiece with a gap beneath the nail and drive the nail through the molding from the front with a nail set and hammer.

Essential Trim Carpentry Skills

From nailing base shoe to cutting crown molding, most trim carpentry jobs require the same basic skill set. First (and probably foremost), you'll need to use reliable measuring techniques and apply them carefully to get accurate results. Simply running out the old tape measure and dashing off a couple of rough numbers won't do the trick. You'll need to learn the limitations of the measuring tools you use as well as some tricks for getting accurate readings in tight or irregular paces.

Taking the measurement is only half the battle: you'll also need to transfer the measurement to your workpiece, either with measuring tools or by using mechanical methods such as tracing. Then you can begin to worry about selecting the best cutting tool and making sure it is set up accurately.

Making the actual cut is not time-consuming, especially if you are using power tools. The best method is to make a creep cut: You secure the workpiece and make a slight cut just outside the cutting line. Then move the workpiece closer and closer to the blade until it is cutting right on the line. Once you've cut all your workpieces, they'll need sanding and perhaps some additional fitting before they are installed. In many cases, it makes sense to paint or finish the pieces prior to installation as well.

In this chapter:
- Measuring & Marking
- Cutting & Fitting Joints
- Finishing Trim
- Sanding Trim
- Painting Trim
- Clear-Coating Trim

Measuring & Marking

There are three keys to measuring accurately: taking the measurement, transferring the measurement, and hitting your mark when you make the final cut. The first two keys depend upon proper use of your measuring tools. You can take measurement upon measurement and doublecheck a dozen times, but if you're not using the correct tool techniques, your prospects for success are greatly diminished.

A retractable tape measure is the most important measuring tool for most trim carpenters (although it is definitely not the most accurate). Depending on whether you are taking an inside measurement or an outside measurement, you have to be aware of how a tape measure works. The hook at the end of the tape is secured by rivets that allow it to move. The amount that the hook moves is the same distance as the thickness of the hook itself. This allows you

to accurately transfer inside measurements to the material you are cutting. When you are measuring an inside measurement, make sure the hook is pushed in. The measurement starts from the outside of the hook. When you hook the tape onto your workpiece, make sure that the hook is pulled out. You are now transferring this measurement from the inside of the hook.

When you are marking your workpiece, use a mechanical pencil or a #2.5 lead pencil. The lead in a #2.5 is harder than a #2 pencil's lead, thus giving you a darker line. Try to make a single line mark. Multiple lines will become fat and you will lose accuracy. For very delicate cuts where great accuracy is required, use a marking knife to score a cutting line.

How to Measure from a Mitered Edge

Position the workpiece to be cut against an auxiliary fence on your miter saw so the inside of the miter is flush with the edge of the fence. Clamp the workpiece to the fence.

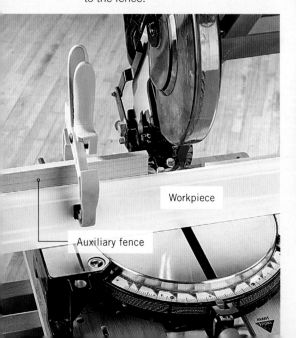

Workpiece

Auxiliary fence

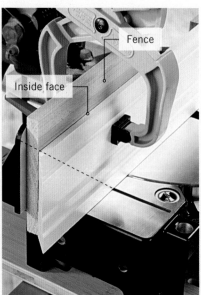

Fence

Inside face

Make sure the short (inside) face of the mitered board is aligned with the edge of the auxiliary fence exactly.

Place the hook of your tape measure against the end of the fence and pull the tape to transfer your measurement to the workpiece.

Using Measuring Tools

To mark a line parallel to the edge of a board, lock the blade at the desired measurement, then hold the tip of the pencil along the edge of the blade as you slide the tool along the workpiece. This is useful when marking reveal lines on window and door jambs.

Purchase a well-made 25-ft. tape measure for general trim projects. With the actual fractions printed on the tape, "easy-read" varieties are more user-friendly and help avoid confusion and cutting errors.

Use the trim piece as a measuring device, marking the cut line directly off the wall. Eliminating the tape measure can reduce errors and make it easier to visualize the cut.

Use a T-bevel to find the appropriate bevel angle for walls that are out of plumb and for many other angle measuring situations. Tighten the T-bevel and transfer the angle to your miter saw to set up for cutting the molding.

Scribe the back of a molding and check the mark with a square to determine whether or not the corner is plumb. If the scribe mark is not square, transfer the angle to your saw with a T-bevel and make a compound miter cut.

Cutting & Fitting Joints

Cutting and fitting joints is a skill that requires patience, knowledge, and well-maintained equipment to achieve effective results. There are a few basic joints that are generally used for most trim applications: butt, inside and outside miter, scarf, and coped joints.

Although cutting trim joints accurately is the key function of a power miter saw, it is not the only tool necessary for quality joinery. Coped joints require a coping saw as well as a set of metal files. For some trim applications such as frame-and-panel wainscot, fitting butt joints is simplified with the use of a biscuit jointer or a pocket hole jig. These are specialty tools designed for joining wood.

Cutting and fitting joints during installation can be very frustrating, especially when it involves difficult walls that are not plumb and corners that are out of square. Take the time to read through the proper techniques of using a miter saw as well as the correct method for cutting each individual joint. These techniques are described in detail to help you work through the imperfections found in every house and to avoid common problems during installation.

The first step to achieving an accurate cut is to set up your saws so they are true. On a power miter saw, check that the blade is perpendicular to the base and to the fence. The second step to making an accurate cut is to ensure that your workpiece is flat on the base and tight against the fence. This will not only ensure accurate cuts but will hold the workpiece firmly in place. Be sure to refer to the manufacturer's instructions when adjusting the saw.

Careful cutting is the hallmark of good joinery, be it for making furniture or installing trim moldings. Used correctly, a power miter saw offers the speed and precision to make your project look like it was done by a pro.

Cutting with a Power Miter Saw

There are two general types of power miter saw. The basic type cuts mitered angles when material is placed against the fence or beveled angles when material is placed flat on the work surface. The second type is called a compound miter saw. Compound saws allow you to cut a miter and a bevel simultaneously. The compound angle is extremely helpful in situations where a corner is out of plumb and a mitered angle requires a bevel to compensate. Some compound saws are available with a sliding feature that allows you to cut through wider stock with a smaller blade size. This option raises the cost of the saw considerably.

Waste side

Creep cuts. To avoid cutting off too much, start out by making a cut about ¼" to the waste side of the cutting line. Then nibble at the workpiece with one or more additional cuts until you have cut up to the cutting line. Wait until the blade stops before raising the arm on every cut.

Use stops on your saw base or saw stand to make uniform cuts of multiple pieces. If your saw or stand doesn't have adjustable stops or if the workpiece is longer than the saw stop capacity, clamp a wood block to the saw table or worksurface to function as a stop.

How to Cut Wide Stock

With a power miter saw: Make a full downward cut. Release the trigger and let the blade come to a full stop, then raise the saw arm. Flip the workpiece over and finish the cut.

Blade guard removed for clarity

With a sliding compound miter saw: Equipped with a saw carriage that slides away from the fence, these saws have greater cutting capacity than a nonsliding saw so they can cut wider stock. They're also more expensive, but you may find it worth renting one.

Mitering Outside Corners

Cutting outside miters is one of the main functions of a power miter saw. Most saws have positive stops (called detents) at 45° in each direction, so standard outside corners are practically cut for you by the saw. Keep in mind that your saw must be accurately set up to cut joints squarely. Read the owner's manual for setting up your saw as well as for safety precautions. Before you begin, check the walls for square with a combination square or a framing square. If the corner is very close to square, proceed with the square corner installation. If the corner is badly out of square, follow the "Out of Square" procedure on the following page.

TOOLS & MATERIALS

Combination square or framing square	Pneumatic finish nail gun
Miter saw	T-bevel
Pencil	Molding
Tape measure	Masking tape
Air compressor	1 × 4
Air hose	Eye protection

How to Miter Outside Corners

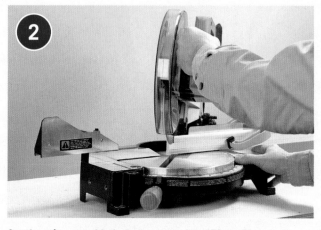

Set the miter saw to 45°. Position the first piece on edge, flat on the miter box table, flush against the fence. Hold the piece firmly in place with your left hand, and cut the trim with a slow, steady motion. Release the power button of the saw, and remove the molding after the blade stops.

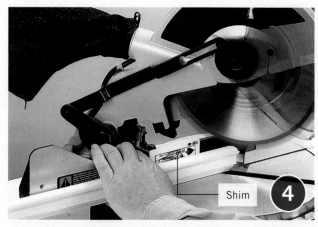

Set the miter saw blade to the opposing 45° positive stop. Place the second piece of molding on edge, flat on the saw table, flush against the fence. Fasten the piece tightly in place with a hold-down or clamp. Cut the molding with a slow, steady motion.

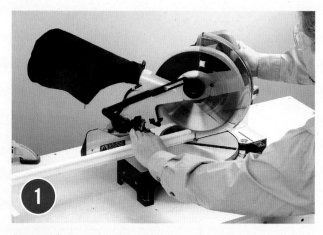

Stud location   Stud location

First piece

Second piece

With the first piece of molding tacked in place, hold the second piece in position and check the fit of the joint. If the joint is tight, nail both pieces at stud locations.

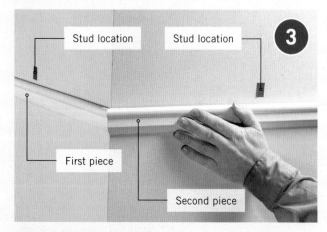

Shim

If the corner joint does not fit tightly, shim the workpiece away from the fence to make minor adjustments until the joint fits tightly. Shims should be a uniform thickness. Playing cards work well.

How to Miter Out-of-Square Outside Corners: Method 1

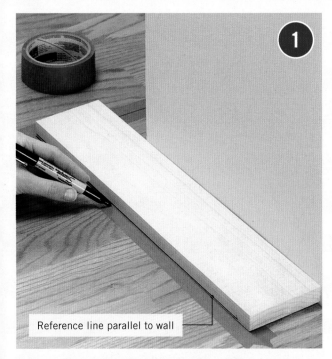

Reference line parallel to wall

Draw a reference line off each wall of the corner using a straight 1 × 4. Put masking tape down on the finished floor to avoid scuffing it and to see your lines clearly. Trace along each wall, connecting the traced lines at a point out from the tip of the corner.

To find the angle you need to miter your moldings, place a T-bevel with the handle flush against one wall, and adjust the blade so that it intersects the point where your reference lines meet. Lock the blade in place at this angle.

 # How to Miter Out-of-Square Outside Corners: Method 2

Use a digital angle finder to record the exact outside corner angle. These tools are sold in a wide price range, with some costing as little as $30.

Digital angle finder

Do some math. If the outside corner angle is not a whole number (most angle finders give readings in 0.1° increments), then round up. For example, if the angle finder measures the outside angle at 91.4°, round up to 92° and cut the miter at 44° (180° - 92° = 88° and the miter is half of this, which is 44°). A big mistake is to divide the angle in half without subtracting it from 180. In this case, a 92° angle readout divided in half would yield 46°, which at 2° off the mark would easily cause a visible mistake in the miter.

Mitering Inside Corners

Although most professionals prefer to cope-cut inside corners, it is common to see moldings that are mitered to inside corners. These joints are more likely to separate over time and to allow gaps to show. For that reason it is not advised to use inside corner miters when installing a stain-grade trim product. The gaps will be visible and are very difficult to fill with putty. For paint-grade projects, mitering inside corners makes more sense because joints can be filled and sanded before the top coats of paint are applied.

TOOLS & MATERIALS

Miter saw	Air compressor
Pencil	Air hose
Tape measure	Molding
Utility knife	T-bevel
Pneumatic finish nail gun	Eye protection

How to Miter Square Inside Corners

Set the miter saw to 45° and place the first piece of trim on edge, flat on the miter box table and flush against the fence. Hold the piece firmly in place with your left hand and cut the trim with a slow, steady motion. Release the power button and remove the molding after the blade stops.

Back-cut the inside edge of the trim piece with a utility knife so that the top corner will sit flush against the wall corner.

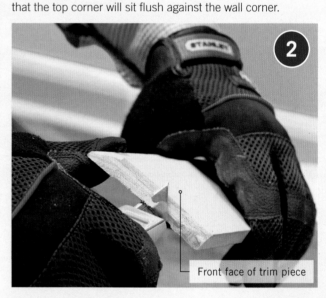

Front face of trim piece

Test the fit of the joint, adjusting the miter angle if necessary. Once the fit is tight, nail both pieces at stud locations.

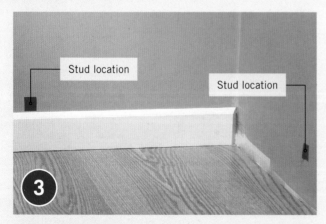

Stud location

Stud location

Butt the molding tightly against the wall and tack it into place. Adjust the blade of the miter saw to the opposite 45° angle, and cut the mating piece.

Out-of-Plumb Corner Cuts

Out-of-plumb walls are concave, convex, or simply not perpendicular to the floor and ceiling at one or more points. It is a common condition. In some cases, the condition is caused by the fact that drywall sheets have tapered edges to make taping joints easier and the tapers fall at the edge of a work area where trim is installed. In other cases, the condition may be caused by wall-framing issues. In either case, you'll find that it's easier to adapt your trim pieces to the wall than to try and straighten the finished wall surface. To do this, the trim pieces need to be cut to match the out-of-plumb area, to compensate for the taper in the panel. Another option is to install a running spacer along the bottom edge, and then to cut your molding square, as shown on the previous page.

TIP

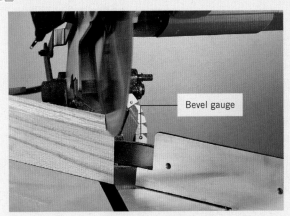

Bevel gauge

Occasionally, a compound cut is necessary for cutting miters on out-of-plumb corners. When this situation arises, set the bevel of the miter saw to match the out-of-plumb wall, and miter the angle at the appropriate degree. Compound cuts can be difficult to get right the first time, so test the fit with a piece of scrap material first.

How to Make Out-of-Plumb Corner Cuts

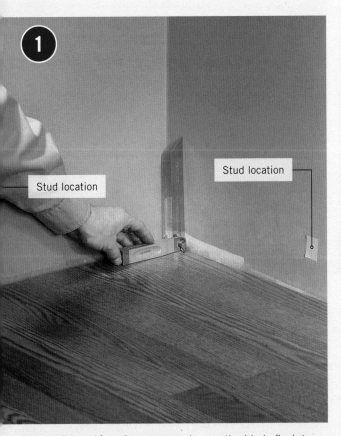

Stud location

Stud location

Place a T-bevel into the corner and press the blade flush to the wall surface. Tighten the adjustment knob so the blade conforms to the angle of the profile of the wall.

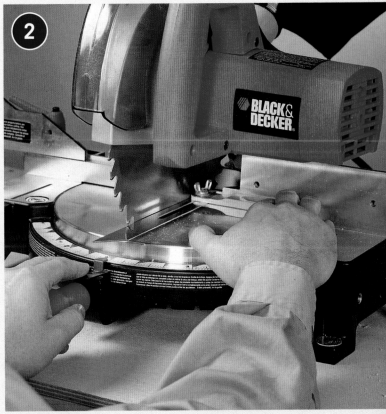

Transfer the angle of the T-bevel to the miter saw blade by locking the saw in the down position and adjusting the angle to match the angle of the T-bevel. Cut the molding to match the angle.

Making Coped Cuts

At first glance, coping moldings appears to be difficult work that only a professional would attempt. But in actuality, coping only requires patience and the right tools. Whether a molding is installed flat against the wall or is sprung to fill an inside corner junction, as with crown molding, the concept of coping is the same. It is essentially cutting back the body of a trim piece along its profile. This cutting is done at an angle so that only the face of the molding makes direct contact with the adjoining piece.

For beginners, coping a molding requires a coping saw, a utility knife, and a set of metal files with a variety of profiles. The initial cope cut is made with the coping saw, and the joint is fitted with a utility knife and files. This fitting can be a long process, especially when working with intricate crown moldings, but the results are superior to any other method.

TOOLS & MATERIALS

Miter saw	Pneumatic finish
Metal files or rasp set	nail gun
Utility knife	Air compressor
Pencil	Air hose
Tape measure	Molding
Coping saw	Eye protection

Coping is a tricky skill to learn, but a valuable capability to possess once you've got the process down. With very few exceptions, a coped cut can be made only with a handsaw (usually, a coping saw like the one shown above).

 How to Make Coped Cuts

Measure, cut, and install the first trim piece. Square-cut the ends, butting them tightly into the corners, and nail the workpiece at the marked stud locations.

Cut the second piece of molding at a 45° angle as if it were an inside miter. The cut edge reveals the profile of the cope cut.

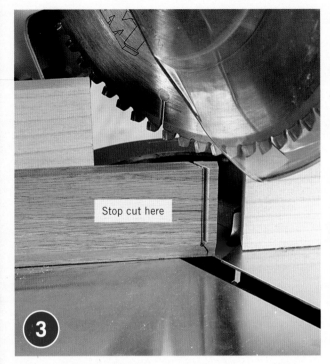

3

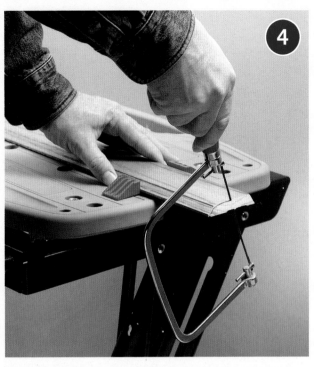

4

Make the long, straight cut along the edge of the molding. An easy, accurate way to do this is to use a power miter saw set at about a 2° miter. Use a spacer between the workpiece and the saw fence and cut through the workpiece, stopping just short of the profile.

The more traditional way to make this cut is to use a coping saw cutting at a 45° bevel. Finish cutting the profile with a coping saw.

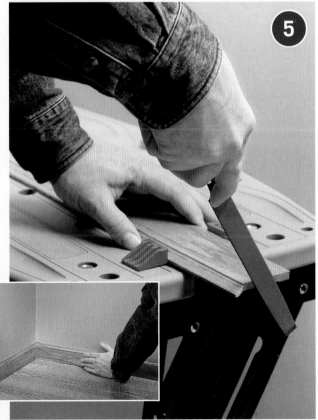

5

TIP: RASPS & FILES

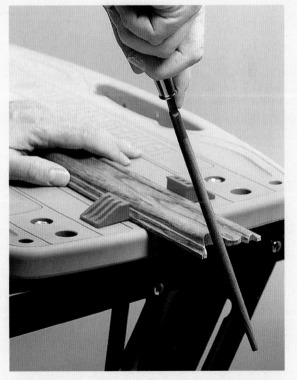

Test-fit the piece (inset photo) and use a metal file to fit the joint precisely. When the joint is properly fitted, nail the coped piece in place.

Trim components such as this chair rail can be complex to cope properly. A variety of rasps or metal files with different profiles is the key to fitting these joints tightly.

Cutting Mitered Returns

Mitered returns are a decorative treatment used to hide the end grain of wood and provide a finished appearance when molding stops prior to the end of a wall. Mitered returns range from tiny pieces of base shoe up to very large crown moldings. They are also commonly used when installing a stool and apron treatment or on decorative friezes above doors.

Bevel returns are another simple return option for chair rails, baseboards, and base shoe. A bevel return is simply a cut at the end of the molding that "returns" the workpiece back to the wall at an angle. The biggest advantage to using mitered returns rather than bevel returns is that mitered returns already have a finish applied. Bevel returns require more touchups.

Cutting mitered returns for small moldings, such as quarter round, or for thin stock, such as baseboard, can be tricky when using a power miter saw. The final cut of the process leaves the return loose where it can sometimes be thrown from the saw by the air current of the blade. Plan on using a piece of trim that is long enough to cut comfortably, or you will find yourself fighting the saw.

TOOLS & MATERIALS

Combination square	Air compressor
Utility knife	Air hose
Power miter saw	T-bevel
Miter box and back saw	Molding
Pencil	Wood glue
Tape measure	Eye protection
Pneumatic finish nail gun	

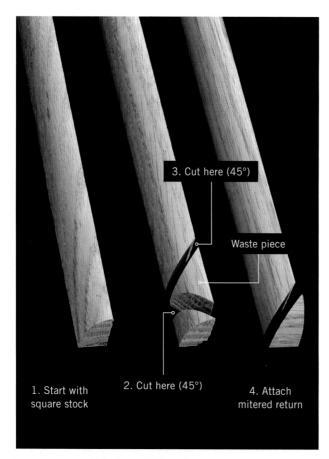

3. Cut here (45°)

Waste piece

1. Start with square stock

2. Cut here (45°)

4. Attach mitered return

Returns are made from two 45° angle cuts. The scrap piece is removed and the return piece is glued into place.

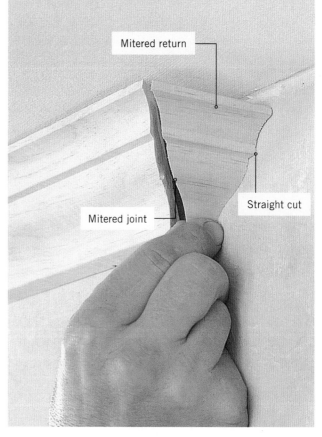

Mitered return

Straight cut

Mitered joint

Mitered returns finish molding ends that would otherwise be exposed. Miter the main piece as you would at an outside corner. Cut a miter on the return piece, then cut it to length with a straight cut so it butts to the wall. Attach the return piece with wood glue.

How to Cut Mitered Returns in Shoe

Cut the shoe molding to length, leaving an inside 45° miter at the end that is open or butts against door casing. Install the shoe (always nail shoe to the base trim, not to the floor). The shoe, at its longest point, should be aligned with the edge of the casing.

Mitered return

Mark the return: Cut a piece of shoe with the opposite miter to the installed piece. Draw a straight cutting line across the workpiece so it is the same thickness as the installed piece of shoe. Cut carefully along the cutting line.

Mitered return

Glue the return piece to the end of the installed piece of shoe to create a clean mitered return end that butts neatly against the casing.

Beveled return

OPTION: Instead of making a mitered return, make a partial miter cut to clip the corner of the square-cut base shoe, softening the line where it meets the casing.

Cutting Scarf Joints

Scarf joint is a technical term for the miter joint used to join two pieces of trim over a long length. This joint is not difficult to cut, but should always be laid out over a stud location so it can be properly fastened.

Whenever possible, position scarf joints so they point away from the main entry to the room (or another area from which the joint is most likely to be viewed). Doing so will hide the joint from view at a quick glance.

When forming scarf joints in moldings that will be painted, lightly sand the mating surfaces of the joint to flush out any imperfections, and fill any resulting gaps with filler. Prefinished stain-grade materials need to be tightly fitted and the nail holes filled with putty.

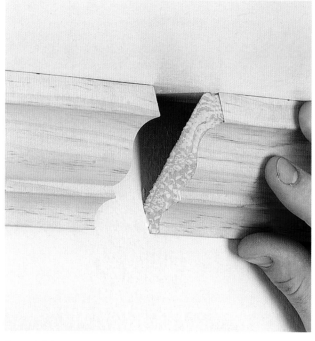

TOOLS & MATERIALS

Miter saw	Air compressor
Pencil	Air hose
Tape measure	Molding
Pneumatic finish nail gun	Eye Protection

A scarf joint is a glorified butt joint that's used to join two pieces of trim that are the same profile and are in line with one another. Scarf joints are easier to conceal than butt joints and also less prone to opening and showing gaps when humidity or temperature change.

TIP

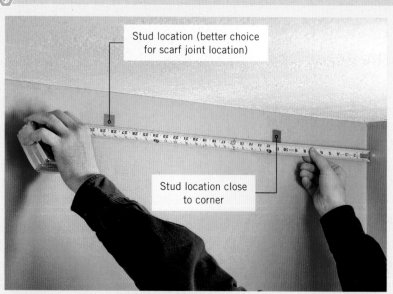

Stud location (better choice for scarf joint location)

Stud location close to corner

Determine the stud where the scarf joint will be located along the length of the run before cutting any of your stock. Divide the run as evenly as possible while optimizing material yield. In other words, avoid creating a joint too close to the end of the run because it can look unbalanced. Measure the length for the first piece of molding from the corner to the center of the stud location.

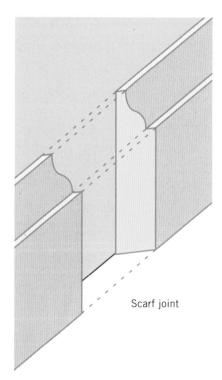

Scarf joint

Any type of molding can be joined into a longer segment with an angled scarf joint.

How to Cut a Scarf Joint

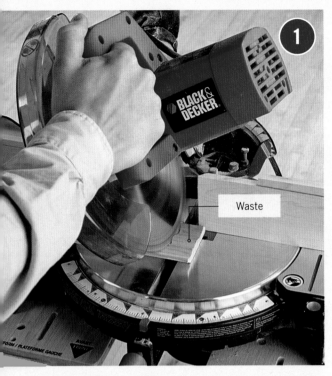

Lay the first mating board flat on a compound miter saw table with the top edge pressed against the fence and the waste portion of the workpiece on the right side of the blade. Make a 30° bevel cut.

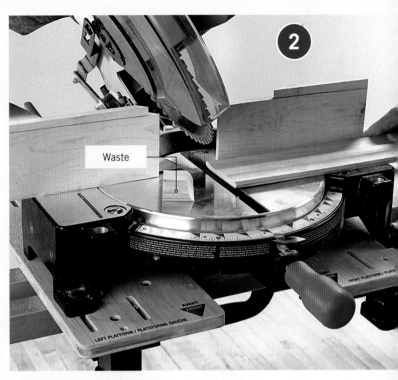

Set the second mating board onto the saw table with the waste portion left of the blade. Do not change the saw setup. Cut the workpiece with the same 30° bevel.

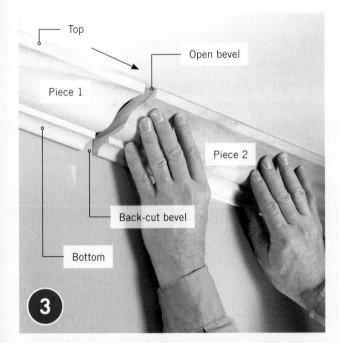

Test-fit the scarf joint on the wall (a helper is a great asset here). Have one person hold the piece with the open bevel (Piece 2 above) in position while the other person places the piece with the back-cut bevel over it. Check for a tight joint and then mark the back-cut piece for trimming to final length. If both ends of the run are inside corners, you'll have to overlap the open-cut piece and mark for cutting to length.

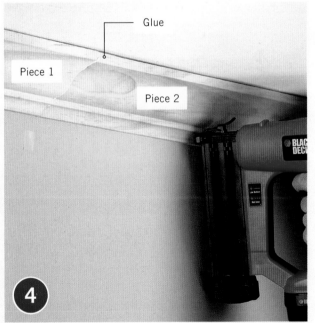

Tack the piece with the open bevel in position and apply wood glue (high-tack trim and molding glue is perfect here) to the open bevel. Re-form the scarf joint and tack the back-cut piece in position. Finish nailing around the joint and then work your way toward each end with the nailer.

Finishing Trim

Even the best trim installation can look bad if the finishing is done poorly. That's why the type of finish and the quality of that finish make such a big difference in the overall appearance of a room. Often, the finish of a trim project is overlooked entirely or done as an afterthought, and the installer may be so tired of working on the project that he or she does a lackluster job. To avoid this problem, finish as much of your trimwork as possible before you start to install. Paint-grade moldings should be primed on both sides and have one finish coat applied to the face. Stain-grade moldings should be stained and have two coats of polyurethane on the face and one coat on the backside. This way, after the moldings are installed, all you need to do is fill the nail holes and apply a final coat (and sometimes you can get away without the final coat).

Before you buy your material, you need to decide what type of finish you will be using. The basic choice is between a painted finish and a clear finish over natural wood.

If you are a novice do-it-yourselfer, consider making your first trim project one with a painted finish. Installing decorative crown molding with a lustrous wood finish might have great appeal for you, but starting out with a painted baseboard installation in a bedroom or utility-type room is more realistic. This project will allow you to practice cutting joints and dealing with trimwork that can be easily filled and puttied, before attempting the more difficult stain-grade project.

Although stain-grade trim projects usually are more expensive and take longer to finish than painted projects, the natural warmth and appearance of wood grain cannot be recreated with paint. Stained projects show off the quality of the trim material rather than covering it up.

To properly prepare your moldings for finish, place them on sawhorses or a workbench where they are easy to reach. When finish sanding, always sand with the grain of the wood, stepping your way up to the coarser grits as you work (each finer grit smooths out the sanding marks from the previous grit). After sanding all the pieces smooth, wipe them down with a dry cloth (or better yet, a tack cloth) to remove dust.

After applying each coat of polyurethane, primer, or paint, examine each piece of trim for surface problems like dribbles, pooling, or skip marks. These areas need to be dealt with in a timely fashion so they do not telegraph through the final coat.

Regardless of the type of finish you choose, take the time to prepare and properly finish your moldings. In the end, you'll be glad you did; your trim will look better, and the overall quality of your installation will improve.

Prefinish your moldings. Always apply one coat to the backs of the moldings to seal the entire piece and help balance wood movement.

Finishing Trimwork

Painted trim projects are easier for the novice do-it-yourselfer because nail holes and gaps in joinery (and other mistakes) are easier to conceal.

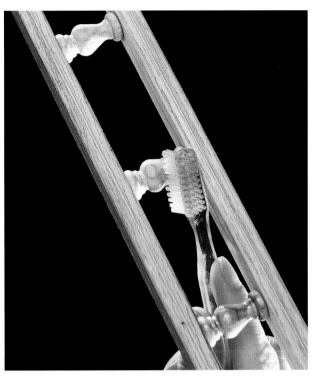

Use a soft toothbrush to apply brush-on finishes to hard-to-reach areas, like spindle-and-rail moldings and other ornamental trim pieces.

Gently but thoroughly stir clear topcoating products like polyurethane before and during application. Do not shake the product or air bubbles will develop in the liquid, leaving burst marks behind on the finished surface.

1. Attach waxed paper to wall before trim is nailed.

2. Pull waxed paper out after trim finish is applied and dry.

If you don't have time to prefinish your casings before installing, tape waxed paper to the walls before attaching the trim. Then when you apply your finish, the walls will already be masked off. Lap the seams so that any drips on the paper stay off the wall.

Sanding Trim

No matter what type of finish you apply, every piece of wood furniture requires sanding to ensure a smooth surface. Preparing trim pieces to accept stain, primer, or polyurethane is essentially the same process. The only difference is at which grit level you call the sanding complete.

Before you start sanding, do a visual check of each trim piece. Inspect the edges for splintering. Most splintering is easily sanded smooth, but larger splinters may need to be glued down. If you're installing clear-finished trim, look for large imperfections in the wood. The sections of trim containing these blemishes should not be used whenever possible. Mark the area of the molding around the blemish with pencil lines, and don't bother to sand it.

Most factory-made moldings are smooth enough off the shelf to start sanding at 100- or 120-grit. Grits below 100 are generally made for rough material removal, not sanding smooth. Trim used in painted projects generally is ready for primer after sanding at 120-grit. Stain-grade projects look better when the wood is sanded up to 150- or 180-grit.

Remember that the purpose behind sanding is to remove marks left from the machining process and leave a smooth surface to finish. Be careful to avoid rounding over the edges and any joint surfaces.

Choose tools and methods for sanding your trim pieces, and use them consistently for all grit levels. Sand the trim with long, even strokes running in the grain direction, and reposition the paper frequently to expose new grit to the material. When you are finished sanding, wipe the pieces down with a dry cloth or tack cloth before applying the finish.

Use foam-backed sandpaper for curved or intricate trim pieces to avoid sanding down the high points of the molding.

Mark large blemishes with a pencil, designating them as scrap material. Don't bother to sand these areas smooth.

Sanding Trim

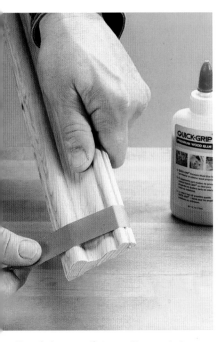

Repair large splinters with wood glue. Use masking tape to "clamp" the piece until the glue sets. Then remove the tape and sand the area smooth to remove excess glue.

Use a sanding block to smooth out flat surfaces evenly. Sanding blocks can also be made from scrap wood, such as a 2 × 4.

Wipe away the dust after the final sanding with a clean, dry cloth. Inspect the face of each piece one final time before applying the finish.

Sand very lightly between finish coats with 220-grit paper. This scratches the surface just enough for the next coat to adhere properly and also removes minor imperfections in the first finish coat.

Painting Trim

Paint-grade trim projects are easier to complete when the moldings have been prefinished. Although you will still need to apply the final topcoat after installation, this simplified method ensures that paint goes on evenly and helps avoid paint marks on finished walls and ceilings.

In their rush to get going on a trim project, many do-it-yourselfers completely skip coating the trim with primer and move right to finish paint. Primer is important. It creates a stronger bond with the raw material than paint alone, greatly reducing cracking and bubbling of the top coats. Primer also costs less than good-quality finish paint and can be tinted to match the finish color, reducing the number of necessary finish coats.

Trimwork is generally primed on both the front and back to seal the entire piece, balancing the wood movement from humidity and temperature changes. After the primer is dry, two finish coats are applied to the face. When the finish coats are dry, the molding can be installed. After installation, gaps in joints and fastener holes need to be filled. The final step is to apply a touchup coat to the filler areas.

Pour a paint additive into the mix to reduce brush marks on the finished product. A "cut bucket" like the one above is easier to handle than a gallon pail and creates a convenient way to mix the products.

Paint trim moldings with a higher-sheen paint than the surrounding walls. Paint with higher gloss is more durable and highlights the trim, drawing attention to interesting details.

Use a high-quality bristle brush to paint trimwork. Straightedge brushes around 2 inches are the tool of choice for many professional painters when painting moldings. Quality brushes have a shaped wooden handle and a sturdy, reinforced ferule made of noncorosive metal. Many also have flagged, or split, bristles with chiseled ends for precise work. If bristle marks are a concern, consider putting an additive in the paint. Paint additives thin the paint without affecting its durability or sheen. The result is a paint that flows on smoother and lays out flatter when dry. Using an additive may require that you apply at least one additonal coat.

After each coat of primer or paint is applied, carefully inspect each piece for drips or clots. These problems need to be dealt with quickly, or they will mirror through the final coat. Remember that multiple thin layers of paint look better and last longer than one heavy coat. Heavy layers will also hide any intricate details or crisp edging, and could possibly make installation more difficult.

Painting Trim

Dip the brush into the paint, loading one-third to one-half of its bristle length. Tap the bristles against the inside of the can to remove excess paint. Do not drag the bristles against the top edge or rub them against the lip of a one-gallon can.

Paint moldings with thin, even coats starting along the deeper grooves of the trim and moving on to the smooth areas. This sequence will minimize drips into the detail of the molding.

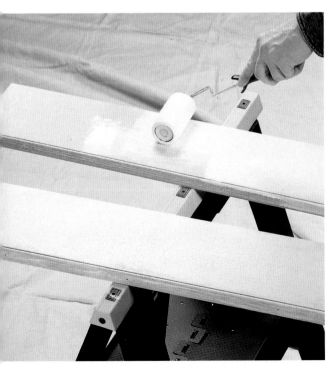

Use a small paint roller to coat long, straight strips of trim material. Rollers make for fast work and don't leave brush marks. If the paint is too thick or you roll too quickly, however, the roller can create an orange-peel effect that you may not like.

Clean the brush with mineral spirits when using oil-based paint or with warm water when using water-based. Shake out the brush and let it dry. Always start subsequent coats with a clean, dry brush.

Clear-Coating Trim

TOOLS & MATERIALS

Bristle brush or foam brush	Sawhorses
Latex gloves	Plastic bag (optional)
Stir sticks	Trim material
Paint can opener	Polyurethane
Drop cloth or cardboard	Stain (optional)

Water-based and oil-based finishes have a few basic differences in application and results that you should be aware of so that you can make the best decision about which product is right for you.

Not long ago, oil-based polyurethanes were regarded as much more durable and capable of providing more even coverage than water-based products. Today, this is not always the case. The major differences between modern oil and water urethanes are not related to finish quality as much as secondary (but important) characteristics such as odor, finish appearance, and drying times. The durability of water-based products is no longer an issue. In fact, the most durable urethanes available are water-based.

Oil products emit fumes during drying that can linger for weeks. Pregnant women and young children should avoid these fumes altogether. Water-based products create minimal fumes and are not dangerous under normal conditions with adequate ventilation.

According to most manufacturers, water-based products offer faster drying times than oil varieties. This literally means less time spent between coats. Water-based urethanes also clean up with soap and warm water, rather than mineral spirits. Easy cleanup can come in handy for large spills.

The biggest factor to consider when choosing a type of polyurethane is finish appearance. Although water-based products offer many more conveniences than oil, the results can be quite different. When oil-based urethanes are applied, they add a warm amber color to trimwork that creates more visual depth and variety.

Water-based products dry crystal clear. The color of the trim before the product is applied is similar to the finished product. Only a light color change appears. Keep in mind that most of the clear-finished trim in an older house is oil-based, and water-based finishes will not match.

The following examples run through the steps of successful clear-coat finishing. These steps are a guideline to finishing only. Always follow the manufacturer's specific application directions. Drying times will vary, depending on temperature and humidity.

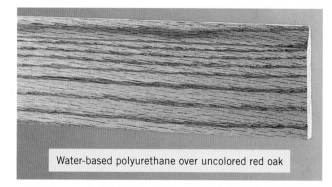

Water-based polyurethane over uncolored red oak

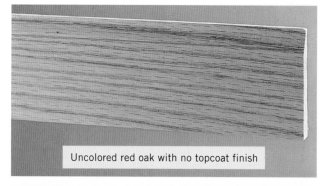

Uncolored red oak with no topcoat finish

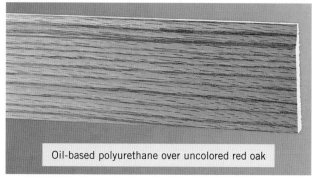

Oil-based polyurethane over uncolored red oak

The finished appearance of oil-based and water-based urethanes often differs. Oil-based products (bottom photo) tend to darken or yellow the trim, which can have the positive effect of highlighting grain characteristics. Water-based products (top photo) offer easier cleanup and faster drying times.

TIPS FOR WORKING WITH URETHANES

Always stir urethan products to properly mix them. Never shake them. Shaking creates tiny air bubbles in the product that will follow to your project. Before opening the can, roll it gently upside down a few times to loosen the settled material from the bottom.

Apply urethane in a well-ventilated area. Lack of ventilation or heavily applied product will result in longer drying times. If you use a fan to increase ventilation, aim it away from the project: do not blow air directly on the project or dust and other contaminants will adhere to your finish.

 How to Apply a Clear Finish

Set up the work station area with two sawhorses and a drop cloth or sheet of cardboard on the floor. Place the trim pieces to be finished on the horses. Inspect each piece for large blemishes or flaws, repairing any large splinters (see page 209).

Sand each piece as necessary, finishing with a fine-grit paper. Wipe the moldings with a clean, dry cloth to remove any leftover dust.

(continued)

If desired, apply a coat of stain to the moldings with a foam or bristle brush. For more even coverage of the stain, apply a pre-stain wood conditioner. Follow the manufacturer's instructions for stain drying time, and remove the excess with a clean rag.

Let the stain dry sufficiently and apply the first thin coat of polyurethane with a brush. Stir the polyurethane frequently before you begin, between coats, and during application. Let the finish dry for four to six hours.

After the finish has dried, lightly sand the entire surface with 220-grit sandpaper. This will ensure a smooth finish with a strong bond between layers. If the sandpaper gums up quickly, the moldings need more time to dry.

6 Wipe the moldings with a clean, dry rag to remove any dust. Apply a second layer of polyurethane. Check each piece for skipped areas and heavy drips of urethane. These areas need to be corrected as soon as possible or they may show through the final coat.

Let the moldings dry for four to six hours and lightly sand the entire surface with 220-grit sandpaper.

Apply a third and final coat of polyurethane to the moldings. Keep the third coat very thin, using only the tip of the brush to apply it. Lightly drag the tip across the molding on the flat areas. If the moldings have deep grooves or intricate details, skip these areas; two coats will be sufficient. Try to maintain constant pressure and avoid smashing the brush as this will create air bubbles in your finish. Allow the moldings to dry for a minimum of 12 hours (check the manufacturer's recommended drying times).

Low Battery

Nail Jam

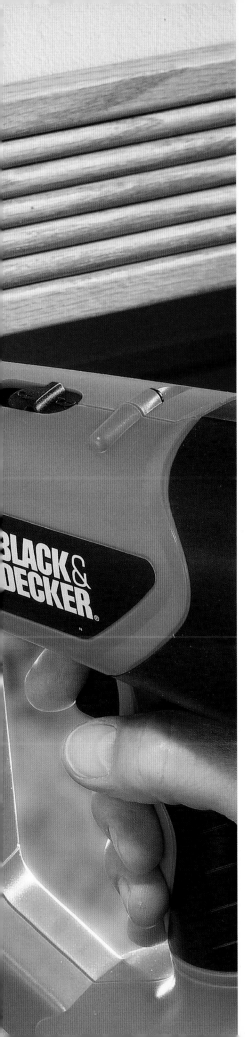

Trim Carpentry Projects

With a full set of trim carpentry skills safely under your tool belt, it's time to get to work. Simpler projects make good jumping off points. For example, install case molding around a window or door. Depending on the method you choose, even this simple project will involve cutting 45° miters—not hard, but if you're off you'll see it right away.

As you gain experience and confidence, tackle some more challenging trim carpentry projects, such as installing frame-and-panel wainscot or adding built-up crown molding to dress up a plain room. Once you've convinced yourself that your tools are not a complete menace to your materials, try upgrading to some hardwood trim stock. It's less forgiving and more expensive than paint-grade trim, but the warmth of real wood is well worth it in many homes.

In this chapter:

- One-piece Base Molding
- Built-up Base Molding
- Picture Rail
- Chair Rail
- Built-up Chair Rail
- Crown Molding
- Built-up Crown Molding
- Polymer Crown
- Basic Casing
- Window Stool & Apron
- Arts & Crafts Casing
- Basement Window Trim
- Wall Frame Moldings
- Wainscot Frames

One-piece Base Molding

Baseboard trim is installed to conceal the joint between the finished floor and the wallcovering (a necessary feature of a house). Installing plain, one-piece baseboard such as ranch-style base or cove base is a straightforward project. Outside corner joints are mitered, inside corners are coped, and long runs are joined with scarf cuts.

The biggest difficulty to installing base is dealing with out-of-plumb and nonsquare corners. However, a T-bevel makes these obstacles easy to overcome.

Plan the order of your installation prior to cutting any pieces, and lay out a specific piece for each length of wall. It may be helpful to mark the type of cut on the back of each piece so you don't have any confusion during the install.

Locate all studs and mark them with painter's tape 6 inches higher than your molding height. If you need to make any scarf joints along a wall, make sure they fall on the center of a stud. Before you begin nailing trim in place, take the time to pre-finish the moldings. Doing so will minimize the cleanup afterward.

Baseboard doesn't need to be fancy to be effective. Without a shoe or a cap, a plain, one-piece base molding makes a neat transition from floor to wall.

TOOLS & MATERIALS

Pencil	Pneumatic finish nail gun
Tape measure	& compressor
Power miter saw	Pneumatic fasteners
T-bevel	Carpenter's glue
Coping saw	Finishing putty
Metal file set	Eye protection
Moldings	

How to Install One-piece Base Molding

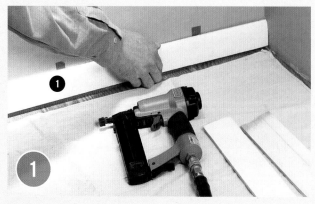

Measure, cut, and install the first piece of baseboard. Butt both ends into the corners tightly. For longer lengths, it is a good idea to cut the piece slightly oversized (up to ¹⁄₁₆" on strips over 10 ft. long) and "spring" it into place. Nail the molding in place with two nails at every stud location.

Cut the second piece of molding oversized by 6 to 10", and cope-cut the adjoining end to the first piece. Fine-tune the cope with a metal file and sandpaper. Dry-fit the joint, adjusting it as necessary to produce a tight-fitting joint.

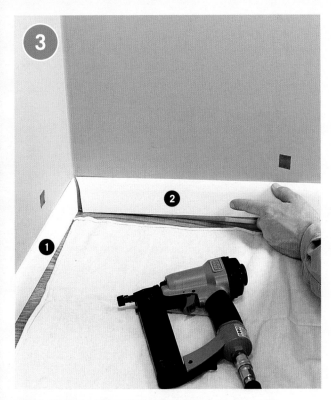

Check the corner for square with a framing square. If necessary, adjust the miter cut of your saw. Use a T-bevel to transfer the proper angle. Cut the second piece (coped) to length, and install it with two nails at each stud location.

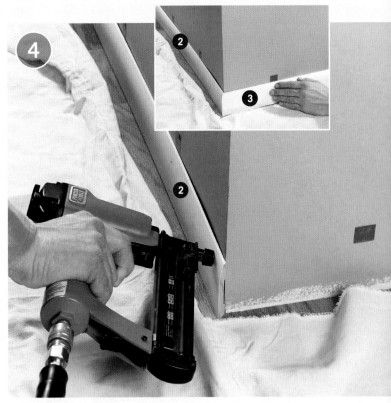

Adjust the miter angle of your saw to cut the adjoining outside corner piece. Test fit the cut to ensure a tight joint (inset photo). Remove the mating piece of trim, and fasten the first piece for the outside corner joint.

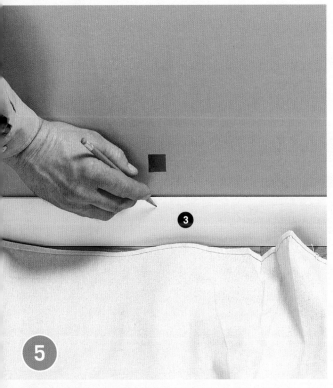

Lay out any scarf joints by placing the piece in position so that the previous joint is tight, and then marking the center of a stud location nearest the opposite end. Set the angle of your saw to a 30° angle, and cut the molding at the marked location (see pages 224 to 225).

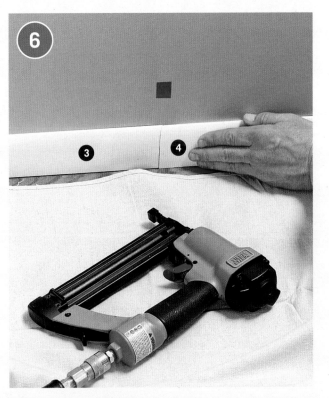

Nail the third piece in place, making sure the outside corner joint is tight. Cut the end of the fourth piece to match the scarf joint angle, and nail it in place with two nails at each stud location. Add the remaining pieces of molding, fill the nail holes with putty, and apply a final coat of finish.

Built-up Base Molding

Built-up base molding is made up of several strips of wood (usually three) that are combined for a particular effect. It is installed in two common scenarios: (1) to match existing trim in other rooms of a house or (2) to match a stock one-piece molding that is not available.

Installing a built-up base molding is no more difficult than a standard one-piece molding, because the same installation techniques are used. However, built-up base molding offers a few advantages over standard stock moldings. Wavy floors and walls are easier to conceal, and the height of the molding is completely up to you, making heat registers and other obstructions easier to deal with.

In this project, the base molding is made of high-grade plywood rather than solid stock lumber. Plywood is more economical and dimensionally stable than solid lumber and can be built up to any depth as well as cut down to any height. Keep in mind that plywood molding is less durable than solid wood and is only available in 8- and 10-foot lengths, making joints more frequent.

TOOLS & MATERIALS

Pneumatic finish nail gun	Nail set	Sandpaper	Base shoe molding
Air compressor	Tablesaw or straightedge guide and circular saw	Power sander	Cap molding
Air hose		¾" finish-grade oak plywood	2" finish nails, wood putty
Miter saw	Pencil		Eye protection
Hammer	Tape measure		

Built-up base trim is made by combining baseboard, base shoe, and another molding type, typically cap molding.

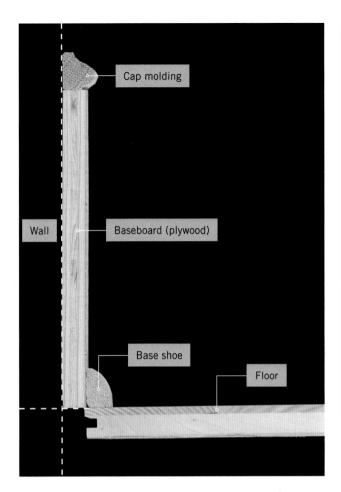

- Cap molding
- Wall
- Baseboard (plywood)
- Base shoe
- Floor

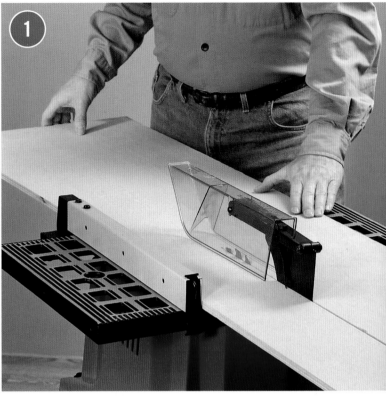

Cut the plywood panel into 6" strips with a tablesaw or a straightedge guide and a circular saw. Lightly sand the strips, removing any splinters left from the saw. Then apply the finish of your choice to the moldings and the plywood strips.

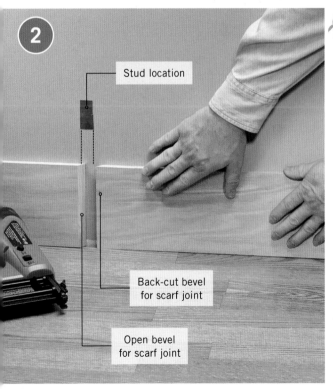

- Stud location
- Back-cut bevel for scarf joint
- Open bevel for scarf joint

Install the plywood strips with 2" finish nails driven at stud locations. Use scarf joints on continuous runs, driving pairs of fasteners into the joints. Cut and install moldings so that all scarf joints fall at stud locations.

BASE TRIM SPACERS

Baseboard can be built up on the back with spacer strips so it will project farther out from the wall. This can allow you to match existing casings or to create the impression of a thicker molding. However, the cap rail needs to be thick enough to cover the plywood edge completely, or the core of the panel may be visible.

Installing Built-up Base Molding

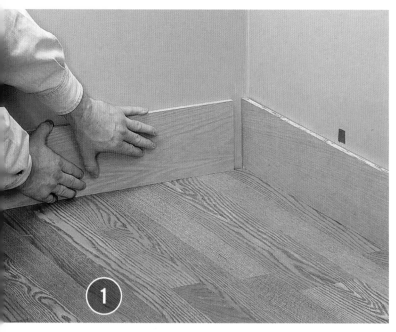

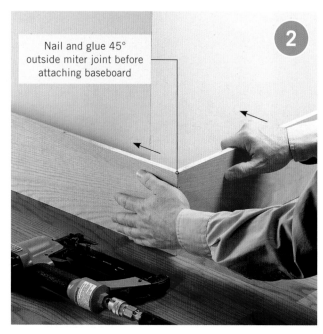

Nail and glue 45° outside miter joint before attaching baseboard

②

Test-fit inside corner butt joints before cutting a workpiece. If the walls are not square or straight, angle or bevel the end cut a few degrees to fit the profile of the adjoining piece. The cap molding will cover any gaps at the top of the joint. See illustration, page 220.

Miter outside corners squarely at 45°. Use wood glue and 1¼" brad nails to pull the mitered pieces tight, and then nail the base to the wall at stud locations with 2" finish nails. Small gaps at the bottom or top of the base molding will be covered with cap or base shoe.

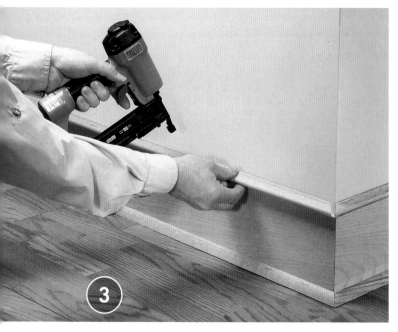

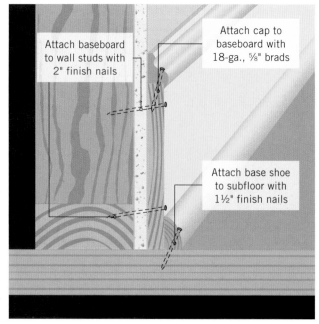

Attach baseboard to wall studs with 2" finish nails

Attach cap to baseboard with 18-ga., ⅝" brads

Attach base shoe to subfloor with 1½" finish nails

Use a brad nailer with 18-gauge, ⅝" brads to install the cap and base shoe moldings along the edges of the plywood base. Fit scarf joints on longer lengths, coped joints on inside corners, and miter joints on outside corners. Stagger the seams so that they do not line up with the base molding seams. Set any protruding nails with a nail set, and fill all nail holes with putty.

Built-up baseboard requires more attention to the nailing schedule than simple one-piece baseboards. The most important consideration (other than making sure your nails are all driven into studs or other solid wood), is that the base shoe must be attached to the floor, while the baseboard is attached to the wall. This way, as the gap between the wall and floor changes, the parts of the built-up molding can change with them.

Options with Heat Registers

Installing base molding around heat registers and cold-air returns can sometimes be challenging. Register thickness and height vary, complicating installation. Here are a few methods that can be employed for trimming around these obstructions.

Adjust the height of your baseboard to completely surround the heat register opening. Then cut a pocket out of the base for the heat register to slide into. Install the base shoe and cap trim molding continuously across the edges of the base board.

Install a taller backer block to encompass larger register openings. Cut a hole the same size as the duct opening in the backer block and cover the edges of the plywood with cap rail, mitering the rail at the corners. Butt the base molding into the sides of the register. Cut and install returns for the base shoe flush with the ends of the register.

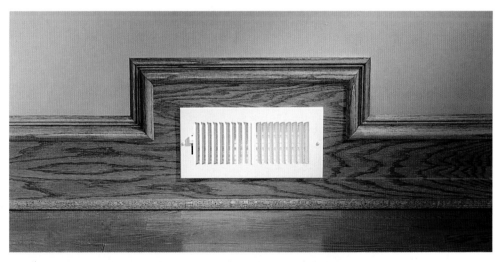

Install a wooden heat register for a less noticeable appearance. Wooden registers can be finished to match your trim and are available through most hardwood floor retailers. Butt the base molding into the ends of the register cover, and bevel the front edges of the base shoe to match the depth of the register.

Picture Rail

Picture rail molding is a specialty molding that was installed in many older homes so the homeowners could avoid making nail holes in the finished walls. Picture rail molding is a simple but elegant way to add style to any room. Special picture hanging hooks slide over the molding and artwork may be hung with a cord over the hook. Picture rail molding also provides its own decorative touch, breaking up the vertical lines from floor to ceiling. For this reason, it is also installed as a decorative touch by itself.

Picture rail molding is easy to install but should be reinforced with screws, not brads or nails, especially if you are hanging large, heavy items. Depending on the style of your home, picture rail can be hung anywhere from 1 foot to a few inches down from the ceiling. In some homes, picture rail is added just below the cornice or crown molding for an additional layer of depth. When applied this way, it is commonly referred to as a "sub-rail."

In the example shown, the picture rail is installed using a level line to maintain height. If your ceiling is uneven, you may choose to install picture rail a set distance from the ceiling to avoid an uneven appearance.

Picture rail may still be used as a support strip for hanging artwork, although more often it is installed solely for its decorative appeal.

How to Install Picture Rail Molding

Measure down the desired distance from the ceiling, and draw a level reference line around the room using a pencil and a 4-ft. level. Or use a laser level. Use a stud finder to locate the framing members, and mark the locations on the walls with blue painter's tape.

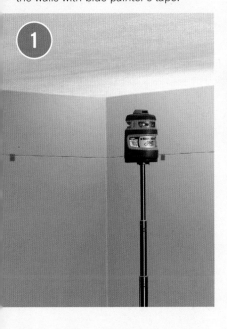

Calculate the cutting angle. First, adjust the saw blade so it is parallel to the arm of the T-bevel when the handle is flush against the saw fence. Note the number of degrees, if any, away from zero that the blade location reads. Subtract this number from 180 and divide by 2; this is your cutting angle.

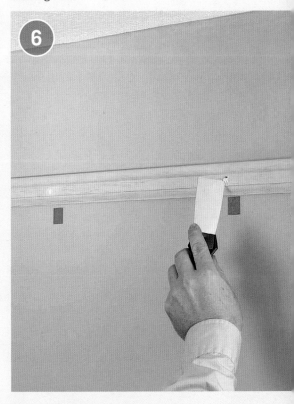

Use a T-bevel to measure the angle of the corner, tightening the lock nut with the blade and the handle on the reference line. Place the T-bevel on the table of your power miter saw, and adjust the miter blade so that it matches the angle.

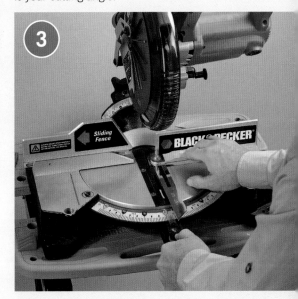

Cut both mating parts at the same bevel angle arrived at in step 3. When cutting picture rail, the molding should be positioned with the bottom edge resting on the table and the back face flat against the saw fence.

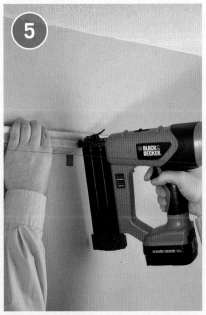

Nail the molding at the stud locations covering the level line around the room (if you're using a laser level, you simply keep it in position and turned on to cast a reference line you can follow). After each molding is completely nailed in place, go back to each stud location and drive 1⅝" drywall screws into the molding through counter-bored pilot holes.

Fill nail holes with wood filler. Let the filler dry and sand it smooth. Then apply a final coat of paint over the molding face.

Chair Rail

Chair rail molding typically runs horizontally along walls at a height of 32 to 36 inches (the rule of thumb is to install it one-third of the way up the wall). Originally installed to protect walls from chair backs, today chair rail is commonly used to divide a wall visually. Chair rail may cap wainscot, serve as a border for wallpaper, or divide two different colors on a wall. Or more interesting chair rail profiles can be effective alone on a one-color wall.

Stock chair rail moldings are available at most lumberyards and home centers. However, more intricate and elaborate chair rails can be crated by combining multiple pieces of trim.

Chair rail once was installed to protect fragile walls from chair backs, but today it is mainly installed as a decorative accent that visually breaks up dull walls.

TOOLS & MATERIALS

Pencil	4-ft. level	Metal file set	Carpenter's glue
Stud finder	Air compressor	Moldings	Finishing putty
Tape measure	Finish nail gun	Pneumatic fasteners	Finishing materials
Power miter saw	Coping saw	Painter's tape	Eye protection

How to Install Chair Rail

On the starting wall of your installation, measure up the desired height at which you plan to install the chair rail, minus the width of the molding. Mark a level line at this height around the room. Locate all studs along the walls, and mark their locations with painter's tape below the line.

Measure, cut, and install the first piece of chair rail with the ends cut squarely, butting into both walls (in a wall run with two inside corners). Nail the molding in place with two 2" finish nails at each stud location.

Miter-cut the second piece of molding with a power miter saw and then cope the end with a coping saw. Clean up the edge of the cope cut with a metal file to ensure a tight fit. Dry-fit the piece to check for any gaps in the joint.

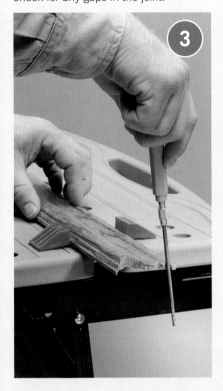

③

Coped joint

Coped piece

Butted piece

④

When the coped joint fits tightly, measure, mark, and cut the opposing end of the second piece of trim squarely with a miter saw. Nail the second piece in place with two nails at each stud location. Follow the level line with the bottom edge of the molding.

⑤

Install the third piece of chair rail with a cope cut at one end. Use a butt joint where the molding runs into door and window casings. Fill all nail holes with putty, and apply a final coat of finish to the molding.

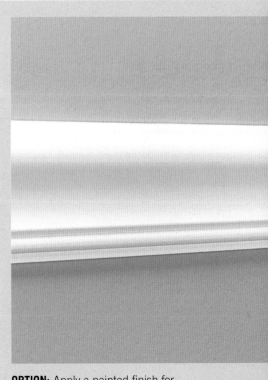

OPTION: Apply a painted finish for a more casual appearance. White semi-gloss is a safe choice.

Built-up Chair Rail

Designing and installing a built-up chair rail can be a very creative project that adds a considerable amount of style to any room. For the project shown, five smaller pieces of trim are combined with a 1 × 4 filler strip to create a bold, strong chair rail. If you are considering a larger built-up chair rail, make sure the existing base and crown moldings of the room will not be overshadowed. A good rule of scale to remember is that chair rail should always be smaller than the crown or base.

If you plan to design your own molding, the choices are just about endless. It is a good idea to mimic the style of your existing moldings so that the new chair rail will not look out of place. If the room you are installing in currently has no chair rail, consider new wall finishes as well. Two-tone painted walls will emphasize the transition of a chair rail, as will changing the finish from paint to wallpaper or wainscot.

A built-up chair rail is made of several styles of moldings, so the design options are virtually unlimited. The profile shown here features a strip of screen retainer on top of two pieces of profiled door stop. The stop molding is attached to a 1 × 4 filler that is then softened at the top and bottom edges with cover molding.

TOOLS & MATERIALS

Ladder	Drill with bits
Pencil	Painter's tape
Stud finder	Moldings
Tape measure	Pneumatic fasteners
Power miter saw	1⅝" drywall screws
Coping saw	Hole filler
Pneumatic finish nail gun & compressor	Finish materials
	Eye protection
4-ft. level or laser level	

Before you begin installing the molding pieces of the built-up chair rail, decide what type of return you will use. Returns are finish details that occur in areas where different moldings meet at perpendicular angles or quit in the middle of a wall. On some built-up chair rail, you can take advantage of the depth of the molding by butting the back moldings up to the obstructions but running the cap moldings onto the surface.

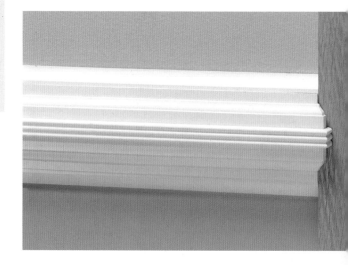

How to Install a Built-up Chair Rail

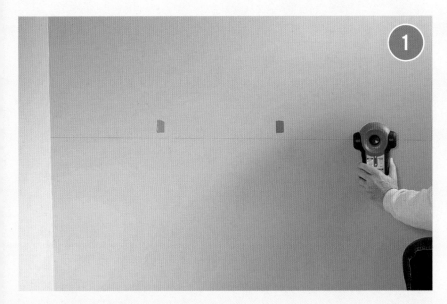

On the starting wall of your installation, mark the desired height of the first chair rail component you will install (here, the 1 × 4 filler strip). At this height, mark a level line around the room. Locate all studs along the walls, and mark their locations with painter's tape above the line.

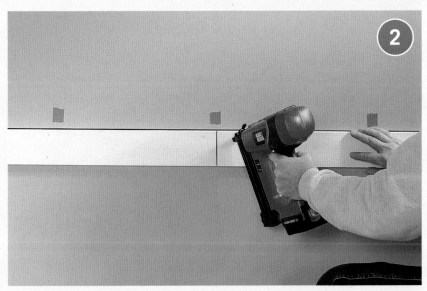

Cut and install the 1 × 4 filler strip so that the top edge of the strip follows the level line around the room. Fasten the strip with two 2½" finish nails driven at every stud location. Butt the ends of the filler strip together, keeping in mind that the joints will be covered by additional moldings.

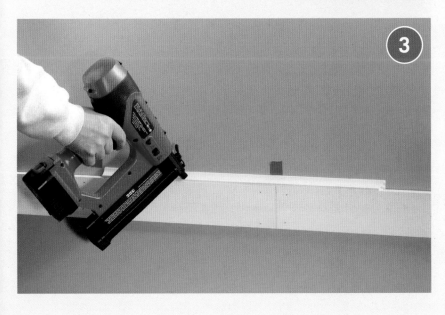

Cut and install the upper piece of cove molding around the room, nailing it flush to the top edge of the 1 × 4 filler strip. Use scarf joints on long runs, coped joints at inside corners, and mitered joints on outside corners. Drive one nail at every stud location into the wall and one nail between each stud down into the filler strip.

(continued)

Install the lower piece of cove molding
flush with the bottom edge of the filler
strip. Use the same nailing sequence
as with the upper cove molding. Cut
scarf joints on long runs, coped joints
at inside corners, and mitered joints on
outside corners.

Measure, cut, and install the upper
piece of stop molding around the room,
driving two 1½" finish nails at each stud
location. Cut scarf joints, coped joints,
and mitered joints as necessary for
each piece. Stagger the seams of the
scarf joints on the stop molding so that
they do not line up with the scarf joints
of the cove moldings.

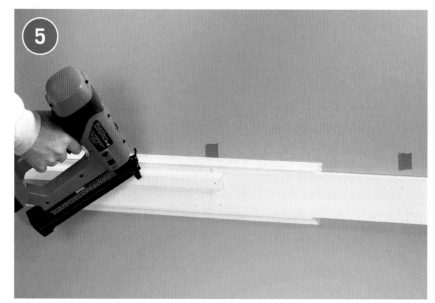

Install the lower piece of stop molding
around the room, keeping the edge of
the molding flush with the bottom edge
of the filler strip. Fit each joint using the
appropriate joinery method. Drive two
nails at each stud location.

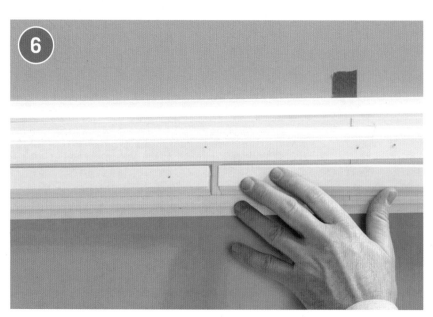

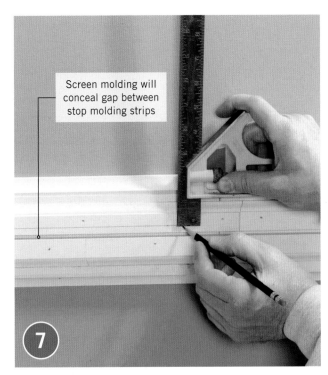

Screen molding will conceal gap between stop molding strips

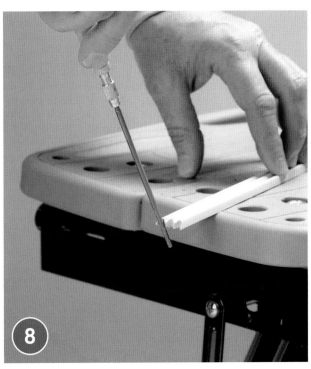

Set a combination square to 1⅜". Rest the body of the square on the top edge of the upper stop molding and use the blade of the square as a guide to mark a reference line around the room. This line represents the top edge of the screen molding.

Install the screen retainer molding, as with the other moldings, using the appropriate joints necessary. Fine-tune the cope cuts using a round metal file. Nail the molding in place with a brad nailer and 1⅝" brad nails. Keep the top edge of the molding flush with the reference line from Step 7.

Use a paintbrush to apply a final coat of paint to the moldings. Cover the finished floor with a drop cloth, and protect the lower portion of the wall from drips by masking it off with plastic if necessary.

Set any nail heads with a nail set, and fill all the nail holes with paintable wood filler. Check for any gaps in the joinery, and fill them as well. Let the filler dry, and sand it smooth with 180-grit sandpaper. Wipe the moldings with a dry cloth to remove any dust.

Crown Molding

Simply put, crown molding is angled trim that bridges the joint between the ceiling and the wall. In order to cover this joint effectively, crown moldings are "sprung." This means that the top and bottom edges of the molding have been beveled, so when the molding is tilted away from the wall at an angle, the tops and bottoms are flush on the wall and ceiling surfaces. Some crown moldings have a 45° angle at both the top and the bottom edges; another common style ("38° crown") has a 38° angle on one edge and a 52° angle on the other edge.

Installing crown molding can be a challenging and sometimes confusing process. Joints may be difficult for you to visualize before cutting, and wall and ceiling irregularities can be hard to overcome. If you have not worked on crown molding joints before, it is recommended that your first attempt be made with paint-grade materials. Stain-grade crown is commonly made of solid hardwood stock, which makes for expensive cutting errors and difficulty concealing irregularities in joints.

Inside corner joints of crown molding should be cope-cut, not mitered, except in the case of very intricate profile crown that is virtually impossible to cope (and must therefore be mitered). While mitering inside corners may appear to save time and produce adequate results, after a few changing seasons the joints will open up and be even more difficult to conceal.

Installing crown molding in a brand-new, perfectly square room is one thing, but what happens when the walls and ceilings don't meet at perfect right angles? In most houses that have been around for more than a couple of seasons, walls have bulges caused by warped studs or improper stud placement that's causing the drywall to push out into the room. Ceilings have issues caused by warped joists or drywall that has loosened or pulled away from the ceiling joists. Corners may be best finished with extra-thick layers of joint compound that has been applied a bit heavily, causing an outside corner piece to sit further away from the corner bead. These are just a few of the issues that can work against you and cause even an experienced carpenter to become frustrated.

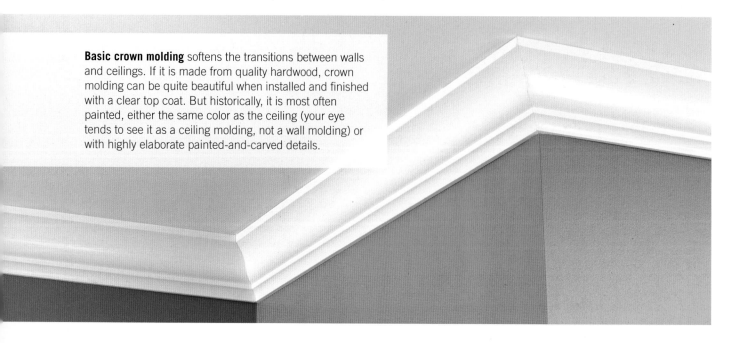

Basic crown molding softens the transitions between walls and ceilings. If it is made from quality hardwood, crown molding can be quite beautiful when installed and finished with a clear top coat. But historically, it is most often painted, either the same color as the ceiling (your eye tends to see it as a ceiling molding, not a wall molding) or with highly elaborate painted-and-carved details.

HOW TO MAKE A GAUGE BLOCK

Make and use a gauge block to ensure that crown molding is installed uniformly. A gauge block is used to show where the bottom edge of the crown will sit on the wall. This is especially important for laying out inside and outside corners. To make a gauge block, place the profile of crown upside down against the fence of your saw. The top edge of the crown should lay flat against the base. The fence represents the wall, and the base represents the ceiling. The crown will be situated in the same position as it would sit on the wall. Run a pencil line across the bottom edge of the crown. Tape can be placed against the fence to help see the pencil marks. Measure from the base to this line and subtract $\frac{1}{16}$". Cut a block to this measurement, and label it to match the profile of crown that you're installing.

Cutting compound miters is tricky. Throughout this book, crown molding is shown being mitered with the workpiece held against a fence or fence extension. This hand-held approach is quick and effective but takes some getting used to. A practically foolproof option is to use an adjustable jig, such as the compound miter jig shown here.

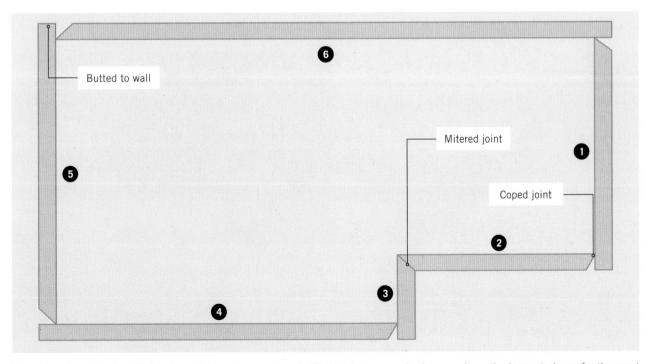

Plan the order of the installation to minimize the number of difficult joints on each piece, and use the longest pieces for the most visible sections of wall. Notice that the left end of first piece is cope-cut rather than butted into the wall. Cope-cutting the first end eliminates the need to cope-cut both ends of the final piece and places the cuts in the same direction. This simplifies your installation, making the method to cut each piece similar.

How to Use Backers to Install Crown Molding

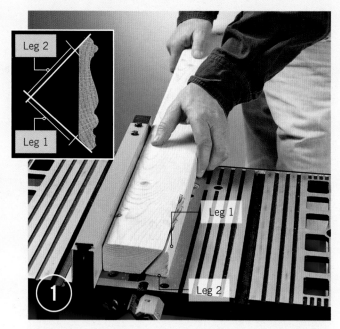

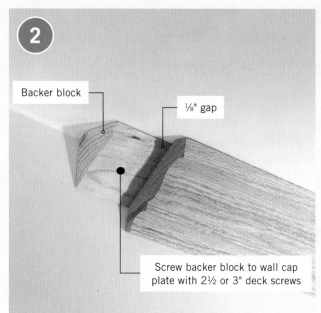

Installing crown molding is greatly simplified if you first attach triangular backers in the crotch area between the walls and ceilings. You can run the backers continuously along all walls, or you can space them at regular intervals for use as nailers. To measure the required length for the triangle legs, set a piece of the crown molding in the sprung position in a square in an orientation like the inset photo above. Rip triangular backer strips from 2× stock on your tablesaw, with the blade set at 45°.

Locate the wall studs with a stud finder, and mark the locations on the wall with blue painter's tape. Secure the backer block to the wall by driving 2½ or 3" deck screws at an angle through the block and into the top plate of the wall. Now, your crown molding can be attached to the backers wherever you'd like to nail it. Install crown according to the following instructions.

 # How to Install Basic Crown Molding

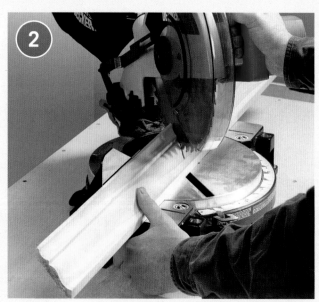

Cut a piece of crown molding about 1-ft. long with square ends. Temporarily install the piece in the corner of the last installation wall with two screws driven into the blocking. This piece serves as a template for the first cope cut on the first piece of molding.

Place the first piece of molding upside down and sprung against the fence of the miter saw. Mark a reference line on the fence for placement of future moldings, and cut the first coped end with an inside miter cut to reveal the profile of the piece.

Measure, cut to length, and install the first piece of crown molding, leaving the end near the temporary scrap loose for final fitting of the last piece. Nail the molding at the top and bottom of each stud location.

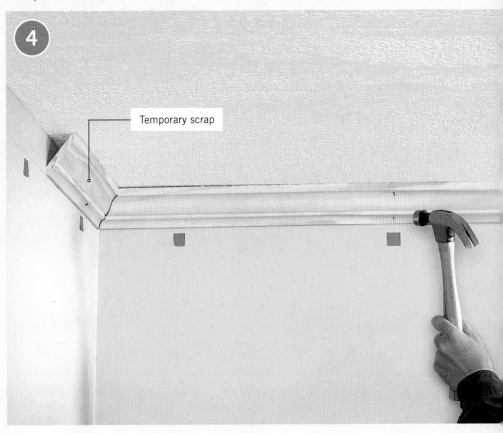

Temporary scrap

Cope-cut the end of the first piece with a coping saw. Carefully cut along the profile, angling the saw as you cut to back-bevel the cope. Test-fit the coped cut against the temporary scrap from step 1. Fine-tune the cut with files and fine-grit sandpaper.

Position the actual stock so a cut end is flush against the wall at one end and, at the other end, mark the outside corner on the back edge of the molding. Miter-cut the piece at the mark, according to the angles you noted on the test pieces.

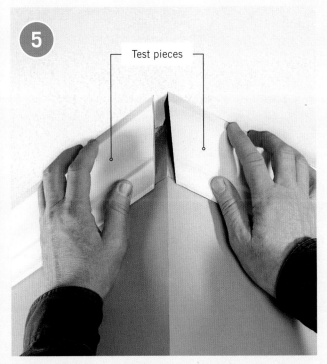

Test pieces

Cut two test pieces to check the fit of outside corners. Start with each molding cut at 45°, adjusting the angles larger or smaller until the joints are tight. Make sure the test moldings are properly aligned and are flush with the ceiling and walls. Make a note of your saw settings once the joint fits tightly.

(continued)

7

Measure and cut the third piece with an outside corner miter to match the angle of your test pieces. Cut the other end squarely, butting it into the corner. Install the piece with nails driven at stud locations. Install the subsequent pieces of crown molding, coping the front end and butting the other as you work around the room.

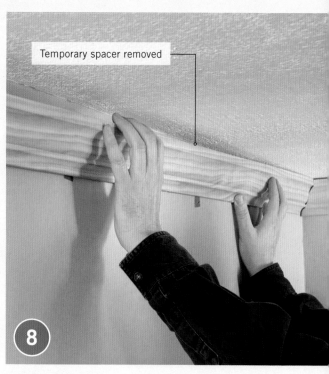

8

Temporary spacer removed

To fit the final piece, cope the end and cut it to length. Remove the temporary scrap piece from step 3, and slide the last molding into position. Nail the last piece at the stud locations when the joints fit well, and finish nailing the first piece.

9

Fill all nail holes. Use spackling compound if painting; wait until the finish is applied, and fill with tinted putty for clear finishes. Use a putty knife to force spackling compound or tinted wood putty into loose joints, and caulk gaps ⅛" or smaller between the molding and the wall or ceiling with flexible, paintable, latex caulk.

10

Lightly sand the filled nail holes and joint gaps with fine sandpaper. Sand the nail hole flush with the surface of the moldings, and apply a final coat of paint to the entire project.

How to Install Crown at a Sagging Ceiling

Gauge block

Make light pencil marks on the wall to show where the bottom of the crown will sit.

TIP: Make and use a gauge block for this (see page 233). This is especially important on outside corners.

Score the drywall slightly in the sagging portion of the ceiling. Set the crown along the lines made by the gauge block and the top of the point where the drywall is scored. Mark the edges of the sagging area in a visible spot on the walls.

Use a small wood block to drive the sagging drywall up where it meets the wall. Don't get too aggressive here.

Install the crown so the bottom edge is flush with the gauge line. The molding will conceal the damage to the drywall.

Built-up Crown Molding

Built-up crown molding is a multi-piece assembly created by joining several trim boards, usually including at least one crown profile, on the wall and the ceiling. Often referred to as cornice molding, these built-up combinations can be truly striking in appearance, especially at and around outside corners. By using careful layout techniques and building simple mock-ups, this complex-looking process can become relatively simple. In large part, this is because the material that is installed both on the ceiling and on the wall can function as a backer, giving the crown molding that's featured in the assembly a secure surface area for nailing. Be creative and experiment with different combinations of trim to come up with a unique design of your own.

BUILT-UP OPTIONS

Create a mock-up of the built-up molding assembly you're planning to install. Fasten 12"-long pieces of each type together in the intended orientation. If you are undecided among multiple combinations, make a mock-up of each so you can compare them.

TOOLS & MATERIALS

Power miter saw	1½" finish (8d) or pneumatic (16-gauge) nails	Wood glue
Finish nailer		Utility knife
Measuring tape	#2.5 pencil	Eye protection

Built-up crown molding creates a bit of old-world charm in any setting. The three-piece interpretation seen here is made with two pieces of baseboard and a piece of crown.

How to Install a Built-up Crown

1

Remove any old crown molding in the cornice area. Use a utility knife to cut through old paint and caulk between the molding and the wall or ceiling. Then use a pry bar to work the crown molding loose in small sections. Be sure to brace the end of the pry bar on the inside of the crown and pull downward. Do not pry upwards; this can damage the ceiling.

2

Use a mock-up of the built-up molding as a marking gauge to establish a baseline for the bottom of the assembly on the wall. Start in the corners and work your way around the room. This will allow you to see how the ceiling rises and falls so you know where to install the first piece.

3

Make a reference line for the top of the built-up assembly, using the mock-up as a gauge.

TIP

To measure a wall when working alone, first make a mark on the wall or ceiling exactly 10" out from one corner. Then, press the tab against the wall at the other end, measure to the marked line, and add 10" to the measurement.

(continued)

Install the base (lowest) molding around the entire room first. The bottoms of the base pieces should be flush against the bottom line that was scribed using the mock-up as a gauge. Do not try to push the trim up against the ceiling; it must be flush with the base line. Any gaps at the top will be hidden by subsequent trim pieces.

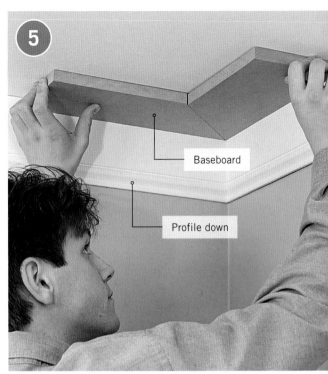

Find the correct miter angles for installing the flat ceiling trim. Cut two scraps of stock at 45°, and test how well they fit together in the corner. Adjust the cuts as needed to form a corner that has a neat miter with both sides flush against the wall.

Install the second trim profile parts all around the perimeter of the room. Typically, this will be flat moldings (with or without an edge profile) installed flat against the ceiling and mitered at the corners.

Install the final piece, which is usually crown molding that fits against the flat wall molding and the ceiling molding. It is best to use coped joints at the inside corners (see page 200). Sand, fill the nail holes, and finish the built-up cornice as desired (if you have not prefinished all the parts).

Use picture rail (page 224) to enhance a cornice molding. Standard height for picture rail is about 10 to 12" below the ceiling, but you can place it at any level. For a simple variation of the project shown, use square-edged stock for the band (since the bottom edge will mostly be hidden), and add picture rail just below the band. Be sure to leave enough room for placing picture hooks.

Install blocking to provide a nailing surface and added bulk to a built-up cornice. In this simple arrangement, a 2 × 2 block, or nailing strip, is screwed to the wall studs. A facing made from 1 × 2 finish lumber is nailed to the blocking and is trimmed along the ceiling with quarter-round. The crown molding is nailed to the wall studs along the bottom and to the nailer along the top.

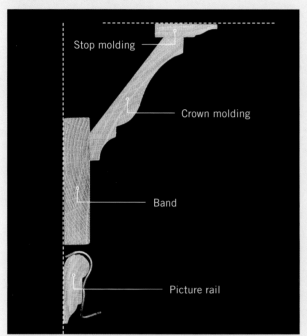

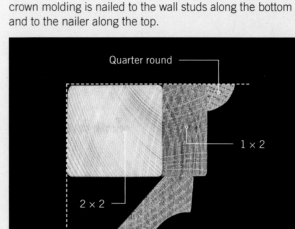
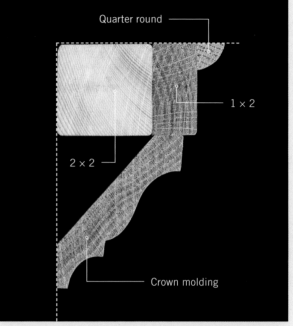

Built-up cornice treatments can be as simple or complex as you would like. This Arts & Crafts variation is made of flat solid stock ripped down to specific dimensions. Two pieces of 1 × 2 stock are fastened together to form an L-shaped angle. The angle is then screwed to the wall at the stud locations. An additional piece of 1" wide stock is nailed in place so the top edge is flush with the installed angle. This configuration creates a stepped cornice with a simpler appearance than the traditional sprung moldings. Notice that the L angle is nailed together with a slight gap at the back edge. This is done to compensate for irregularities in the corner joint.

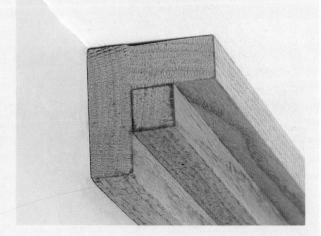

This highly detailed Victorian-style built-up cornice is made of several pieces of stock trim and solid stock ripped down to different widths. The right-angle component of this cornice may be screwed directly to the wall, to serve both a decorative function as well as serve as a nailer for the other trim elements. The screw holes are covered when the crown molding is installed.

Polymer Crown

TOOLS & MATERIALS

Drill with countersink-piloting bit

Power miter saw or hand miter box and fine-tooth saw

Caulk gun

Putty knife

Crown molding

Finish nails

150-grit sandpaper

Rag

Mineral spirits

Polymer adhesive

2" drywall screws

Vinyl spackling compound

Paintable latex caulk

Eye protection

Polymer moldings come in a variety of ornate, single-piece styles that offer easy installation and maintenance. The polystyrene or polyurethane material is as easy to cut as softwood, but unlike wood, the material won't shrink and it can be repaired with vinyl spackling compound.

You can buy polymer molding preprimed for painting, or you can stain it with a nonpenetrating heavy-body stain or gel. Most polymers come in 12-foot lengths, and some have corner blocks that eliminate corner cuts. There are even flexible moldings for curved walls.

How to Install Polymer Crown Molding

Plan the layout of the molding pieces by measuring the walls of the room and making light pencil marks at the joint locations. For each piece that starts or ends at a corner, add 12 to 24" to compensate for waste. If possible, avoid pieces shorter than 36" because short pieces are more difficult to fit.

Hold a section of molding against the wall and ceiling in the finished position. Make light pencil marks on the wall every 12" along the bottom edge of the molding. Remove the molding, and tack a finish nail at each mark. The nails will hold the molding in place while the adhesive dries. If the wall surface is plaster, drill pilot holes for the nails.

To make the miter cuts for the first corner, position the molding faceup in a miter box. Set the ceiling side of the molding against the horizontal table of the miter box, and set the wall side against the vertical back fence. Make the cut at 45°.

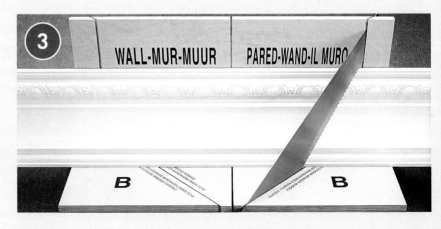

WALL-MUR-MUUR   PARED-WAND-IL MURO

B   B

(4) **Check the uncut ends** of each molding piece before installing it. Make sure mating pieces will butt together squarely in a tight joint. Cut all square ends at 90°, using a miter saw or hand miter box.

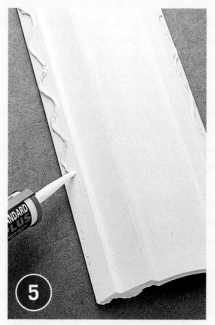

(5) **Lightly sand the backs of the molding** that will contact the wall and ceiling, using 150-grit sandpaper. Slightly dampen a rag with mineral spirits, and wipe away the dust. Run a small bead of polymer adhesive (recommended or supplied by the manufacturer) along both sanded edges.

(6) **Set the molding in place** with the mitered end tight to the corner and the bottom edge resting on the nails. Press along the molding edges to create a good bond. At each end of the piece, drive 2" drywall screws through countersunk pilot holes through the flats and into the ceiling and wall.

(7) **Cut, sand, and glue the next piece of molding.** Apply a bead of adhesive to the end where the installed molding will meet the new piece. Install the new piece, and secure the ends with screws, making sure the ends are joined properly. Install the remaining molding pieces, and let the adhesive dry.

(8) **Carefully remove the finish nails** and fill the nail holes with vinyl spackling compound. Fill the screw holes in the molding and any gaps in the joints with paintable latex caulk or filler, and wipe away excess caulk with a damp cloth or a wet finger. Smooth the caulk over the holes so it's flush with the surface.

Basic Casing

TOOLS & MATERIALS

Tape measure	Straightedge
Drill	Miter saw
Pencil	Casing material
Nail set	Baseboard molding and
Hammer or	corner blocks (optional)
pneumatic nailer	4d and 6d finish nails
Level	Wood putty
Combination square	Eye protection

Stock wood casings provide an attractive border around window and door openings while covering the gaps between the wall surface and the window jamb. Install casings with a consistent reveal between the inside edges of the jambs and the edges of the casings.

In order to fit casings properly, the jambs and wall surfaces must be in the same plane. If one of them protrudes, the casing will not lie flush. To solve this problem, you may need to shave the edges of the jambs down with a block plane. Or you may need to attach jamb extensions to the window or door to match the plane of the wall. For small differences where a drywall surface is too high, you can sometimes use a hammer to compress the drywall around the jambs to allow the casings to lie flush.

Drywall screws rely on the strength of untorn face paper to support the panel. If the paper around the screws becomes torn, drive additional screws nearby where the paper is still intact.

Simple case molding installed with mitered corners is a very common approach to trimming windows and doors. While it lacks visual interest, it is easy to install and relatively inexpensive.

How to Install Mitered Casing on Windows & Doors

On each jamb, mark a reveal line ³⁄₁₆ to ¼" from the inside edge. The casings will be installed flush with these lines.

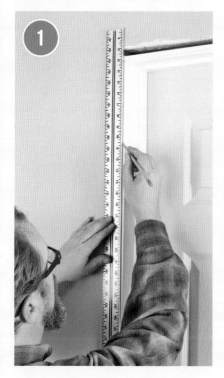

Make 45° miter cuts on the ends of the moldings. Measure and cut the other vertical molding piece, using the same method.

Place a length of casing along one side jamb, flush with the reveal line. At the top and bottom of the molding, mark the points where horizontal and vertical reveal lines meet. (When working with doors, mark the molding at the top only.)

Drill pilot holes spaced every 12" to prevent splitting, and attach the vertical casings with 4d finish nails driven through the casings and into the jambs. Drive 6d finish nails into the framing members near the outside edge of the casings.

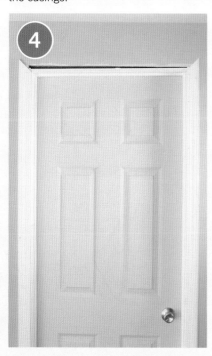

Locknail the corner joints by drilling pilot holes and driving 4d finish nails through each corner, as shown. Drive all nail heads below the wood surface, using a nail set, then fill the nail holes with wood putty.

Measure the distance between the side casings and cut top and bottom casings to fit, with ends mitered at 45°. If the window or door unit is not perfectly square, make test cuts on scrap pieces to find the correct angle of the joints. Drill pilot holes and attach with 4d and 6d finish nails.

Window Stool & Apron

Stool and apron trim brings a traditional look to a window and is most commonly used with double-hung styles. The stool serves as an interior sill; the apron (or the bottom casing) conceals the gap between the stool and the finished wall.

In many cases, such as with 2 × 6 walls, jamb extensions made from 1× finish-grade lumber need to be installed to bring the window jambs flush with the finished wall. Many window manufacturers also sell jamb extensions for their windows.

The stool is usually made from 1× finish-grade lumber, cut to fit the rough opening, with "horns" at each end extending along the wall for the side casings to butt against. The horns extend beyond the outer edge of the casing by the same amount that the front edge of the stool extends past the face of the casing, usually under 1 inch.

If the edge of the stool is rounded, beveled, or otherwise decoratively routed, you can create a more finished appearance by returning the ends of the stool to hide the end grain. A pair of miter cuts at the rough horn will create the perfect cap piece for wrapping the grain of the front edge of the stool around the horn. The same can be done for an apron cut from a molded casing.

As with any trim project, tight joints are the secret to a successful stool and apron trim job. Take your time to ensure all the pieces fit tightly. Also, use a pneumatic nailer; you don't want to spend all that time shimming the jambs perfectly only to knock them out of position with one bad swing of a hammer.

The window stool and apron give the window a finished appearance while offering the practical advantage of a window sill.

 **SAFETY TIP**

Back-cut the ends of casing pieces where needed to help create tight joints, using a sharp utility knife.

 TOOLS & MATERIALS

Tape measure	1× finish lumber
Straightedge	Casing
Circular saw or jigsaw	Wood shims
Handsaw, plane, or rasp	4d, 6d, and 8d finish nails
Drill	Utility knife
Hammer	Eye protection
Pneumatic nailer (optional)	

How to Install Stool & Apron Window Trim

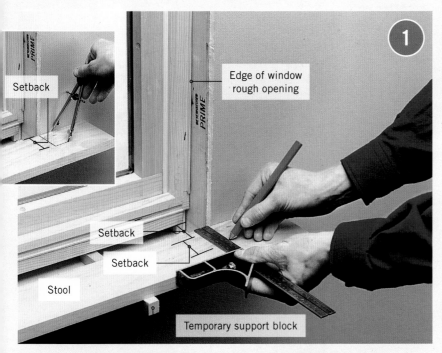

Setback

Edge of window rough opening

Setback

Setback

Stool

Temporary support block

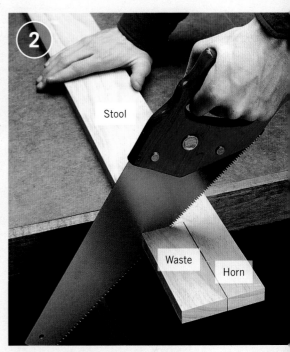

Stool

Waste

Horn

Cut the board for the stool to length, with several extra inches at each end for the horns. Temporarily position the stool in the window opening, pressed against the wall and centered on the window. Use a combination square to measure the setback distance from the window frame to the near edge of the stool. Mark the setback onto the stool at each edge of the window rough opening (if the measurements are different, use the greater setback distance for each end). Then use a compass and pencil to scribe the profile of the wall onto the stool to complete the cutting line for the horn (inset photo).

Cut out the notches to create the stool horns. For straight lines, you can use a large handsaw, but for the scribed line use a more maneuverable saw like the jigsaw or a coping saw. Test-fit the stool, making any minor adjustments with a plane or a rasp so it fits tightly to the window frame and flush against the walls.

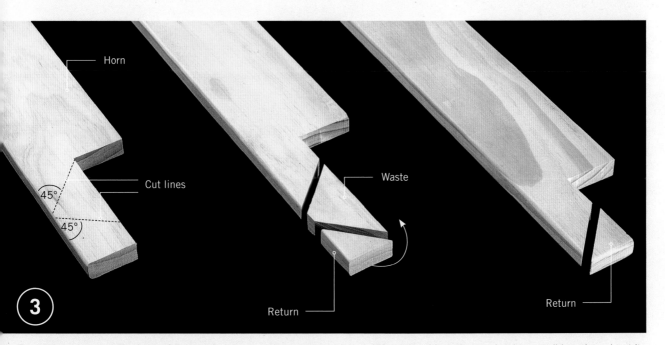

Horn

Cut lines

Waste

45°

45°

Return

Return

To create a return at the horn of the stool, miter-cut the return pieces at 45° angles. Mark the stool at its overall length and cut it to size with 45° miter cuts. Glue the return to the mitered end of the horn so the grain wraps around the corner.

NOTE: Use this same technique to create the returns on the apron, but make the cuts with the apron held on edge, rather than flat.

(continued)

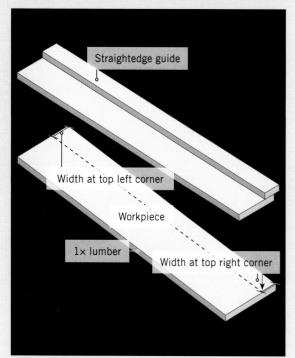

Straightedge guide

Width at top left corner

Workpiece

1× lumber

Width at top right corner

Where jamb extensions are needed, cut the head extension to its finished length—the distance between the window side jambs plus the thickness of both side extensions (typically 1× stock). For the width, measure the distance between the window jamb and the finished wall at each corner; then mark the measurements on the ends of the extension. Use a straightedge to draw a reference line connecting the points. Build a simple cutting jig, as shown.

Clamp the jig on the reference line, and rip the extension to width. Using a circular saw, keep the baseplate tight against the jig and move the saw smoothly through the board. Reposition the clamp when you near the end of the cut. Cut both side extensions to length and width, using the same technique as for the head extension (see TIP at left).

④

Apply wood glue to the back edge of the frame, and position it against the front edge of the window jambs. Use wood shims to adjust the frame, making sure the pieces are flush with the window jambs. Fasten the frame at each shim location, using 8d finish nails driven through pilot holes. Loosely pack insulation between the studs and the jambs, or use minimal-expanding spray foam.

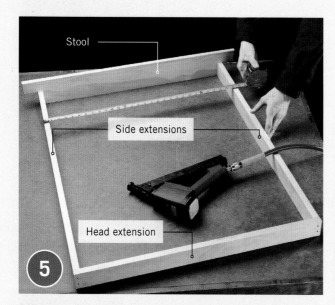

Stool

Side extensions

Head extension

⑤

Build a box frame with the extensions and stool, using 6d finish nails and a pneumatic nailer. Measure to make sure the box has the same dimensions as the window jambs. Drive nails through the top of the head extension into the side extensions and through the bottom of the stool into side extensions.

⑥

Reveal mark

Reveal

7

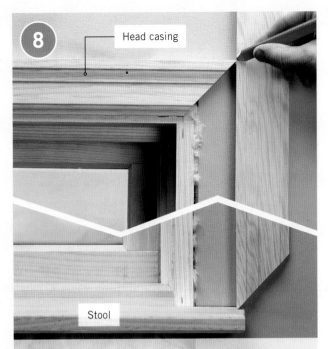

8

Head casing

Stool

On the edge of each jamb or jamb extension, mark a ³⁄₁₆ to ¼" reveal. Place a length of casing along the head extension, aligned with the reveal marks at the corners. Mark where the reveal marks intersect, then make 45° miter cuts at each point. Reposition the casing at the head extension and attach, using 4d finish nails at the extensions and 6d finish nails at the framing members.

Cut the side casings to rough length, leaving the ends slightly long for final trimming. Miter one end at 45°. With the pointed end on the stool, mark the height of the side casing at the top edge of the head casing.

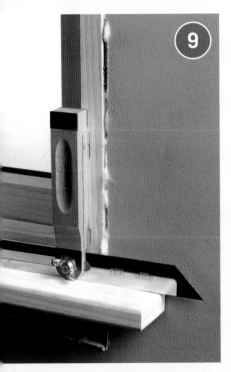

9

Test-fit the casings, making any final adjustments with a plane or rasp. Fasten the casing with 4d finish nails at the extensions and 6d finish nails at the framing members.

10

11

To get a tight fit for side casings, align one side of a T-bevel with the reveal, mark the side extension, and position the other side flush against the horn. Transfer the angle from the T-bevel to the end of the casing, and cut the casing to length.

Cut the apron to length, leaving a few inches at each end for creating the returns (step 3). Position the apron tight against the bottom edge of the stool, and then attach it, using 6d finish nails driven every 12".

Arts & Crafts Casing

Traditional Arts & Crafts casings are made of simple, flat materials with little to no decorative molding trimmed out of the stock. Add nonmitered corners to the mix, and this casing becomes as plain as possible. The back band installed on the perimeter of this project is optional, but it adds depth to the window treatment while maintaining a simple style.

Traditionally, the wood used for this style of trim is quartersawn oak. The term "quartersawn" refers to the method of milling the material. Quartersawn oak is easily distinguishable from plain-sawn oak by its tight grain pattern laced with rays of lighter color also known as rifts. Quartersawn oak is more expensive than plain oak and may only be available at lumberyards or hardwood supply stores, depending upon your area. Either plain-sawn or quartersawn oak will fit the style of this casing.

To begin the installation of this trim style, refer to pages 246 and 249 to read the step-by-step process for installing jamb extensions, if necessary, and the stool portion of this project.

The Arts & Crafts style is similar to the overall look and feel of Mission furniture, as can be seen in this relatively simple oak window casing.

TOOLS & MATERIALS

Tape measure	Handsaw	Compass	Wood shims
Straightedge	Plane or rasp	Nail set	4d, 6d, and 8d finish nails
Power miter saw	Drill hammer	1 × 4 finish lumber	Finishing putty
Circular saw or jigsaw	Pneumatic nailer	Back band trim	Eye protection
	Combination square		

How to Install Arts & Crafts Casing

Follow the step-by-step process on pages 247 to 249 to install the stool and jamb extensions. Set a combination square to $\frac{3}{16}$ or $\frac{1}{4}$" and mark a reveal line on the top and side jambs.

1

2

To find the length of the head casing and apron, measure the distance between the reveal lines on the side jambs, and add twice the width of the side casings. Cut the head casing and the apron to length. Install the head casing flush with the top reveal line. Use a scrap piece of trim to line up the head casing horizontally.

3

Measure and cut the side casings to length. Install them flush with the reveal lines. Make sure the joints at the top and bottom are tight. Measure the distance to the end of the stool from the outer edge of the side casing. Install the apron tight to the bottom of the stool at the same dimension from the end of the stool.

Back band

4

Measure, cut, and install the back band around the perimeter of the window casings, mitering the joints at the corners. Continue the back band around the edge of the apron, mitering the corners. Nail the back band in place with 4d finish nails.

Basement Window Trim

TOOLS & MATERIALS

Pencil
Tape measure
Tablesaw
Drill with bits
2-ft. level
Framing square
Utility knife
Straightedge
Miter saw
Router and router table
Clamps
Spray-foam insulation
Finish-grade ¾" oak plywood
Composite or cedar wood shims
1¼, 2" finish nails
1⅝" drywall screws
Carpenter's glue
Eye protection

Basement windows bring much-needed sunlight into dark areas, but even in finished basements they often get ignored on the trim front. This is partly because most basement foundation walls are at least 8 inches thick, often a lot thicker. Add a furred-out wall and the window starts to look more like a tunnel with a pane of glass at the end. But with some well-designed and well-executed trim carpentry, you can turn the depth disadvantage into a positive.

A basement window opening may be finished with drywall, but the easiest way to trim one is by making extrawide custom jambs that extend from the inside face of the window frame to the interior wall surface. Because of the extra width, plywood stock is a good choice for the custom jambs. The project shown here is created with veneer-core plywood with oak veneer surface. The jamb members are fastened together into a nice square frame using rabbet joints at the corner. The frame is scribed and installed as a single unit and then trimmed out with oak casing. The casing is applied flush with the inside edges of the frame opening. If you prefer to have a reveal edge around the interior edge of the casing, you will need to add a solid hardwood strip to the edge of the frame so the plies of the plywood are not visible.

Because they are set into thick foundation walls, basement windows present a bit of a trimming challenge. But the thickness of the foundation wall also lets you create a handy ledge that's deep enough to hold potted plants or even sunning cats.

Check to make sure the window frame and surrounding area are dry and free of rot, mold, or damage. At all four corners of the basement window, measure from the inside edge of the window frame to the wall surface. Add 1" to the longest of these measurements.

Set your tablesaw to make a rip cut to the width arrived at in step 1. If you don't have a tablesaw, set up a circular saw and straightedge cutting guide to cut strips to this length. With a fine-tooth panel-cutting blade, rip enough plywood strips to make the four jamb frame components.

Cross-cut the plywood strips to correct lengths. In our case, we designed the jamb frame to be the exact same outside dimensions as the window frame, since there was some space between the jamb frame and the rough opening.

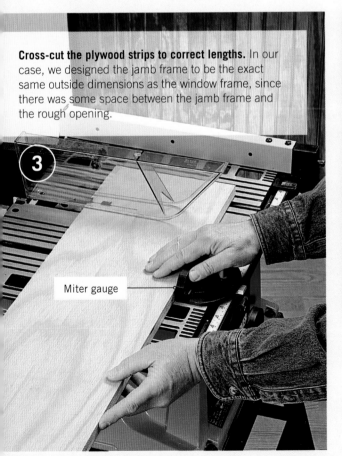

Miter gauge

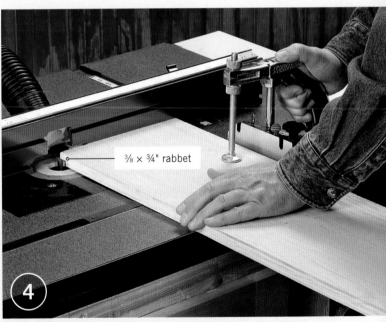

⅜ × ¾" rabbet

Cut ⅜-deep × ¾"-wide rabbets at each end of the head jamb and the sill jamb. A router table is the best tool for this job, but you may use a tablesaw or handsaws and chisels. Inspect the jambs first, and cut the rabbets in whichever face is in better condition. To ensure uniformity, we ganged the two jambs together (they're the same length). It's also a good idea to include backer boards to prevent tearout.

(continued)

Glue and clamp the frame parts together, making sure to clamp near each end from both directions. Set a carpenter's square inside the frame, and check it to make sure it's square.

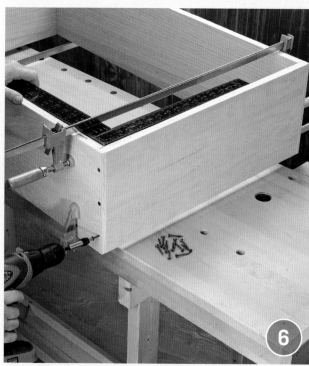

Before the glue sets, carefully drill three perpendicular pilot holes, countersunk, through the rabbeted workpieces and into the side jambs at each corner. Space the pilot holes evenly, keeping the end ones at least ¾" in from the end. Drive a 1⅝" drywall screw into each pilot hole, taking care not to overdrive. Double check each corner for square as you work, adjusting the clamps if needed.

Let the glue dry for at least one hour (overnight is better). Then remove the clamps and set the frame in the window opening. Adjust the frame so it is centered and level in the opening and the exterior-side edges fit flush against the window frame.

Taking care not to disturb the frame's position (rest a heavy tool on the sill to hold it in place if you wish), press a steel rule against the wall surface and mark trimming points at the point where the rule meets the jambs at each side of all four frame corners, using a sharp pencil.

Remove the frame and clamp it on a flat work surface.
Use a straightedge to connect the scribe marks at the
ends of each jamb frame side. Set the cutting depth
of your circular saw to just a small fraction over ¾".
Clamp a straightedge guide to the frame so the saw
blade will follow the cutting line, and trim each frame
side in succession. (The advantage to using a circular
saw here is that any tearout from the blade will be on
the nonvisible faces of the frame).

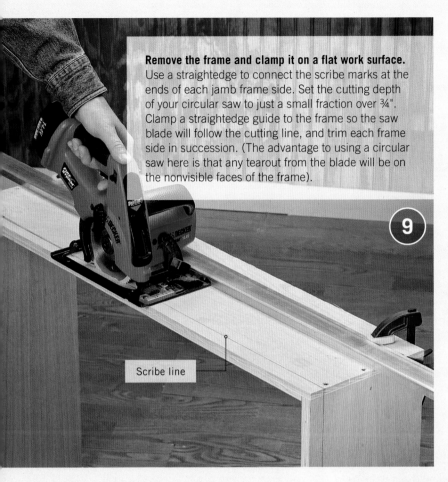

Scribe line

Replace the frame in the window
opening in the same orientation as when
you scribed it, and install shims until it is
level and centered in the opening. Drive
a few finish nails (hand or pneumatic)
through the side jambs into the rough
frame. Also drive a few nails through the
sill jamb. Most trim carpenters do not
drive nails into the head jamb.

Insulate between the jamb frame and the rough frame with
spray-in polyurethane foam. Look for minimal-expanding foam
labeled "window and door," and don't spray in too much. Let
the foam dry for a half hour or so, and then trim off the excess
with a utility knife.

TIP: Protect the wood surfaces near the edges with wide
strips of masking tape.

Remove the masking tape, and clean up the mess from the
foam (there is always some). Install case molding. We used
picture-frame techniques to install fairly simple oak casing.

Wall Frame Moldings

Adding wall frame moldings is a traditional decorative technique used to highlight special features of a room, divide large walls into smaller sections, or simply add interest to plain surfaces. You can paint the molding the same color as the walls or use a contrasting color. For even greater contrast, paint or wallcover the areas within the frames.

Decorative wood moldings with curved contours work best for wall frames. Chair rail, picture rail, base shoe, cove, quarter-round, and other suitable molding types in several wood species are readily available at home centers and lumberyards.

To determine the sizes and locations of the frames, cut strips of paper to the width of the molding and tape them to the wall. You may want the frames to match the dimensions of architectural details in the room, such as windows or a fireplace.

Install the molding with small finish nails driven at each wall stud location and at the ends of the pieces. Use nails long enough to penetrate the studs by ¾ inch. If there aren't studs where you need them, secure the molding with dabs of construction adhesive.

Wall frame moldings use ordinary trim pieces to create frames with mitered corners that give the illusion of frame-and-panel construction.

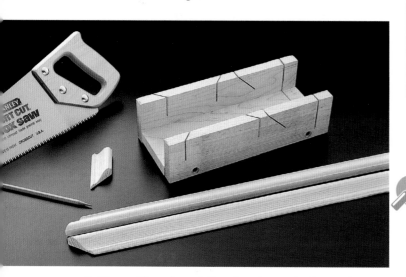

Cut the molding pieces to length, using a miter box and a backsaw (or power miter saw) to cut the ends at 45°. The top and bottom pieces should be the same length, as should the side pieces. Test-fit the pieces, and make any necessary adjustments.

TOOLS & MATERIALS

Level	Tape
Framing square	Wood finishing materials
Miter box and backsaw	Construction adhesive
Drill and bits	Paintable latex caulk
Nail set	or wood putty
Paper strips	Eye protection

How to Install Wall Frame Moldings

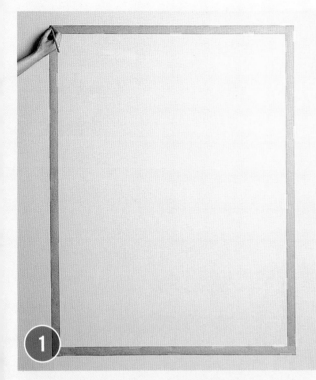

1

Cut paper strips to the width of the molding, and tape them to the wall. Use a framing square and level to make sure the frame is level and the strips are square to one another. Mark the outer corners of the frame with light pencil lines.

2

Paint or stain the moldings as desired. Position the top molding piece on the placement marks, and tack it in place with two finish nails. If necessary, drill pilot holes for the nails to prevent splitting.

3

Tack the side moldings in place, using the framing square to make sure they are square to the top piece. Tack up the bottom piece. Adjust the frame, if necessary, so that all of the joints fit tightly, and then completely fasten the pieces.

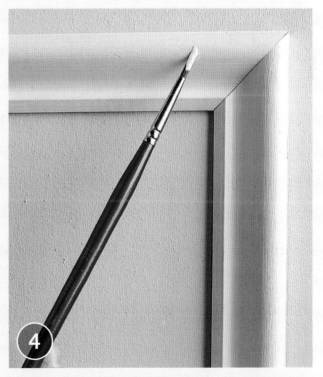

4

Drive the nails slightly below the surface, using a nail set. Fill the nail holes (and corner joints, if necessary) with wood putty. Touch up the patched areas with paint or stain.

Wainscot Frames

TOOLS & MATERIALS

Laser level
Pencil
Tape measure
Circular saw or tablesaw
Straightedge guide
Power miter saw
Drill with bits
Carpenter's square
Pocket hole jig with screws
Pry bar
Hammer

Pneumatic finish nail gun
with compressor
Caulking gun
¾"-thick MDF sheet stock
1¹⁄₁₆" cove molding
½ × ¾" base shoe
⁹⁄₁₆ × 1⅛" cap molding
(10 ft. per panel)
Panel adhesive
Paint and primer
Eye protection

Frame-and-panel wainscot adds depth, character, and a sense of old-world charm to any room. Classic wainscot was built with grooved or rabbeted rails and stiles that captured a floating hardwood panel. In the project shown here, the classic appearance is mimicked, but the difficulties of machining precise parts and commanding craftsman-level joinery are eliminated. Paint-grade materials (mostly MDF) are used in the project shown; however, you can also build the project with solid hardwoods and finish-grade plywood if you prefer a clear-coat finish.

Installing wainscot frames that look like frame-and-panel wainscot can be done piece by piece, but it is often easier to assemble the main frame parts in your shop. Not only does working in the shop allow you to join the frame parts together (we use pocket screws driven in the backs of the rails and stiles); it generally results in a more professional look.

Once the main frames are assembled, they can be attached to the wall at stud locations. If you prefer to site-build the wainscot piece by piece, you may need to replace the wallcovering material with plywood to create nailing surfaces for the individual pieces.

We primed all of the wainscot parts prior to installing them and then painted the wainscot (including the wall sections within the wainscot panel frames) a contrasting color from the wall above the wainscot cap.

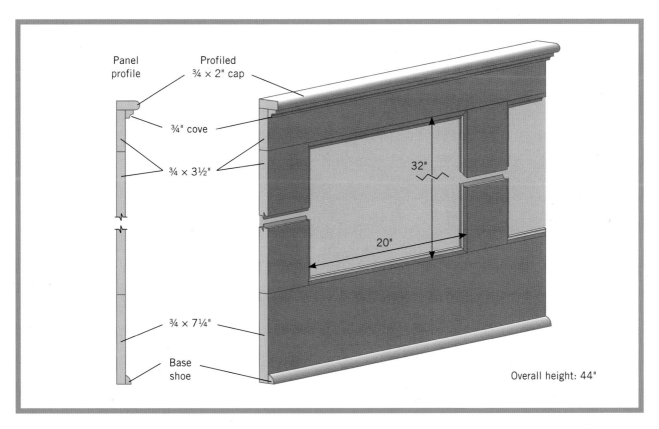

How to Install Wainscot Frames

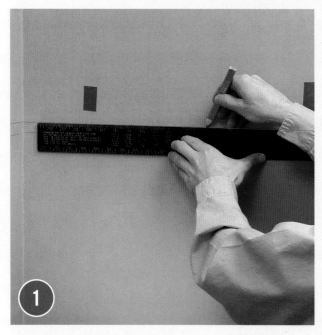

Use a laser level and a pencil to mark the height of the wainscot installation directly onto all walls in the project area. Also mark the height of the top rail (¾" below the overall height) since the cap rail will be installed after the rest of the wainscot is installed. Mark stud locations, using an electronic stud finder.

Plot out the wainscot layout on paper, and then test the layout by drawing lines on the wall to make sure you're happy with the design. Try to use a panel width that can be divided evenly into all project wall lengths. In some cases, you may need to make the panel widths slightly different from wall to wall, but make sure to maintain a consistent width within each wall's run.

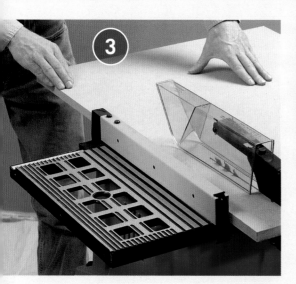

Based on your plan, rip a sheet of MDF into strips to make all of the wainscot parts except the trim moldings. In our case, that included the cap rail (2" wide), the top rail and stiles (3½" wide), and the base rail (7¼" wide).

NOTE: These are standard lumber dimensions. You can use 1 × 4 and 1 × 4 dimensional lumber for the rails and stiles. Use 1 × 2 or rip stock for the cap rail.

Cut top rails, base rails, and stiles (but not cap rails) to length, and dry-assemble the parts into ladder frames based on your layout. Plan the layouts so wall sections longer than 8 ft. are cut with scarf joints in the rails meeting at a stud location. Dry-assemble the pieces on a flat work surface.

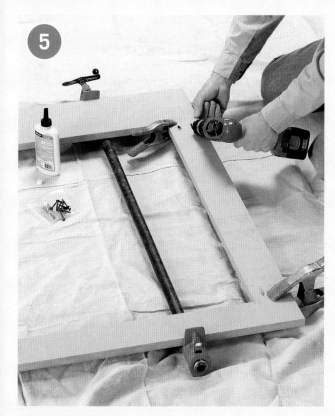

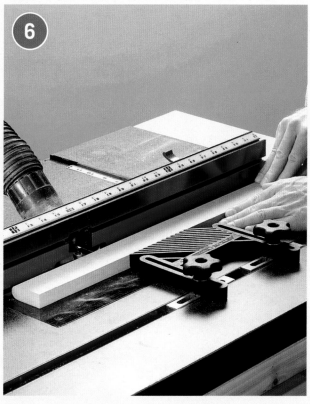

Assemble the frames using glue and pocket screws or biscuits. Clamp the parts together first, and check with a carpenter's square to make sure the stiles are perpendicular to both rails.

Mount a ¾" roundover bit in your router or router table, and shape a bullnose profile on the front edge of your cap rail stock.

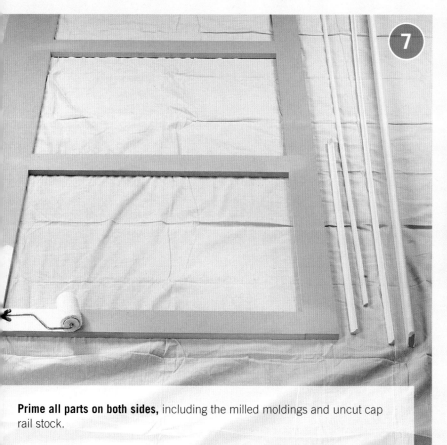

Prime all parts on both sides, including the milled moldings and uncut cap rail stock.

Position the frames against the wall, and shim underneath the bottom rails as necessary to bring them flush with the top rail marks on the wall (¾" below the overall height lines). Attach the wainscot sections by driving 3" drywall screws, countersunk, through the top rail and the bottom rail at each stud location. If you are using scarf joints, be sure to install the open half first.

(continued)

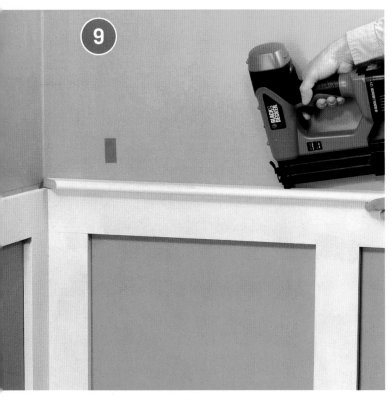

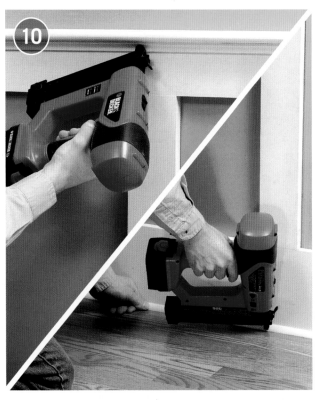

Cut the cap rail to length, and attach it to the top rail with panel adhesive and finish nails. Drive a 3" drywall screw through the cap rail and into the wall toenails style at each location. Be sure to carefully drill pilot holes and countersink holes for each screw. Miter-cut the cap rails at the corners.

Install cove molding in the crotch where the cap rail and top rails meet, using glue and a brad nailer. Then nail base shoe to conceal any gaps between the bottoms, rails, and the floor. Miter all corners.

Cut mitered frames to fit around the perimeter of each panel frame created by the rails and stiles. Use cap molding.

Mask the wall above the cap rail, and then prime and paint the wainscot frames. Generally, a lighter, contrasting color than the wall color above is most effective visually.

Simple Base Molding

Base moldings and other moldings with profiled edges are perfect projects for making in your home workshop. You can produce them very efficiently by employing the following method. Start by choosing an edge-profiling bit that you like for the top profile, such as the ogee bit and the roundover bit shown below. Then, select wood stock that is a little more than twice the width of your planned molding height (for example, to make 5½-inch-tall molding, select 12-inch-wide stock). Then rout the edge profiles into both edges of the stock on a router table. Now all you need to do is rip the stock down the middle, and you'll have two identical strips of molding.

TOOLS & MATERIALS

Router table with midsize router
Edge-profiling bit
Tablesaw
Prepared stock
Eye protection

Custom base molding is relatively easy to make. It can be simple and made from common lumber like the base molding seen here (you'll save a lot of money making it yourself), or it can have a unique profile and be made from any wood you choose, even an exotic wood.

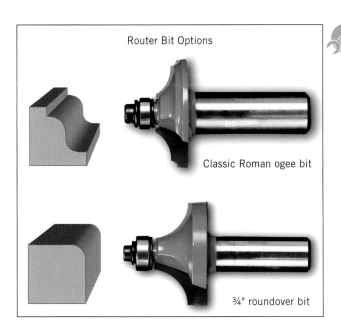

Router Bit Options

Classic Roman ogee bit

¾" roundover bit

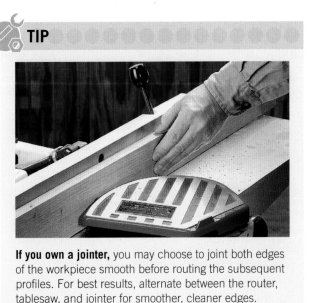

TIP

If you own a jointer, you may choose to joint both edges of the workpiece smooth before routing the subsequent profiles. For best results, alternate between the router, tablesaw, and jointer for smoother, cleaner edges.

How to Make Simple Base Moldings

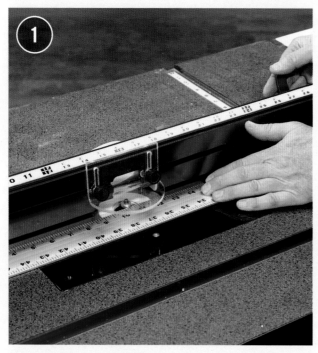

Prepare ¾" thick material to the maximum board width possible with two straightedges. Set the fence on the router table so that it is flush with the front edge of the bearing guide. Use a straightedge to help align the fence. If your stock is rough, set the fence slightly in front of the bearing guide so the fence guides the cut.

Use scrap material to fine-tune the height of the router bit. Adjust the height until you achieve the desired profile. Check the workpiece for troublesome tearout areas, and determine optimum test-feed rates when running scrap material.

Rout the edges of your prepared material one side at a time, maintaining an even feed rate and applying adequate downward and lateral pressure to the workpiece. Profile both edges.

Set the tablesaw fence to rip the profiled molding stock in half, and then rip-cut the stock to release two sections of molding that have a profile on one edge and are square-cut on the other edge. Sand the square edge of the molding to remove rough saw blade marks.

Metric Conversions

ENGLISH TO METRIC

TO CONVERT:	TO:	MULTIPLY BY:
Inches	Millimeters	25.4
Inches	Centimeters	2.54
Feet	Meters	0.305
Yards	Meters	0.914
Square inches	Square centimeters	6.45
Square feet	Square meters	0.093
Square yards	Square meters	0.836
Ounces	Milliliters	30.0
Pints (U.S.)	Liters	0.473 (Imp. 0.568)
Quarts (U.S.)	Liters	0.946 (Imp. 1.136)
Gallons (U.S.)	Liters	3.785 (Imp. 4.546)
Ounces	Grams	28.4
Pounds	Kilograms	0.454

TO CONVERT:	TO:	MULTIPLY BY:
Millimeters	Inches	0.039
Centimeters	Inches	0.394
Meters	Feet	3.28
Meters	Yards	1.09
Square centimeters	Square inches	0.155
Square meters	Square feet	10.8
Square meters	Square yards	1.2
Milliliters	Ounces	.033
Liters	Pints (U.S.)	2.114 (Imp. 1.76)
Liters	Quarts (U.S.)	1.057 (Imp. 0.88)
Liters	Gallons (U.S.)	0.264 (Imp. 0.22)
Grams	Ounces	0.035
Kilograms	Pounds	2.2

CONVERTING TEMPERATURES

Convert degrees Fahrenheit (F) to degrees Celsius (C) by following this simple formula: Subtract 32 from the Fahrenheit temperature reading. Then multiply that number by $\frac{5}{9}$. For example, 77°F - 32 = 45. $45 \times \frac{5}{9} = 25$°C.

To convert degrees Celsius to degrees Fahrenheit, multiply the Celsius temperature reading by $\frac{9}{5}$. Then, add 32. For example, 25°C $\times \frac{9}{5} = 45.$ $45 + 32 = 77$°F.

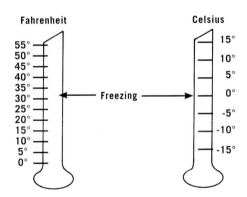

METRIC PLYWOOD PANELS

Metric plywood panels are commonly available in two sizes: 1,200 mm × 2,400 mm and 1,220 mm × 2,400 mm, which is roughly equivalent to a 4 × 8-ft. sheet. Standard and Select sheathing panels come in standard thicknesses, while Sanded grade panels are available in special thicknesses.

STANDARD SHEATHING GRADE		SANDED GRADE	
7.5 mm	(5/16 in.)	6 mm	(4/17 in.)
9.5 mm	(3/8 in.)	8 mm	(5/16 in.)
12.5 mm	(1/2 in.)	11 mm	(7/16 in.)
15.5 mm	(5/8 in.)	14 mm	(9/16 in.)
18.5 mm	(3/4 in.)	17 mm	(2/3 in.)
20.5 mm	(13/16 in.)	19 mm	(3/4 in.)
22.5 mm	(7/8 in.)	21 mm	(13/16 in.)
25.5 mm	(1 in.)	24 mm	(15/16 in.)

LUMBER DIMENSIONS

NOMINAL - U.S.	ACTUAL - U.S. (IN INCHES)	METRIC
1 × 2	3/4 × 1 1/2	19 × 38 mm
1 × 3	3/4 × 2 1/2	19 × 64 mm
1 × 4	3/4 × 3 1/2	19 × 89 mm
1 × 5	3/4 × 4 1/2	19 × 114 mm
1 × 6	3/4 × 5 1/2	19 × 140 mm
1 × 7	3/4 × 6 1/4	19 × 159 mm
1 × 8	3/4 × 7 1/4	19 × 184 mm
1 × 10	3/4 × 9 1/4	19 × 235 mm
1 × 12	3/4 × 11 1/4	19 × 286 mm
1 1/4 × 4	1 × 3 1/2	25 × 89 mm
1 1/4 × 6	1 × 5 1/2	25 × 140 mm
1 1/4 × 8	1 × 7 1/4	25 × 184 mm
1 1/4 × 10	1 × 9 1/4	25 × 235 mm
1 1/4 × 12	1 × 11 1/4	25 × 286 mm
1 1/2 × 4	1 1/4 × 3 1/2	32 × 89 mm
1 1/2 × 6	1 1/4 × 5 1/2	32 × 140 mm
1 1/2 × 8	1 1/4 × 7 1/4	32 × 184 mm
1 1/2 × 10	1 1/4 × 9 1/4	32 × 235 mm
1 1/2 × 12	1 1/4 × 11 1/4	32 × 286 mm
2 × 4	1 1/2 × 3 1/2	38 × 89 mm
2 × 6	1 1/2 × 5 1/2	38 × 140 mm
2 × 8	1 1/2 × 7 1/4	38 × 184 mm
2 × 10	1 1/2 × 9 1/4	38 × 235 mm
2 × 12	1 1/2 × 11 1/4	38 × 286 mm
3 × 6	2 1/2 × 5 1/2	64 × 140 mm
4 × 4	3 1/2 × 3 1/2	89 × 89 mm
4 × 6	3 1/2 × 5 1/2	89 × 140 mm

LIQUID MEASUREMENT EQUIVALENTS

1 Pint	= 16 Fluid Ounces	= 2 Cups
1 Quart	= 32 Fluid Ounces	= 2 Pints
1 Gallon	= 128 Fluid Ounces	= 4 Quarts

(continued)

Metric Conversions (continued)

COUNTERBORE, SHANK & PILOT HOLE DIAMETERS

SCREW SIZE	COUNTERBORE DIAMETER FOR SCREW HEAD (IN INCHES)	CLEARANCE HOLE FOR SCREW SHANK (IN INCHES)	PILOT HOLE DIAMETER	
			HARD WOOD (IN INCHES)	SOFT WOOD (IN INCHES)
#1	.146 (9/64)	5/64	3/64	1/32
#2	1/4	3/32	3/64	1/32
#3	1/4	7/64	1/16	3/64
#4	1/4	1/8	1/16	3/64
#5	1/4	1/8	5/64	1/16
#6	5/16	9/64	3/32	5/64
#7	5/16	5/32	3/32	5/64
#8	3/8	11/64	1/8	3/32
#9	3/8	11/64	1/8	3/32
#10	3/8	3/16	1/8	7/64
#11	1/2	3/16	5/32	9/64
#12	1/2	7/32	9/64	1/8

NAILS

Nail lengths are identified by numbers from 4 to 60 followed by the letter "d," which stands for "penny." For general framing and repair work, use common or box nails. Common nails are best suited to framing work where strength is important. Box nails are smaller in diameter than common nails, which makes them easier to drive and less likely to split wood. Use box nails for light work and thin materials. Most common and box nails have a cement or vinyl coating that improves their holding power.

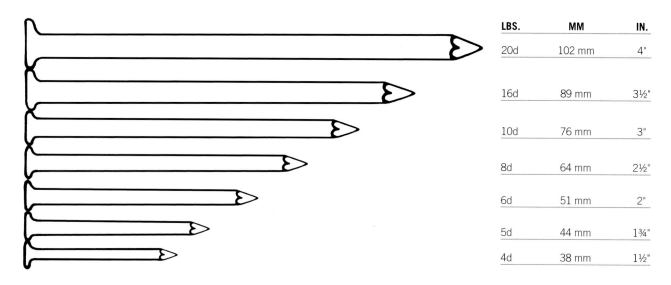

LBS.	MM	IN.
20d	102 mm	4"
16d	89 mm	3½"
10d	76 mm	3"
8d	64 mm	2½"
6d	51 mm	2"
5d	44 mm	1¾"
4d	38 mm	1½"

Resources

Black & Decker Corp.
Power tools and accessories
800-544-6986
www.blackanddecker.com

Red Wing Shoes Co.
Work boots and shoes
800-733-9464
www.redwingshoes.com

Moulding & Millwork Producers Association (MMPA)
General information on wood trim
800-550-7889
www.wmmpa.com

Fypon, Ltd.
Non-wood trim and millwork
800-446-9373
www.fypon.com

The Steel Network, Inc.
Curved Steel Track, page 81
888-474-4876
www.steelnetwork.com

Photo Credits

p. 22 Shutterstock

p. 37 iStock Photo

p. 55 Shutterstock

p. 81 (lower) iStock Photo

p. 90 Fypon

p. 108 iStock Photo

p. 190, 191 Shutterstock

Index